the cinema of BÉLA TARR

DIRECTORS' CUTS

the cinema of BÉLA TARR

the circle closes

András Bálint Kovács

 **WALLFLOWER PRESS** LONDON & NEW YORK

A Wallflower Press Book
Published by
Columbia University Press
Publishers Since 1893
New York • Chichester, West Sussex
cup.columbia.edu

A complete CIP record is available from the Library of Congress

ISBN 978-0-231-16530-3 (cloth : alk. paper)
ISBN 978-0-231-16531-0 (pbk. : alk. paper)
ISBN 978-0-231-85037-7 (e-book)

Series design by Rob Bowden Design

Cover image of Béla Tarr courtesy of the Kobal Collection

Columbia University Press books are printed on permanent
and durable acid-free paper.
This book is printed on paper with recycled content.
Printed in the United States of America

c 10 9 8 7 6 5 4 3 2 1
p 10 9 8 7 6 5 4 3 2 1

CONTENTS

ACKNOWLEDGEMENTS

As a matter of fact the people to whom I am deeply thankful for their helping me writing this book are the same people this book is about: Béla Tarr, Ágnes Hranitzky, László Krasznahorkai, Mihály Víg, Gyula Pauer and Gábor Medvigy. Over the past twenty years or so they have shared every detail of their work related to the films of Béla Tarr that was of interest to me. Some of them I hadn't seen for many years, but when we met they were as open and helpful as when we were in close collaboration.

It is needless to say that my close friendship with Béla Tarr and Ágnes Hranitzky gave me a perspective on their work I wouldn't have otherwise. Their friendship and support has been an invaluable contribution to this book. However, never did they give any indication as to what they expected me to say or to write. They always respected my opinion, even when we disagreed.

Tarr and Hranitzky were the only ones I showed the manuscript of this book. They both read it and meticulously corrected factual errors and commented on my statements. Sometimes disapprovingly. There was an issue, however, they could not get past. We argued a lot over it, and finally they said, 'This is your book, write what you think'. Out of respect for their point of view, I summarised this controversy in the last chapter.

I have always felt that I owed this book to them, and I can only hope that it will be worthy of their huge work.

INTRODUCTION

This book is a critical analysis of the work of Hungary's most prominent and internationally best-known film director, Béla Tarr. Anyone who is acquainted with his work will see immediately the consistency with which Tarr develops his themes, characters and style throughout his career. His films are like variations on a number of basic themes and formal motifs where the themes themselves become intertwined, or absorbed, in one another. We can best approach his films by learning how they relate to each other, how they vary these elements. As far as I can see, Tarr's films are the result of a conscious and sustained development of a style in order to make it more and more expressive of a specific vision Tarr has about the people and the world around him. This form changes only slightly from film to film as the stories change, but since the stories are based on the same elements, the form and the style basically modify the same motifs. In this process it is possible to observe a filmmaker trying out different solutions, experimenting with aesthetic effects so as to make his statement more transparent. My main approach will thus be to show an internal evolution detectable in the films' stylistic and thematic systems through which Tarr has arrived at a degree of expressivity, one which seems impossible to increase within this system.

Tarr follows a very particular method in developing his works, which I will call *the permutation principle*. I will show that almost all the important stylistic and narrative elements were already present in Tarr's early films, and with the help of a conscious and meticulous recombination of and experimentation with these elements, Tarr arrived at what I will call the 'Tarr style'. This permutation principle concerns not only the stylistic level, but higher, narrative and thematic levels too. Once he found the successful ingredients and their combinations, he continued developing this style in various radical ways. This is how he arrived at a point where only two possibilities seemed viable: returning to a more classical formal system, or abandoning his formal and thematic world altogether. The first choice required too many compromises and seemed impossible, although *The Man from London* (2007) seems to be a step in this direction. He chose the second way, but made this choice in a radical manner. This is what he said after the release of the film in several interviews and private conversations: 'I want to make one more film about the end of the world, and then I will stop making films.'[1]

The announcement of his potential withdrawal from filmmaking, which is not unheard of in the world of show business (especially in the case of rock bands), left many people perplexed. Even though we have seen filmmaking careers end, it is very unusual that someone at the peak of international recognition, in the middle of his life (Tarr was fifty-two when he said this), suddenly stops doing what he can do best and for which he has attracted the widest international attention. Even Ingmar Bergman did not stop making films after he announced that *Fanny and Alexander* would be his last film, and he was seventy-four years old. Yet the answer is simple. When people ask for an explanation for this decision in private, Tarr always says something along the lines of 'If I don't feel the urge to say something new, I quit, because I don't want to repeat myself, and I don't want to make films just because I have been a filmmaker for the last thirty-five years.' Well, if we have not seen many filmmakers quitting their jobs at the apogee of their careers, we have seen more than one who continued making films even after their own audience lost interest in them and the films themselves became nothing more than repetitions of the same old forms and ideas. Apparently, Tarr lost faith in what he could achieve within the confines of the form he created, believing it could not ever be more striking and radical. Tarr takes filmmaking as seriously as possible. It is not a 'living' or a 'profession' for him. It is important only as long as he feels that he has something to say, and what he has to say has to be radical and has to look radical. The eventuality that he will nevertheless continue to make films has no real bearing on this book. Even if Tarr changes his mind a couple of years from now, making an account of what he has accomplished in the period lasting from his debut until *The Turin Horse* makes sense. In this case, this book will be about his 'first period'. In the alternative case (if he really stops filmmaking for good, which I hope he does not), this book will be about the time when Béla Tarr made films.

Tarr's poetics rest on the history of the European and Hungarian art-film tradition, and so the positioning of Tarr's films in a historical context seems unavoidable, and ultimately all the questions raised by this oeuvre should be answered in this context as well. This seems all the more important because Tarr has represented Hungarian cinema over the last twenty years, which is why one has to ask why Béla Tarr has become the only internationally widely known Hungarian film director in this period. I will deal with this question in the last chapter.

The time when Béla Tarr made his films is a peculiar period of film history. He started his career when the European modernist art film was in decline. But he had been raised on this kind of cinema. Jean-Luc Godard was his hero when he was a teenager, and he was immersed in the leftist avant-garde movements of the early 1970s. Tarr was convinced that making films was a political act, and as such had to be taken very seriously. He became well-known internationally in the middle of the 1980s, when very few filmmakers still shared this view. In the meantime, the homogeneity of the modernist art-film movement dissolved, and cinema lost its political radicalism, but its stylistic solutions have continued to be the main patterns for art cinema. Modernism as a movement went out of fashion, but its individual stylistic patterns did not.

The 1980s and 1990s brought the new era of international art cinema. Since the end of modernism, we cannot speak about a set of 'available' stylistic options that are mainstream, with others out of fashion. With the global proliferation of various modernist trends, virtually every solution that has ever been employed is and remains an available option for everyone. A given film's style is a combination of different options. Béla Tarr is a particularly good cinematic example of an artist in the globalised art-world era to which the spectacular post-modern eclecticism of the late 1970s and 1980s was just the overture. In this era one cannot speak of auteurism in the sense that someone invents an original stylistic or narrative solution that will be the mark of his/her authorship. Instead, different peculiar combinations of already existing solutions become the signature of an author or even a group of authors, as we can see in the case of the 'Dogme' style. There is nothing in the Dogme style that could be called an 'original' stylistic invention in the sense that we can speak of the 'originality' of Fellini, Antonioni or Godard. Likewise, technically speaking, there is nothing new in the Tarr style either, except the idiosyncratic combination of various already existing stylistic patterns: their fine-tuning, their calibration for the sake of specific topics and aesthetic effects.

There are no stylistic period markers in this kind of art cinema (yet specific combinations may be more fashionable in given periods than others, which, among other features, may associate them with this period). There are no homogeneous national stylistic markers either (yet certain combinations may be more fashionable in certain regions than others). There are no more national styles like *German* expressionism, *French* impressionism, *Italian* neorealism or *Russian* montage. National and regional markers exclusively come from the topics and from the represented exterior world. Stylistic markers are international and authorial only in the sense that specific topics are associated with an idiosyncratic combination of various stylistic solutions. Again, technically speaking, the Dogme style is not a Danish style. None of it was invented in Denmark in the 1990s by Lars von Trier or any other filmmaker of the group. What really is 'Danish' in these films are the landscapes, the stories, the behaviour of the characters, and the physical environment. Likewise, stylistically nothing is 'Hungarian' in the second-period Béla Tarr films other than the environment represented in them. The particular combination and ultimately the unique aesthetic effect are the author's signature rather than individual solutions or topics. To be sure, certain successful forms will still most likely be imitated on the national level. After the release of *Damnation* in 1987 a whole series of black-and-white films with a depressed atmosphere appeared in Hungarian cinema in the early 1990s (György Fehér: *Szürkület*, 1990; Árpád Sopsits: *Céllövölde*, 1990; Attila Janisch: *Árnyék a havon*, 1991; Ildikó Szabó: *Gyerekgyilkosságok,* 1993; János Szász: *Woyzeck*, 1994), and the extreme long take has remained since then a fashionable marker of young Hungarian filmmakers such as Kornél Mundruczó, Benedek Fliegauf, Ágnes Kocsis and Bálint Kenyeres.

The international modernism of the 1960s was the modernisation of various national art cinema practices. That is how national variants were born out of some basic stylistic and narrative principles. Modernism was the encounter of a set of universal stylistic solutions and different national cultural traditions. Today's film artists' challenge is not to reconcile, say, *nouveau roman* narrative style and Russian Orthodox spiritualism as it was a challenge for Tarkovsky in the 1960s. The challenge for film artists today is, for example, to reconcile Tarkovsky's modernist solutions with those of Fellini and with some influence from Dreyer and maybe Renoir so that the resulting film does not look like a senseless eclectic mixture of anything. This is how art film became an international practice. Accordingly, its audience is international and probably socially heterogeneous too. There are probably no more Béla Tarr fans in Hungary than there are in the United States or Germany.

Damnation's novelty at the end of the 1980s was to bring back a number of stylistic solutions considered out of fashion for about a decade, and to use them to create a vision of the world, rather than just an image of a region, country or period. At the same time its visual qualities together with its handling of time ran radically and spectacularly counter to the fashion of short-take, fast-paced non-linear editing, influenced mainly by music videos, which was about to become the mainstream. Meditation stemming from radical continuity and slowness was the mark of a kind of non-mainstream alternative art-film style in the early 1990s. But there was more to it than that. It was also the period when a new form of video art began to take shape and to 'infiltrate' art galleries, a form which, thanks to new media and new imaging technology (not least cheap flat LCD screens), has become important in the fine arts. The work of Bill Viola was influential in this process because of its static long-take meditative style. One can clearly detect a tendency in the Tarr films made after *Damnation* to include sequences that could be easily taken out and contemplated and enjoyed separately due to their visual and acoustic compositions, which are closed and self-contained. *Damnation* already abounds in sequences of this kind. The scene in the 'Titanik Bar' is like a slow music video, and the first love-making scene, with its theatrical staging and acoustic texture, and the introductory tracking shot of the ball scene are striking examples of this tendency. The extreme duration of *Satantango* (1994) made this effect even more palpable in many of its sequences; and it is certainly this effect in *Werckmeister Harmonies* (2000) that inspired Gus Van Sant to replicate it exactly in his film *Gerry* (2002). Tarr found his way between international narrative art cinema and non-narrative video art, which represented in the 1990s a new aesthetic quality.

But he also found a way to express powerfully a sentiment about a historical period without ever directly referring to this period specifically, which made his expression open to universal interpretation. This sentiment concerns a general decline which had a very concrete meaning in Eastern Europe at that time, although it became meaningful globally. Beyond their aesthetic and historical value, the significance of the films of Béla Tarr is that they provided the most powerful vision of a whole region and its historical situation. Even though his films are seen by only a limited audience, they express in their universalistic language the feelings of millions of ordinary people living in Eastern Europe. This is a feeling of disappointment, of having been tricked, because the work of a lifetime has been wasted, because they have become the victims of petty intrigues; they were duped by political adventurers, and they can see the same corrupt world with different actors in a different set, with a different ideology. No one can be trusted, and it is not possible to believe in anything, since all ideals have been utilised to abuse the helpless. This very negative image of the world has become the epitome of a vision shared in other parts of the world. To advance some of the conclusions of this book I could say that the expression of this human situation represented as a trap from which there is no escape is the focus of Tarr's films, and circular narrative structure and extreme narrative slowness are the most conspicuous stylistic tools Tarr uses in service of this expression. Circularity expresses the trap situation, slowness gives birth to something I would call *the time of hope*, hope that after all there is a way out of the circle when there is not.

The nature of the ensemble of Tarr's films puts some constraints on the methodology of their analysis too. Some readers might raise an eyebrow at seeing the quantitative methods I will use at some points. They may ask: how can we get closer to the essence of a film by counting the close-ups in it? Well, for the sake of those who find quantitative methods repugnant in the study of art I want to argue that quantitative analysis is not good for talking about interpretation or aesthetic value. Quantitative analysis is useful in comparing individual works of a corpus in order to find out if there is any significant change, and if there are any significant trends in the change. As a matter of fact that is what every critic does intuitively when comparing formal characteristics of different films, except they do not do it with the exactitude necessary for solid theorising. But exactitude is not the main point in quantitative analysis; it may surprise us too. It illuminates trends that cannot obviously be seen in a single work, not even by comparing two or three films, but can be seen by comparing all the films or a big enough sample from a specified period. These may remain hidden even to the author of the films. No author, not even Tarr, compares exactly the rate of close-ups in his films to determine what rate he should use in the next one. He has a general idea of the length of shots he wants to use, but he has no idea how one film compares with another in this respect. And when we discover a consistent trend over thirty years we may have to answer questions which otherwise could not even be raised. A quantitative analysis can tell us neither *why* something changes nor what this change *means*. Causes of changes and the meaning of the changes will always remain the domain of the intuitive critic. But in order to make sure that what we see as a change is in fact one, and that it is significant enough to be taken into consideration, quantitative methods are very helpful in providing the data which we must interpret with our critical intuition.

An interesting issue regarding Tarr's work as a whole is the possibility of periodisation. For most critics this is quite obvious. Almost everybody who knows the films thinks that his work can be divided into two periods: one before *Damnation* and one starting with this film. However, Tarr himself contests this opinion whenever the issue is raised. He is very determined in his claim that it is not possible to discern different periods in his work, only a gradual evolution, since all the important stylistic and thematic elements of his later films are already present in one way or another in his early ones too. According to this approach Tarr's oeuvre can be viewed as a single continuous path leading to the crystallisation of a personal cinematic expression. This crystallisation process went through various stages until those elements that can now be considered as fundamental characteristics became articulated and integrated into the Tarr style. I hope that with the help of quantitative analysis I will be able to show to what extent this series of works can be regarded as a unified evolutionary process leading from the first Tarr film to the last, and at the same time supply enough arguments to support this periodisation.

The chapters of this book are organised according to the stylistic and thematic motifs of the Tarr films. I had to also follow a chronological order, as the main focus of the book is the evolution of these motifs in Tarr's oeuvre. I believe it is important to start the book with a chapter on Béla Tarr as a person, as an artist. His very peculiar position in the Hungarian film industry is due, to a great extent, to his working methods and not least to his eccentric personality, which assures him an outsider position which seems to be the only thing that makes him feel comfortable. An equally important personal aspect of Tarr's work concerns his relationship with his colleagues: actors, camera operators, writer, set designer, composer and above all his partner in life, co-director and editor, Ágnes Hranitzky. Chapters two through four deal with stylistic features and their evolution. Chapter five discusses the narrative forms and themes of the Tarr films in chronological order. Chapter six looks at the characters of the films. I will also discuss Tarr's short films and works made in film school, which still can be found. They are not discussed separately, and not in chronological order either. I inserted each of them where I thought they fitted into the thematic logic of the book.

Much of the information the reader will find in this book derives from my personal acquaintance with Béla Tarr. Many of his statements and opinions that I cite in the text are not taken from bibliographical materials. They arose from personal conversations and my watching him working over the past twenty-five years. Even though this friendship would not have endured if our ideas about films and certainly about his own films had not been close, my perspective on his films in this book is that of a member of his audience, and not that of someone from his crew. The opinions and thoughts expressed in this book are mine and do not correspond necessarily with what he would say about his own films, something that will be discussed in more detail in the last chapter.

Notes

1   Vincent Malusia (2008) 'J'ai perdu toutes mes illusions', *Transfuge*, September, p. 25.

CHAPTER ONE

The Persona

Because this chapter is about Béla Tarr as a person, I will not refrain from evoking a personal memory. The first time I met with Tarr was in 1979, at a screening of Ermanno Olmi's *The Post*. The screening was organised by filmmakers, Béla Tarr among them, who not much later organised their own filmmaking studio, called Társulás. Their goal was to find young film critics who were receptive to supporting their particular goals in creating documentary-style fiction films. As we left the screening room and walked toward some club in which we would discuss the film, Béla started to talk about the film, while most of us, including myself, were just trying to make some sense of what we had just seen. I was amazed by his crystal clear, strong, sharp and unambiguous comments formulated five minutes after he had finished watching a film for the first time. I was amazed how someone could have such an assured approach to the world as to be able to form so quickly an uncompromising, and accurate, opinion about anything. By the time we arrived at the club I was convinced that there was no other way of interpreting this film than the way Béla Tarr did. At least this is how I remember the story; Tarr has a different recollection of it. He says he was not present at the screening, and has never seen this film. He joined us only when we left the screening room, and made his comments only after he had listened to our conversation about the film. Whatever is the case, my impression of what he said was the same. Whether or not he saw it, he gave me a key to this film through the unambiguous, straightforward words he used.

This first impression has never changed since then. I think that the key to his character can be found in the power of his approach to the world, the uncompromising stubbornness of pursuing his goals, and the intelligence and sophistication by which he formulates his vision in both words and images.

Béla Tarr was born in Pécs, in southern Hungary, in 1955. For his fourteenth birthday he received an 8mm camera from his father. Very soon, at the age of seventeen, this camera got him into trouble. During his high school years he got involved with some radical leftist movements ideologically not far from Maoism. These groups, although consisting of intellectuals and artists, made a cult around physical work and around being among workers. They grouped around music groups like Monszun and theatre groups such as Orfeo. Tarr, while still a high school student, also went regularly to work in a shipyard and followed these groups on their regular excursions to workers' districts and workers' hostels. On one of these occasions he met a group of gypsy workers who wrote a letter to János Kádár, first secretary of the Hungarian Socialist Workers Party, asking him to grant them permission to leave the country to work in Austria, because they could not find enough work at home. The whole idea seemed so absurd in 1971 in a country where even visiting a relative living abroad required obtaining special permission, which proved an ordeal to anyone who tried, and this story inspired the sixteen-year-old Tarr to ask these workers to talk about their situation and motivation for his camera. With two of his friends they formed a filmmaking group they named after Dziga Vertov (referring to Jean-Luc Godard and Jean-Pierre Gorin's 'Dziga Vertov Group'). Tarr's Dziga Vertov Group made a documentary about these men, and sent this film, *Guest Workers* (lost since then), to an amateur film festival, where it won first prize. The success made Tarr very proud of his film, which he wanted everybody, especially workers, to see. So he took his projector and tape recorder, and several times a week he would visit workers' hostels, where he would set up his equipment and screen the film to workers arriving home from the factory. He even made posters by hand to advertise these projections at the workers' hostels.

The workers took this well, but the Communist Party did not. One day at school, Tarr was ordered to go to the local party office to explain what he was doing and to screen the film to the party officials. They watched the film but didn't say anything. They let him go, and no direct retaliation was undertaken. But a year later, when, after finishing high school, he wanted to study at university, he was told not even to think about it. He was denied admission to every higher educational institution in the country. So he went to work in the shipyard. He worked there for two years, but his frail, thin build wasn't meant for the hard physical labour. He sent an application to the department of philosophy of Budapest's ELTE University. At the admission exam he shocked the examining professor by asserting that Marx's *Communist Manifesto* was like a work of art rather than a political programme, and that communism was a movement rather than some institutionalised political formation. He was refused admittance. He took the job of doorman at a cultural centre in one of Budapest's workers' districts. In the meantime he continued making amateur films, one of which won another prize at a subsequent amateur film festival. Members of the jury included István Dárday and Györgyi Szalai, two prominent representatives of a group of documentary filmmakers working in a kind of semi-documentary, semi-fictional genre. They invited Tarr to work as an assistant on their next major project, *Film Saga (Film-*

regény, 1977). At the age of twenty, Tarr had his first real contact with professional filmmaking.

In the meantime, Tarr already had a film project in the works, part of which was the film he won the prize for at the amateur film festival. This was about a young woman named Irén Szajki, whom Tarr met when he was filming in a workers' district on the outskirts of Budapest that has been demolished since then. Irén was squatting in an apartment for a period, but eventually the city council had her evicted by force. Tarr, who was working alone at that time, decided to film the act of eviction. He found a hideout in a neighbouring building from which he could film the action quietly, and settled there half an hour before the city council agents arrived, accompanied by the police. Somehow the police found out about his being there and began the whole procedure by arresting him first and taking him to police headquarters. He was kept there half of the day, during which time the agents accomplished their mission. After that he was let go. Irén had nowhere else to go from this apartment but to his father-in-law's place, where she was the twelfth person in residence. This was the origin of Tarr's first full-length feature film, *Family Nest* (*Családi tűzfészek*, 1977), where Irén Szajki played the female protagonist. She also played important roles in later Tarr films, such as *Satantango* and *Werckmeister Harmonies*.

Family Nest was made by the Balázs Béla Stúdió, an independent studio for young filmmakers, and released in 1979. At the age of twenty-two not only did he become the youngest film director in Hungary with a full-length feature film officially released, but thanks to *Family Nest* he earned a national and international reputation, the film also winning the Grand Prize at the 1979 Mannheim International Film Festival. At the same time, the fact that Tarr did not have any professional training did not escape attention. Not only was he very young, but he was also a total outsider in a professional community that was very careful not to allow anyone near film production who did not go through official training. For Tarr to be taken seriously as a filmmaker it was strongly advised he go to an official film school. Although just a couple of years earlier he had been banned from all higher educational institutions in Hungary, after *Family Nest* it would have been very difficult not to admit him to film school. He was accepted into Miklós Szinetár's class, originally a television director training programme, later changed into a film director's programme in 1978.

Tarr was no less an outsider in film school, not bothering to attend many classes. He was making his next feature film, *The Outsider* (*Szabadgyalog*, 1980). He was allowed to do whatever he liked, and was not required to live a regular film student's life. *The Outsider* was already an official professional studio production. After the release of this film he started his third project, *The Prefab People* (*Panelkapcsolat*, 1982). At the same time he made *Macbeth* (1982), originally a film school assignment but later reproduced for television. By the time he graduated from film school he already had three full-length feature films finished, and two international awards, the Locarno Festival special mention for *The Prefab People* being the second. This was quite an unusually intense beginning to a professional career for a filmmaker of his age.

In 1980 Tarr was among the founders of a newly formed studio, called Társulás Stúdió. It was formed by people belonging to a certain 'cinema direct' current, who were joined by some others who had ideas about filmmaking outside of the then-mainstream politically correct realist norm of Hungarian cinema. Officially, its mission was to create and promote the semi-documentary, semi-fictional style the founders of the studio initiated five years earlier. However, filmmakers with clearly avant-garde ambitions could also come and make films in the studio. Very quickly Társulás became Hungarian cinema's most inventive filmmaking studio. But Társulás was short-lived. Right from the outset, filmmakers from other studios did not agree with the formation of Társulás, for the simple reason that they all had to live on the shrinking state funding of the film industry. Another studio meant distribution of the funds between five studios instead of four. After six years' constant struggle, in 1985 Társulás, the only institutional background for the innovative spirit of Hungarian cinema, was dissolved.

Tarr made two films with Társulás, *The Prefab People* and *Almanac of Fall* (*Őszi Almanach*, 1985). In 1985 his next project, *Satantango*, was accepted by the studio, but the production could not start. With the dissolution of Társulás the chances that he could make this film fell considerably. He tried to sell the idea to several of the remaining studios with no success. He was even told by one of the studio heads, a film director colleague, that he was an amateur and he had better quit filmmaking for good. In 1986 Tarr found himself marginalised in the official Hungarian film industry, which he never really belonged to anyway, and it looked like he would not be able to continue as a filmmaker within the existing institutional structure. He started a new project less ambitious than *Satantango*. It was an idea he had had earlier about a small-town singer and her husband, and together with László Kran-sznahorkai, writer of the source novel for *Satantango*, he wrote the script for *Damnation*. He was used to the idea of being an outsider and accepted this marginalised position. He brought together several sponsors not directly involved in filmmaking, like the Hungarian Film Institute and the Hungarian Advertising Agency; Hungarian Television and MOKÉP, the state film distribution company, joined the project later. If Hungarian Television had not been involved in the production, it would have been the first Hungarian feature film after World War II to be produced entirely outside the official filmmaking system.

Thus far Tarr was not a widely known filmmaker. Each of his steps into the realm of filmmaking was irregular and kept him at the margin of the film industry. As Ágnes Hranitzky put it: 'He wasn't taken seriously as a filmmaker. For the studio people, he was just a wannabe.'[1] He was categorised as someone belonging to the by-then extinguished documentary-style fiction film movement, and not even as the most characteristic representative of it, in that his films showed very few direct political concerns. *Almanac of Fall* was already atypical of Tarr's former work and provoked more enthusiasm among critics abroad than among those in Hungary; but this film laid the foundations for his international reputation. The discrepancy between his marginal status in Hungary and his growing international fame became even more pronounced with his next film, *Damnation*. The film provoked harsh or mocking reviews in Hungary and a total rejection by the jury of the Hungarian Film Week of 1988, but at same time, it earned him the Foreign Critics Award on the same occasion, two other international awards (Cannes and Bergamo), a nomination for the European Film Award and a number of other international festival invitations all over the world.

The next year Tarr received a DAAD[2] fellowship for artists to spend a year in West Berlin. Upon return, the Tarr-Hranitzky couple gave up their apartment in the heart of Budapest and moved to a little village about thirty kilometres from the capital city. That is where they started preparations for their gigantic enterprise, *Satantango*. It looked as if Tarr had settled for remaining marginal to the Hungarian professional film world. He did not often participate in professional debates and did not keep in contact with most of the leading figures of Hungary's professional film production. However, he has since become a frequent visiting professor at the Berlin film school, where he has been spending a couple of months each year. Ironically, he has not received any invitation to teach at the Hungarian film school as yet. In 1994 *Satantango* featured at the Hungarian Film Week. The organisers considered this a marginal event, forecasting a weak attendance due to the film's extreme running time (seven and a half hours), and programmed it in a small theatre. Several hundred viewers showed up, loudly expressing their discontent. This film earned Tarr a massive international reputation among cinephiles all over the world. Respected critics praised this film, and a certain cult around it was born.

 Due to the fact that during the preceding fifteen years he himself had to secure the financing for his own films, and played the role not only of the director but also of the executive producer, after the release of his next film, *Werckmeister Harmonies*, Tarr started his own production company, *T. T. Filmműhely*, together with producer Gábor Téni.

By the early years of 2000 Tarr was not a marginal figure any more. He was already well-known for his international successes and was recognised as a somewhat eccentric but important figure of Hungarian cinema. Although bringing together sponsorship for *Werckmeister Harmonies* took a long time, he managed to secure the financing for this film too, including important government grants. In 2003 he obtained the highest national award an artist can get in Hungary. In 2009 he accepted an offer to be a candidate for the future presidency of the Hungarian Film Foundation, but it was not long before he realised that there was very little support for his radical conception of how to run the Foundation, and he stepped back. In 2010 he was elected president of the Hungarian Filmmakers Association.

The lack of success of *The Man from London* was rather disappointing considering the high expectations, and all of this foreshadowed the difficulties surrounding the commencement of Tarr's next project, *The Turin Horse* (2011). This is when Tarr announced that this film would be his last one, after which he would quit filmmaking. He made this announcement when he was already a national and international celebrity, known and respected by many in the international art-film world: T-shirts with his name on are on sale in Los Angeles, his style is imitated by other filmmakers, and he has become a cult figure for art-film audiences all over the world. In short, when Tarr ceased to be a marginalised outsider and became one of the touchstones of the mainstream high-brow art-film culture, he decided it was time to stop.

'When someone makes a film that is seven and a half hours long it means that he just ignores the way the world is.'[3] Being an outsider has been a conscious choice for Tarr for the most part, and provided him with the freedom of not being engaged to any institution or person who would try to make him respect rules he did not want to respect. If Tarr really stops making films, his life as a filmmaker could be seen as a product of a fully dedicated, non-compromising artist who not for one moment in his life was busy building up a 'career'. All he was concerned with at every moment was making the film he wanted to make the way he wanted it to be, no matter in what environment he had to work. At every instance he has done what he wanted, not what he was allowed or advised to do. He was as fully dedicated to his film when, at the age of twenty, he was hiding in the staircase of a building with his 8mm camera, waiting for the police to evict Irén, as when, at the age of fifty, he decided to rebuild the financing for *The Man from London*, and go back to Bastia with new people to restart the production a year after he had to stop. He was the same person at the age of seventeen, visiting workers' hostels with his projector showing his only film to the workers, as he was at the age of thirty-eight, when he went out shooting *Satantango* with the money he borrowed from the cafeteria tender of the studio so that he could pay the technical crew. He was the same person at the age of twenty-four, when instead of attending classes at the film school he made his second feature film, as he was at the age of thirty-two, when after being refused by every studio, he built up funding for *Damnation* independently at a time when this was considered inconceivable to many.

For Tarr, filmmaking has always been a question of inner moral conviction rather than a profession. In the 1970s he was truly convinced that making films was not only a way of life, but a political mission as well. He thought that his films would provoke a revolution merely by their form and by their messages. Tarr had a rather political avant-garde conception of art: radicalism in the artistic form should influence directly the viewer's political ideas. However, his films were neither subversive nor radical enough in their form to be considered politically significant. As much as he took his political mission seriously, his films, among the works of the documentary-fiction current, were not in the least politically explicit. No wonder that they did not provoke any political reactions. (The others did not either, for that matter, and if any of these films had been considered politically dangerous by the political powers they would have been banned right away, as was the case with Gyula Gazdag's *Bástayasétány '74* (1974) and with more than one documentary film of the period.) Tarr's radicalism and his reputation for being a difficult person had a different source than politics.

There is a recurrent motif in Tarr's films which explains much of this paradox. In the majority of the films made after *Almanac of Fall* we find a lonely, marginalised protagonist who takes on an outsider's or an observer's position (Karrer in *Damnation*, the doctor in *Satantango*, Valuska in *Werckmeister Harmonies*, Maloin in *The Man from London*). The character of András in *The Outsider* can be considered as the first manifestation of this character type. I would not go so far as to say that these characters are self-portraits of the filmmaker, but they certainly represent a point of view which he shares. Tarr found his real artistic radicalism when he realised that his radicalism had to do with his position as an outsider rather than with his inner political convictions. He has been radical as a filmmaker rather than as a political thinker or activist. And it was through his absolute self-centredness, stubbornness and unconditional devotion to the cause of his films as an outsider that he could make prevail his real political point of view: his solidarity for the outcast, for those who *really are* at the margins of society, for the *real* outsiders, not outsiders only by choice. In his films Tarr has become a spokesperson for these people with the help of his aesthetic rather than explicit political radicalism. None of his films represents better this attitude than the five-minute sketch called *Prologue*, which is part of the portmanteau film made by twenty-five European film directors called *Visions of Europe* (2004). This film consists of a single take, which is a simple tracking shot near a line of seemingly homeless people standing speechless in line for something. After three and a half minutes, the camera arrives at the head of the queue, where a window is opened by a smiling young woman who starts to hand out little portions of free food to these people. The last sequence, lasting more than a minute of the film, is a list of several hundred names of the homeless people we have just seen standing in the line. This is the most explicit political statement made by Tarr about the enlargement of the European Union, manifesting the same attitude one can find in all of his films. Each of these people has the same dignity as those on the other side of the window, only they are very poor, humiliated and crippled.

In a way this attitude ensured him the possibility of a certain working style. Because Tarr is least concerned with the opinions of people who do not share his dedication to his cinematic cause, he expects devotion from his collaborators that goes beyond mere professionalism. For Tarr no film of his was 'just a film'. Each of them was a 'cause' to which everybody in the crew had to dedicate himself or herself entirely with inner conviction. This is why, starting from *Damnation*, credit lists do not make a distinction visually between important and less important creators. Everybody is shown in the same way with no distinction. The opening credit of *Damnation* does not even read, 'A film by Béla Tarr', but, 'A film by…' – and a list of names. For Tarr his crew formed a community of people dedicated to the same cause outside the mainstream norms. This was a community that had been working together for more than twenty years, and some of them thirty years or more, including Ágnes Hranitzky, of course, actor János Derzsi, Irén Szajki, Miklós Székely B. and composer Mihály Víg.

As much as Tarr tries to keep the same collaborators around him, he has no problem with dismissing anybody who does not fit into his plans. This is a particularly delicate issue when it comes to cinematographers. For his four early films, until *Almanac of Fall*, he worked with several cameramen, usually two or three at a time, as the documentary style required multiple cameras. Cameraman Ferenc Pap was always among them. But problems started with *Almanac of Fall*. Lighting issues and complicated dolly movements drove Tarr to change cameraman twice during the production of the film. With *Damnation* Tarr needed entirely new camerawork, which had nothing to do with the earlier documentary style, based essentially on improvisation and static close-ups. Tarr wanted someone who could help him develop even further the long-take style with complicated and well-designed tracking shots. Because he knew what he wanted to accomplish, he looked for someone inexperienced, rather than someone who already had his own crystallised camerawork style. Gábor Medvigy, who had not made a feature film yet, was his choice. Their cooperation was not without conflicts, but it was good enough for Tarr to ask him to work on *Satantango* too. Their relationship worsened dramatically during the shooting and further after the release of the film, yet Medvigy also worked on *Werckmeister Harmonies*. However, this latter film was filmed by four consecutive cinematographers. The problems with the cinematographers continued with *The Man from London*, only this time several cinematographers were asked and then dismissed at the beginning of or even before the shooting. István Szaladják, who started the film, simply walked away from the production site, and took a plane back to Budapest after the first week. Tarr then tried to ask Medvigy again, but this time he refused. Finally, Tarr found a cameraman he had already worked with on a short film (*Travel on the Plain*): Fred Kelemen, a Hungarian-born German filmmaker and a former student of his.

Not unrelated to the problem with cinematographers, rumours spread that Tarr was a difficult person to work with. His reputation as a difficult person to negotiate with in financial terms and as someone non-compromising in artistic terms was constantly growing. The difficult situation in which *Werckmeister Harmonies*' producer found himself after the film was released reinforced this image, even though the producer's problems were not due to the film. Even more so the suicide of Humbert Balsan, the executive producer of *The Man from London*, in spite of the fact that his death in 2005 could not possibly be related to the film, the financing of which was secured already. Nevertheless, some of the people in the French film industry felt that somehow the difficulties imposed by the production of this film after all might have played a role in causing the suicide of the chairman of the European Film Academy.[4]

Tarr seemed to be a 'difficult person' above all to the sponsors. Tarr has always been a non-compromising perfectionist. Already at the beginning of his career he was known for his excessive use of film stock. He always ran beyond the assigned quantity by using multiple cameras and repeating scenes as many times as necessary for the result he wanted. But problems with financing became really severe with *Damnation*. Tarr set up the financing structure of his film himself, and from this point on it was really him in charge of matters of financing. *Satantango* was already an international co-production, but the length of the film and the fact that Tarr was not willing to cut it to 'normal' length caused problems for one of the co-producers. The international success of *Satantango* opened up more possibilities. Building up the financing for *The Man from London* was relatively easy at the beginning, but after Balsan's death it became a nightmare. Tarr needed both Hungarian and French government support to be able to finish the film.

All of the stories and gossip of this kind contributed to Tarr's image as someone who is very problematic to negotiate with, who is willing to go to the very end in the pursuit of his artistic goals, who squeezes the last drop out of everyone who works with him, and the last penny from all possible sources, but also as someone who is overwhelming, and impossible to resist.

Working methods

> When I taught in Berlin I kept telling the students that making a film is not like first you write the script, then the dialogue, and next you choose the actors from a photo album. I said: you don't write a script first, you don't write the dialogue. Here is your synopsis, and the next step is that you choose your actors and the locations. And when you have them all, knowing who will play and where in the film, only then you write the script. So, what they learned from me was that right after the synopsis they have to look for the actors and the locations, and only after that they can write dialogue and scenes, when they know already that they can put the camera there and who will play it. That is the only way you can write scenes and dialogue that don't feel like a kick of a horse.[5]

There are several characteristics of Tarr's working method that have remained constant over the years, even if his style and themes have changed considerably. One of them is the concentration on actors and locations rather than on the narrative as manifested in the script.

Finding the right location has been of prime importance to Tarr's work. He never uses a studio set, and always works in real locations. A location for him is not just 'an apartment', not just a small-town street or some landscape. Every little detail has to bear the atmosphere and the unmistakable visual characteristics of the world in which the story takes place. The landscape, be it natural or built, is an essential part of the narrative composition in Tarr's films. Part of the effect Tarr intends to evoke is the feeling on the viewer's part that he or she recognises this environment as real. So it has to be real. Even if Tarr modifies the landscape in order to intensify its effects, details of it are mostly real. There are some important exceptions, however. *Almanac of Fall* is played out on an artificial set with no connections to any real-world location, although the apartment was real and not built up in a studio. The tower in *The Man from London* is also an artificial construction at the port of Bastia, and the farm in *The Turin Horse* is an entirely artificial construction. Tarr spends a lot of energy to find the appropriate exterior he needs in his films. Sometimes he finds them close to one another; sometimes he has to construct the landscapes from little pieces, as in the case of *Damnation*, where the town in which the film takes place does not correspond to any existing location. Every street, every corner and every building is taken from a different place. Tarr made a selection of the most deteriorated sceneries of Hungary so that the whole film carries an extremely concentrated atmosphere of shabbiness. And in order to find the exact landscape he imagined for *The Man from London*, Tarr went on a tour of every possible little port town in Europe before he made a decision to choose Bastia in Corsica.

Actors' faces are as important for Tarr as the landscape. That is the reason the same actors recur in his films very often. What he looks for is expressive faces rather than psychologically realist acting. His characters' faces are required to express a certain past and a certain existential situation without any real acting. In this, he is a real follower of Bresson, Antonioni, Jancsó and Tarkovsky. Until *Werckmeister Harmonies* he mostly worked with amateurs or actors who did not appear very often in the films. Again, *Almanac of Fall* is the main exception, featuring only well-known professional actors. By contrast, in *Satantango* most of the main characters were amateurs. In later films, even if international stars such as Hanna Schygulla, Tilda Swinton, Peter Berling and Lars Rudolph appear, amateur actors remain the choice for important roles: Erika Bók in *The Man from London* and in *The Turin Horse*; Miroslav Krobot in *The Man from London*; Alfréd Járai, Péter Dobai, Putyi Horváth and Irén Szajki in *Werckmeister Harmonies*.

Downplaying the importance of the scenario has for a long time been a part of the art-film production mode, especially in a style where the documentary-like effect requires a considerable amount of improvisation. What Tarr learned from direct cinema was that dialogue depends very much on what the amateur actors are able and willing to say, and camera movements can be decided only after they know where they will shoot and how the amateur actor is able to move. They had only a storyboard with situations and a general outline of the development of the dialogue, not the precise words and sentences. This is the general principle of the documentary-fiction style, where much of the film is based on improvisation. Tarr left behind the semi-documentary style, but this principle remained his fundamental working method.

Improvisation dropped back considerably after Tarr started his collaboration with Krasznahorkai. Not only situations, but carefully formulated dialogue was written before shooting, and even if considerable changes sometimes had to be made to the dialogue, they were rarely the result of actors' improvisation, at least not more than in any other film. However, a certain amount of improvisation remained part of Tarr's work. We could roughly say that while in his first period (until *Almanac of Fall*) improvisation was at the centre of his work, because the actors themselves had to improvise their dialogue and movements, in the second period improvisation is imposed by the complicated long-take style in real locations. Tarr has the pattern of the camera movement in mind, but the exact choreography and pace of the movements are determined on location during the rehearsals. Instead of detailed technical scenarios he has drawn up, all that Tarr has in his hands during the shooting is the dialogue book and many photos that he or the cinematographer take continuously of the set from different angles. These photographs have the function of orienting the creators. They serve as starting points for the cameraman and the rest of the crew to envisage the result of the given shot. Sometimes, however, even these pictures are not respected and the shot is entirely changed during shooting. For example, one of the key shots from the plan of *The Man from London*, in which the tower could be seen from Maloin's apartment, was finally left out. Every important detail is decided only on location and no preliminary plans or ideas are respected if they don't seem to provide the required effect.

Tarr explains his improvisational working method by a curious inner motivation: 'The lack of self-confidence has to reach an extent where all you can trust in is that you'll feel what is not good.'[6] It is not that Tarr doesn't know what he wants. This means that he can feel that the effect of a given shot takes place only when it really takes place on location during the shooting. He does know what effect he wants, but he does not know what it feels like until it happens. It is as if directing for Tarr means 'eliminating what is wrong' from a sequence until the 'real thing' comes forward. Tarr treats each shot as an individual sequence, rather than as a sequence functioning in a narrative flow. They must be the way they are in their own right, not because they move the narrative forward. Each shot is a long sequence, a block of time, and it has to have an exact atmosphere, an opening and a closing, and a dramaturgical curve of its own, depending only to a small extent on the next or previous shot. All shots must have their own individual aesthetic essence, and in this respect they are in fact reminiscent of the construction of space in time employed by Tarkovsky in service of the notion of 'sculpting in time'.[7]

Needless to say, editing is a relatively unimportant phase of Tarr's work. When a film consists of thirty to fifty shots, the order of the shots is not a real issue in the editing phase. Each shot consists of an entire narrative sequence and represents a temporal unit that is fixed at the time of the shooting, and cannot be altered later on. It happens very rarely that the order of these sequences is altered during editing or that any of them is left out. Much of the process of editing is dissolved into the process of planning the time sequences of the story, and the rhythm of the film is also fixed in the shooting phase. That is also when the length of the shot is basically fixed, leaving only limited opportunities for some adjustment through editing. This is why the shooting schedule is adapted to the chronology of the story when this is possible. As the possibility to change the order of the shots is limited, and especially because there is no way of changing the order of the scenes within the individual shots, it is essential for Tarr to know how a shot ends in order to know how to start the next sequence. And because most aspects of the shot are determined during shooting, filming in chronology wherever it is technically and logistically possible becomes the optimal solution.

Obviously, extreme long takes raise the question of the possibility of corrections. If something in a ten-minute take is not quite successful, the whole take has to be repeated with the risk of doing something else wrong in the second version. There is no possibility of mixing the two versions by keeping what is good in each. A third, a fourth, or a tenth version has to be made until everything is perfect. Sometimes this becomes impossible, especially when several weeks or months pass between the shooting of the different versions, and in such a case Tarr has to come to accept what he hates most: a compromise.

Making a film is a real collaborative work for Tarr. Anybody in the crew or in his closer environment is welcome to contribute to the creative process with a useful idea. Everybody in the crew has his or her precise role of course, but anybody is free to make comments on things that may seem beyond his or her competence. Tarr never says, 'This is none of your business', as long as the person in question does not speak nonsense too often. Everybody is encouraged to have creative ideas that contribute to realising the film's main conception. This is why Tarr considers his main collaborators as co-authors. Everything depends on the person rather than on the position the person has in the crew. An assistant may propose important changes in the soundtrack at the post-production phase, and Tarr will listen to him; a line producer may suggest shifts in camera movements or framings; and of course the cinematographer is required to be as creative as possible, in line with Tarr's thoughts, naturally.

One person with whom Tarr has a special working relationship is Mihály Víg, his main composer since *Almanac of Fall*. (Courtesy of Béla Tarr)

Mihály Víg was a member of the underground rock group Trabant, formed in 1980. The group did not last long but became incredibly popular in young intellectual and avant-garde circles. In the early 1980s two Hungarian films featured their music or some of their members: Gábor Bódy's *Kutya éji dala* (*Dog's Night Song*, 1982) and *Eszkimó asszony fázik* (*Eskimo Woman Feels Cold*, 1984) by János Xantus. Tarr was also looking for a composer for his film from this environment. His choice of Víg turned out to be a good one; not only has he become one of his most stable collaborators, but Víg's work has become an essential part of the Tarr films. As Tarr explains:

> Without the composer the films wouldn't be what they are. He goes into the studio a month before the actual shooting takes place, composes the music, gives it to us and then we use the music during the shoot. So the music plays an equal role to the actors or the scenes or the story. And we trust him so much that we don't go there into the studio. He composes the music and brings the music to us. It's a very close and very profound, very friendly relationship which has been shaped over the past 15 years, and it's a relationship where we don't need to talk about anything serious. We never talk about art, we never talk about philosophy, we don't discuss aesthetics.[8]

It may sound strange that the music is composed even before the shooting starts. This means that Víg's work is not based on the actual images. Rather, the opposite is true. Tarr uses the composed music while actually shooting the film. He knows which scenes will be accompanied by music, and when they are shooting this particular scene they play the music. Very often the music during shooting helps in creating the

Left: Hranitzky and Tarr on the shoot for *Almanac of Fall* in 1983. Right: Hranitzky on the shoot for *Almanac of Fall* in 1983. (Courtesy of Béla Tarr)

exact rhythm of the long and complicated camera movements. According to Gábor Medvigy, cinematographer of *Damnation* and *Satantango* and main cinematographer of *Werckmeister Harmonies*, the shooting of the second market-place scene was saved by Ágnes Hranitzky's idea to start playing the music out loud in the square so that the Steadicam operator felt the rhythm of the scene.

The person who has overall control in all aspects of Tarr's films is his wife, Ágnes Hranitzky. She trained as an editor and started her film career as an assistant editor in the mid-1960s. From the mid-1970s she became involved with the documentary-fiction current. She also became the editor for *Filmregény* (1977), during the production of which she met Béla Tarr. *Filmregény*'s co-director, Györgyi Szalai, called her attention to a twenty-year-old second assistant. According to Ágnes, Szalai said to her about Béla,

Hranitzky and Tarr preparing *The Turin Horse*. (Courtesy of Béla Tarr)

with an obvious lack of foresight: 'Watch that kid, he is awfully good, but the best thing about him is that he doesn't want to be a filmmaker.' Hranitzky had a different impression; she has been living and working with him ever since. She should have been the editor of *Family Nest* but was busy at the time, so her assistant, Anna Kornis, became chief editor, and Hranitzky was consultant. In *The Outsider* she is credited as co-director and editor of the film.

Since then, she has always been part of the creative process right from the beginning of a project. Tarr discusses with her every little detail of the idea, the scenario, the dialogue, the visual conception, the camera movements, the set, the props, the actors, directing, post-production, and she is of course the editor. She is present at every phase of the production and takes action independently if she feels it is necessary. During the shooting phase, other than keeping a critical eye on everything, she is the one who holds the crew together, keeping up morale in times of crisis. She has the authority to give instruction to anybody in the crew and she does this with an incredible thoughtfulness, so that her instructions do not contradict Béla's. If they have different ideas about something, nobody in the crew notices. They discuss it in private.

One could ask why the Tarr-Hranitzky filmmaking relationship is not considered in the same way as, for example, the Straub-Huillet relationship. Why do we speak about 'Tarr films' rather than about 'Tarr-Hranitzky films'? For the public the name of Ágnes Hranitzky is not known at all, even though she is always credited as co-director in each film. Only their collaborators know exactly Hranitzky's role in the creative process, but as one of their closest collaborators, cinematographer Gábor Medvigy, put it, 'nobody really knows the nature or their work together'. So, we have to accept what they say about it. As she explains: 'I have a say in everything, but it's always Béla who has the creative initiative.'[9]

Notes

1 Personal conversation, 2008.
2 Deutscher Akademischer Austausch Dienst: the German state's academic international exchange programme.
3 Unpublished interview, Budapest, 1994.
4 A French film, *Le père de mes enfants* (*The Father of My Children*), by Mia Hansen-Love produced in 2009 about Balsan's suicide has a character in it, the uncompromising 'young Swedish genius', who is very difficult to handle, and whose behaviour does not make the producer's life easy. However, the film refrains from putting all the blame on him for the producer's suicide.
5 Unpublished interview, Budapest, 2004.
6 Unpublished interview, Budapest, 1994.
7 'What is then the essence of the work of the film director? Sculpting in time. Just like a sculptor, who takes a marble block, and having an idea about its future form, extracts all that doesn't belong to it, the filmmaker takes a time block, an enormous portion of fact of the existence, and eliminates all that he doesn't need, and keeps only that which turns out to be a component of the film image.' Andrei Tarkovsky (1989) *Le temps scellé*. Paris: Cahiers du cinéma, 61.
8 Jonathan Romney, 'Places off the Map', interview with Béla Tarr on the stage of the NFT in London. In: *Béla Tarr*. Published on the occasion of the retrospective of Béla Tarr's films at the MOMA in New York, 15 October 2001, p. 48.
9 Personal conversation, 2010.

CHAPTER TWO

Style in the Early Years

On first sight Tarr's oeuvre may be easily divided into two very different stylistic periods: the first running from *Family Nest* to *The Prefab People* (1977–82) and the second running from *Damnation* to *The Turin Horse* (1988–2011). In between, there is a 'transitional' work, *Almanac of Fall*, which carries important stylistic features of both periods, but could not be said to belong to either of them really. What I would like to draw attention to here is first of all, of course, the differences, but then also, and most importantly, the continuity and the evolution between the two periods. As much as the two periods are clearly distinguishable, Tarr's oeuvre can also be viewed as a single continuous path leading to the crystallisation of a personal cinematic expression. This crystallisation process went through various stages until the elements that can now be considered as fundamental characteristics of Tarr's films became articulated and integrated into the Tarr style. Quantitative-style analysis, applied later in this book, will show exactly to what extent this oeuvre can be considered as unified and divided into periods at the same time.

One can best characterise this style as the wedding of two extremes: concrete representation of poverty, of moral and psychic misery in the social and physical environment on the one hand, and poetry of dreams and desires in the representation of the individual characters on the other. Once Tarr found this form, he ran it through different variations and arrived at its excessively reduced and concise version, which he now considers something that cannot be developed any further. In the following overview I will trace his path from the direct cinema style fashionable in the mid-1970s to the doorstep of his own authorial style based on extreme long takes.

As someone who started out in documentary filmmaking and whose first inspiration was a style somewhere between fiction and documentary, Tarr's first-period films can seen as having some general traits that characterise other films of the same movement in this period. Tarr used certain conventions of a series of films which became an increasingly important stylistic influence in Hungarian cinema between around 1975 and 1985. In order to understand the particularities of Tarr's personal style, we have to first understand against what norm his style can be considered particular.

The documentary look

The techniques of direct filming, *cinéma vérité* or documentary in fiction films became widespread in European modern art cinema in the second half of the 1960s, had their climax around the early 1970s, and vanished gradually thereafter.[1] The New German Cinema – especially of Alexander Kluge, Ulrich Schamoni and Peter Fleischmann – gave considerable momentum to this stylistic phenomenon.[2] There were essentially two ways in which filmmakers in this period referred to the non-fiction reality background of their stories. One was the use of the Brechtian 'estrangement effect', a critical reflection on fictional conventions, and the other was what Kluge called 'realism as protest'.[3] According to Kluge, social reality should be filtered through explicit personal judgement of this reality. Thus subjective stylistic patterns, especially those related to editing on the one hand and documentary stylistic patterns (especially those related to visual representation, acting and narrative) on the other, could be freely mixed in one film. This went beyond the original *cinéma vérité* style, in which subjectivity was strictly limited to the personal commentaries of the protagonists, but the author remained in the background as an observer. In the New German Cinema the author comes to the foreground via straightforward irony and/or overt criticism expressed by means of tendentious juxtaposition of specific images and events. This was, however, not unknown in European cinema before the emergence of the New German Cinema. The Czechoslovak New Wave in the early 1960s made ironic use of this formula in films such as Milos Forman's *Black Peter* (1962) and *Loves of a Blonde* (1964) and Ivan Passer's *Intimate Lighting* (1965). The specificity of the New German Cinema was the overt and sharp social criticism, especially in films like Kluge's *Yesterday Girl* (1966), Schamoni's *It* (1966) and Fleischmann's *Hunting Scenes from Bavaria* (1969).

In Hungarian cinema the idea of mixing fiction with documentary style appeared around the early 1970s but did not become really fashionable before around 1975, the time it started to vanish elsewhere. We can attribute this fact to two reasons. Firstly, Hungarian modern cinema in the 1960s relied on a 'serious', often tragic, approach to Hungarian history which did not incorporate irony or documentary style very easily. Secondly, when Hungarian cinema adopted the documentary-fiction mixing method after all, it was due to the simple fact that a certain documentary film practice could not be continued any longer.

The documentary-fiction current grew out of a documentary film practice existing between 1969 and 1974 in the official Hungarian experimental studio of young filmmakers called the Balázs Béla Stúdió. This documentary practice was aimed at developing a certain sociological approach. Especially at the beginning, they did not deal very much with concrete social issues; rather they showed the everydayness of ordinary life. They filmed characteristic details of ways of life, typical situations of communication and procedures of bureaucracy. It was like ethnographic filming in their own immediate environment. Around the mid-1970s it became increasingly difficult to make these documentaries, as it became widespread for these filmmakers to ridicule the people they filmed, and especially in official circles people were reluctant to allow them into their offices to film what they were doing. To get around these difficulties, the filmmakers started to make feature-length fiction films out of real stories with the same purpose, only the characters were not identical to the ones in the real-life stories.

The main concept was that amateur actors play situations in which only the general outlines are determined. Dialogue is improvised by the actors and also improvised are the gestures and the movements they make. The director and the camera operator never know exactly what will follow in a scene; they cannot make many non-recorded rehearsals, because non-professional actors are seldom able to repeat a scene the same way over and over again, and if a scene goes right, it has to be recorded right away. The camera operator does not know exactly what is going on in the scene, so it is shot mostly with two cameras. The camera operator has to improvise too; he or she has to watch the space off-screen to know when to turn the camera from one character to another. The camera is most of the time hand-held in these films, and camera movements are like those of a documentary film: there is always a certain amount of randomness in it in that the characters' movements are only loosely pre-determined. Shots are not too long, but the average is over twenty seconds – 28 seconds in the case of *Jutalomutazás* (1974), the first work of this movement – with large deviations between ten seconds and two minutes. These films were meant to be as 'professional' as possible, so the directors did not stick to any particular non-mainstream or modernist stylistic patterns. Their goal was clear exposition of the issue, so they used classical shot/reverse-shot patterns, long shots, medium close-ups, and close-ups according to classical analytical editing style. Their narratives were linear and chronological. Stories were concentrated around social issues rather than around personal or psychological matters. The characters were meant to be typical creatures of their environment, and their individual traits were not emphasised. The stories did not depict extraordinary, shocking or indecent situations or behaviours. To emphasise the 'reality effect' they used exclusively unaltered real-world locations. The filmmakers would rather travel around the country to find the appropriate real-life office of a party bureaucrat than create it in a studio. After all, most of the elements were real in such a film: the stories, to begin with; the locations, even though exteriors and interiors were often not in the same town or village; the characters, who often had the same profession in real life as they had in the film, although of course they were not the real-life protagonists of the stories; and the words the characters said, which were their own, and were meant to represent the way 'these kind of people' would speak in real life in such a situation.

Style in Tarr's early films

Most of the above-mentioned features characterise Tarr's early films, but they did to a lesser extent by the end of the period than in the beginning. The main characters of *Family Nest* and *The Outsider* had their origin in real life (in the first film Irén plays herself), but their stories in the films were mostly the creation of Tarr's fantasy. In the opening credits of *Family Nest* Tarr put the following titles: 'This is a real story. It didn't happen to the people in this film, but it could have.' By contrast, the stories of *The Prefab People* and *Almanac of Fall* were pure inventions, even though in the case of *The Prefab People* the story was so unspecific that it could be considered as an illustration of the way thousands of families lived in Hungary at that time. In *Almanac of Fall* neither the story nor the characters had real-life originals.

Actors were all amateurs and therefore acting style was improvised in *Family Nest* and *The Outsider*; by contrast, in *The Prefab People* and *Almanac of Fall* well-known professional actors improvised their dialogue, and in this case improvisation was already less apparent. Locations were real in three of the four films. That is where *Almanac of Fall* is different from all of Tarr's films, not only from the early ones. This film is shot in a set that is utterly artificial.

The first two films were shot using the two-camera method, and from *The Prefab People* onwards Tarr used only a single camera, although with several consecutive cameramen. Average shot length is exactly the same in the first two films – 31 seconds – and corresponds to the documentary-fiction norm. However, shot length gradually increases over the following films: 46 seconds for *The Prefab People* and 51 seconds for *Almanac of Fall*. In the film that stands between the two periods, shots are almost twice as long on average as in Tarr's first film, although we can find extreme long takes in all of his films: one of the last shots in *Family Nest* runs over five minutes, and the last shot of *The Outsider* is six and a half minutes long. There is a clear tendency in at least two important aspects in this period: the increase of fictional elements in the story correlates with the increase in the length of the takes. This correlation, as a trend, already clearly shows the most important aspects of the Tarr style of the second period.

What is clearly different in Tarr's early films from the documentary-fiction norm concerns, rather, the focus of the narrative. Tarr is here concentrating on personal relationships rather than on social aspects of the story. This is the least apparent in *Family Nest*, as there is a recurrent conversation topic in the film: the problems caused by the young couple not having an independent apartment. However, most of the scenes of the film are not about this problem, but about the absolute stupidity of the characters and their lack of respect for one another. In *The Outsider* and in later films one can identify no social issues, not even as pretexts; the films concentrate entirely on personal relations.

Stylistically, all three films are slightly different from the other documentary-fiction films in one common way: the *mise-en-scène*. Because for Tarr the important thing in the film is to show how human relations develop in given circumstances rather than to show how a story develops toward the *dénouement*, his technique of directing scenes emphasises the development of human interactions. Especially in *Family Nest*, there are very few scenes where the goal of the scene is some concrete result which would move the story forward. Every scene represents a twist in the relationship of the characters rather than a turn in the story. There are almost no physical acts in the film, only verbal ones. In all of these films there is only one important turn in the plot. In *Family Nest* Irén decides to leave her husband and her father-in-law's apartment. In *The Outsider* András marries Kata. In *The Prefab People* Robi leaves his wife. The verbal acts move the film forward as they lead toward the one big turn in the story.

This is what determines the *mise-en-scène* of the scenes. Tarr organises the scenes in such a way that the emotional rather than the narrative content of the scene becomes visible. Since he works with non-professional actors, and the dialogue is not written in advance, this takes more time than it would if the function of the scene were to direct it toward a plot turn. The film shows a scene as long as is needed for the characters to arrive at a certain emotional state or to explain the emotional state they are in. The basics of the *mise-en-scène* remain the same: staged conversation situations between two or more people, where the characters do not move too much. The camera shows mainly faces and small groups of people who talk and react. In *Family Nest* Tarr uses mainly relatively short static close-ups in filming these situations, where the only camera movement is panning from one character's face to another's. This technique requires that even if takes are not extremely long in these films, the individual scenes are. In later films of this period he is slightly more open to character movement, and especially to more tracking camera movement. In *Almanac of Fall* long tracking shots abound. The average scene length is five minutes for *Family Nest* and four minutes and forty seconds for *The Prefab People* but only three minutes for *Almanac of Fall*. In other words, while shot length increased considerably during the period – 31 seconds, 31 seconds, 46 seconds and 51 seconds respectively from *Family Nest* to *Almanac of Fall* – scene length became shorter by almost exactly the same rate. This means that while Tarr's *mise-en-scène* technique did not change much between *Family Nest* and *The Prefab People*, his camera style changed slightly, since the same average scene length is achieved with considerably longer takes. By the end of the period, this ratio has changed to the extent that Tarr created scenes almost half as long with the help of takes nearly twice as long, in comparison to *Family Nest*. This means that we can expect that in *Almanac of Fall* both *mise-en-scène* and camerawork changed considerably. And that is what we will find, which is why we can consider this film as a transitional film between two periods and two different stylistic systems.

Family Nest

'Revealing' camerawork

This film depicts a very typical situation in Hungary of the 1970s: a worker's large family living in a one-bedroom apartment. The middle-aged couple has three grown-up children, two of whom – a son and a daughter – live with them, along with the wife, Irén, and the little daughter of the son. This unbearable situation is made even more serious by the bad relationship between the parents and the daughter-in-law. The story starts when the son arrives home from his military service. Everybody has great expectations. The parents hope that finally they will leave the house, and the wife hopes that her husband will protect her from the constant verbal attacks of her father-in-law. None of these expectations are fulfilled. The young couple is unable to find a place to live, and the father-in-law not only continues his verbal attacks but also tries to turn his son against his daughter-in-law. His attempts turn out to be successful, and Irén and her little daughter leave the house without her husband protecting them. They have no other choice than to find an illegal squat from which the police may evict them at any moment. The film focuses less on the problems of the Hungarian housing situation than on the human relationships which make this situation more severe. Its stylistic features stem from this concentration on human interaction.

Stylistically, *Family Nest* is atypical in Tarr's oeuvre, in that he has made no other films constructed so consistently with close-ups. There are only two long shots in the film, one at the end of the opening sequence and one in the amusement park scene. Considering that this latter is an open-air scene with no particular personal interactions and no dialogue, the fact that Tarr shot this scene mainly with medium close-ups and only one real long shot is very telling of the consistency with which he avoids wider frames in this film. Tarr takes this approach to create a peculiar surprise effect in his film.

There is a recurring pattern of camera movement in *Family Nest*, which is just the opposite of the standard Hollywood convention for opening a scene. At the beginning of a shot the camera shows a close-up of an object or a person. Later in the shot the image becomes wider, revealing the whole picture. This is done either by slowly zooming out from the initial detail or by turning away from it with or without zooming out. The initial shot of the film illustrates this point. The film opens on two hens in an indeterminate location. It could be a yard, it could be the side of a road, it could be anything. Someone moves into the close-up frame, and the camera turns to her, and as she is getting farther away (the camera does not follow her), the close-up becomes a medium close-up, and then as the camera zooms out from the medium close-up, the picture becomes a medium long shot, and finally a long shot revealing the environment of the initial close-up. And now we can see that the two hens were in fact pecking their way on an unpaved narrow street lined with dirty and neglected houses and full of garbage: a street in either a poor village or the poor outskirts of a big city (figures 1a–d).

Another form of this revealing procedure is when the frame does not change considerably, and the camera shows the immediate environment of the initial object or person by panning or by editing. This is how the family situation is introduced in the eighth shot. The sequence starts with a close-up of the father-in-law. In the reverse-shot we see his wife in a wider close-up, in which part of his head is visible too. Then as the dialogue starts to involve the daughter-in-law and her colleague the camera pans to the right and widens the frame further so that for a second several characters become visible, at least in part, at the same time (figures 2a–d). However, during the whole sequence we never get an image wider than a medium close-up, let alone an establishing shot of the room they are in.

Most of the time this procedure provokes some surprise. There is a clear surprise effect at the beginning of the film, when the viewer expects the character's location to be specified, only to find that no clear idea can be obtained from the heterogeneous elements of the scenery.

The surprise effect becomes shocking in three scenes later in the film. The first, extremely shocking, is the rape scene. When Irén's friend leaves the house, unexpectedly, the two brothers leave too. The next shot is a close-up of the young woman struggling with two men. We recognise her, but not the two men, whose faces are revealed only thirty seconds later, when the camera gradually gets to the distance of a medium close-up: it is the two brothers, one of whom just got back to his wife and child from military service after two years (figures 3a–d).

The next scene is even more shocking. After the two brothers rape the young

Figures 2a–d

woman, we see Gabi, the elder brother, ordering a drink in a pub. Again, this is a close-up. This shot lasts forty seconds. Then comes another close-up of Laci, the younger brother, and the camera slowly pans to his right, revealing the entire situation: the

Figures 3a–d   Figures 4a–d

Figures 5a & b

raped woman is with them in the pub, turning towards him to light her cigarette. Tarr never shows the three of them in one frame; we see only close-ups (figures 4a–d).

Another instance of the surprise effect Tarr achieves through this revealing procedure is in the scene when we first see the father-in-law talking to someone in an unusually nice tone; the camera pans to another close-up of the face of a woman he wants to seduce, the same woman Irén complains to about him, which also adds to the surprise effect (figures 5a & b). The camerawork significantly contributes to the dramatic tension of the film. Its role is not only to reveal the environment of the individual events, but to create surprise, and, as in the last case, irony. It works in such a way that after a while the viewer suspects every instance of a close-up which initiates a scene to hide some funny or shocking detail in the off-screen space, which is a peculiar way of creating suspense in the film.

Participation

Family Nest's consistent close-up style, together with the revealing camerawork, allows for another stylistic pattern, which is implicit for the biggest part of the film, but becomes explicit at the end. The effect of this pattern is the sense that the camera (or the man behind the camera) is participating in the events, that he – the man behind the camera – is in fact present as the action takes place. The fact that Tarr keeps his close-ups tight forces the cameraman to frequently pan with the camera so as to be able to show who is talking or the reaction of a character. Wider shots would make this unnecessary: the camera could remain static, or could make more subtle and unnoticeable movements. Sometimes, however, the camera makes 'arbitrary' movements too, where panning is not motivated by the intention to show a speaking or listening character. On the contrary, even though a character is speaking, the camera moves away from him, and shows something else. A clear instance of this effect is the scene where the father and his three children are playing cards. There is a one-minute-fifty-second-long shot in the middle of the scene where the camera makes a panning move the entire time. During this time the father tells a story about his wartime memories, and they also talk about the card game. The camera first shows close-ups of faces, hands and playing cards, but after a while it pans away from the players and starts showing the television set behind the father, and while we can hear the father's story, we watch and can also hear the programme on television. This 'off the topic' part lasts 22 seconds, more than twenty per cent of the whole shot, which is clearly significant, and calls attention to the arbitrariness or 'independence' of the camera more explicitly than the simple revealing panning shots.

At the end of the film, there are two explicit indications that the camera and the filmmaker are physically present in the diegetic world. These are, however, also pure stylistic elements evoking a 'real' documentary film. They are the 'interview' scenes with Irén and with her husband, where they talk to the camera as if everything that the spectator has seen were real-life documents to which they are giving their reaction. These scenes are foreshadowed by a conversation during which Irén talks to a friend of hers. This is also an example of the revealing technique Tarr uses in the film. In this case, however, the surprise comes first, before the revelation. Irén talks to someone we do not see in extreme close-up for ninety seconds in one long take. It already feels like this is an interview scene, since no one seen before would fit into this situation, so all we can suppose is that Irén is talking to the camera, which is a surprise. After more than a minute, the counter-shot reveals Irén's party, which brings the situation back to the normal diegetic world. But ten minutes later the scene is repeated. Irén talks in close-up to someone who in this case is never revealed. The next shot shows her husband in the same situation, and there is no party on the opposite side of the camera in this case either. This is where the viewer's only possible supposition is that this is a simple interview by the filmmaker.

With these two (fake) interview scenes *Family Nest* constructs a clear stylistic and genre reference: *cinéma vérité*, the self-reflexive semi-documentary genre Jean Rouch invented in the 1950s, which became extremely popular in the late 1960s and early 1970s in Europe. In the *cinéma vérité* genre the film's narrative can also be fictional, but it is always filmed in a loose documentary style with amateur actors originating from the very environment the story takes place. The specificity of *cinéma vérité* is that the actors reflect from time to time on their roles and explain what they are doing and why. This is a form where the fictional character of the story is not hidden but reflected on, which creates another real documentary layer in the narrative: the commentaries and the reflections of the actors. This is a kind of self-reflective narrative in which the film's realist layer (description of the environment, real-life actors, random, unprepared events in the story) becomes fictional, and what is generally hidden in a fiction film (the presence of the filmmaker, the ideas and reactions of the actors, their interaction with the filmmakers) becomes the object of real documentation. Many filmmakers of the period used *cinéma vérité* even in entirely constructed fiction films, like Godard's many films in this period. Even Ingmar Bergman did it once in *The Passion of Anna* (1969), where well-known professional actors – Liv Ullmann, Erland Josephson, Bibi Andersson, Max von Sydow – comment on their parts and describe their feelings about the characters they play.

Tarr is not making *cinéma vérité*; he fakes it. He makes his film look like a *cinéma vérité* film by using the same stylistic elements, but not only is the whole story entirely fictional, but the actors' commentaries are too. As a result, all the stylistic effects of the film become the author's commentary about a reality that he does not represent, but only evokes with the help of the stylistic texture. Tarr very consciously manipulates the events (by editing or through camerawork) and makes them more dramatic than documentary film events usually are, while keeping the documentary 'look'. Tarr's style and narration are not subjective, yet the spectator can notice the author behind them, thanks to the fake *cinéma vérité* style, wherein the author and eventually the author's commentary are placed within the diegetic world. This very powerful authorial attitude is what distinguishes *Family Nest* from the rest of the documentary-fiction films. In no other film of this current would the author reveal him- or herself, let alone play with stylistic or genre elements. In an interview Tarr speaks about this attitude:

> The truth is, I tell you frankly, that never in my life did I shoot a documentary. I never could. … Somehow I have always been too aggressive, too overbearing to be able to make a documentary. Restraining yourself from manipulating things takes humility and much force. But this is impossible anyway, for if you go into a situation with a camera, you have already changed that situation, and nothing goes the way it would, weren't you there. And if this is the case, why not let it be entirely the way I want it?[4]

And it is in this same interview that Tarr talks about how he uses 'social reality' in his film: 'As far as I am concerned I have always limited myself to dealing with simple human stories. So, in these films society was just a background. It didn't mean much more than, say, the water for the fish.'

What we can see in Tarr's first film is that the documentary style hides a strong authorial dominance and a particular point of view, and this style is strongly informed by this dominance. Despite the rawness of the style and the technique, despite the 'low-budget look', there is a strong authorial conception that overwrites the dominant conventions of documentary representation of social reality of the period for the simple reason that Tarr was not interested in placing the social aspect in the foreground. 'The real' was just raw material for him to make his own agenda about human relations prevail, regardless of the social motifs that other documentary-style fiction films would emphasise.

Let us take an example from an emblematic film from the documentary-fiction movement, *Film Saga*, made by István Dárday and Györgyi Szalai around the same time (in 1978), and on which Tarr also worked as second assistant. There is a scene in the film which is comparable with a similar scene in *Family Nest*. Both scenes represent a family dinner with all the family members around the table. One of the main topics of both films is the housing shortage in Budapest. Both families – in one case four people and in the other, five – live in a very small two-bedroom apartment. In both families the parents are workers, although in *Film Saga* the grown-up children have gone to university. In *Film Saga* we have some close-ups, many medium close-ups and, to give viewers an idea of the space, some establishing shots of the kitchen they are in. In *Family Nest*, as mentioned above, we are never given an overview of the space, and we never get a shot with more than two characters in. In *Film Saga* the camera is mostly static, and changes of image are achieved by editing, while in *Family Nest* there is very little editing. The camera is most of the time panning from one character to the other. But the most important difference can be found in the dramatic construction of the scene. In *Film Saga* the whole conversation revolves around the possibility of finding a solution to the family's housing problem. Everybody gives his or her ideas; they raise solutions, discuss them, listen to each other's opinions, and even if sometimes one of them becomes a little more passionate, the overall atmosphere is serene and peaceful. The scene ends with one of the daughters reading out loud a philosophical citation from a serious theoretical journal. This suggests that even though they cannot possibly resolve their problem, they cooperatively look for a solution and they are willing to settle this for everyone's benefit. There is understanding and cooperation in the family, which is represented also visually when we see the family as a whole. In the case of *Family Nest* the representation of the family as a whole is missing entirely. Family members are visually isolated; we can see only one family member at a time. This visual representation well reflects their uncooperative behaviour. In this case there is no mention of the housing problem; there is only a single reference made by Irén to the fact that everything will be different when they can go and live separately. The whole conversation is an exchange of verbal attacks. The topics of the conversation serve only as pretexts for a fight. Here is a sample from the conversation:

> *Father* (to his wife): It needs salt.
> *Mother*: You salt it, dear. How long does it take? Better undersalted than over.
> *Gábor*: True enough. You can salt it later but if it's oversalted…
> *Father*: The meat?
> *Mother*: You can salt that too a little.
> *Mother*: Stop giving it to me like that.
> *Gábor* (to his daughter, Kriszti): Stop playing around.
> *Kriszti*: I don't want that.
> *Father*: When she was with me while you were away, she ate everything.
> *Gábor*: You want me to beat her up?
> *Irén* (to Kriszti): Did you salt it? Grandma forgot the salt. You tell grandma to learn how to cook.
> *Mother*: For me it is salty enough.
> *Kriszti*: What?
> *Mother*: The potato.
> *Irén*: But you forgot to salt the meat.
> *Mother*: I salted that too.
> *Father* (to Irén): She plays with the food. You let that kid do anything, to splash around, mess it up with her hands.
> *Irén*: Let her, if she enjoys it, it'll put weight on her.
> *Father*: You really know how to bring a child up!
> *Irén*: You were delighted if your kids ate at all.
> *Father*: Don't bring up the old times with me. We are talking about what's happening at my table now!
> *Irén*: That happened at your table too.

Father: Look at what she's doing with the salt! Don't leave everything to that
    child. Bring her up properly the way I did with my three.
Irén: Kriszti, don't mess with the salt, Grandpa's getting angry.

This conversation goes on like this until they raise their voices and Irén leaves the
dinner table with Kriszti. Then the father turns to his son and starts scolding him. All
of them mention the fact that they cannot finish a lunch without starting an argument; they are unable not to start it, and unable to finish it.

Clearly, the housing problem is not the main problem here. It is their attitudes
that make the housing problem acute; whereas in the other case the housing problem
stands out as an independent factor, and it is not made more unbearable by the family
members' attitudes.

The Outsider

Tarr's second film follows a single protagonist, András, in the life he lives without
specific goals. András is working in a mental hospital as a nurse. He also plays violin in
the evenings in restaurants. Two important events occur at the beginning of the story.
We learn that a woman had his baby and he doesn't want to care for it, and he is fired
from the hospital because of his irresponsible behaviour. He has to leave his service
apartment too. He finds another job, and meets another woman, who he marries later
in the film. His brother pops up unexpectedly, after three years of absence. None of
these events has much influence on András's life. He continues to live from one day
to another, without having plans for the future. Finally, he is drafted into the army.

The style of this film reminds one more of an ordinary documentary-fiction work,
and overall, this film can be considered an attempt to approach the professional stand-
ards of the time, at least in the sense professionalism was meant in the circle of the
fictional documentary filmmakers. He follows this trend also in that this is a colour
film, which is a rarity in Tarr's oeuvre. He has made only two colour films in his career,
which includes nine released feature films. In *The Outsider* the only reason for the
colour film stock was to adopt the conventions of the time, and to make the film look
more professional. He tried colour film one more time in *Almanac of Fall*. This time it
was part of an experiment with various visual stylistic elements. After that Tarr realised
that black and white was more appropriate for his kind of stylisation, and he has not
made any colour footage in a feature film since. (The fact that *Macbeth* was a colour
production too tells us nothing about Tarr's own choice, since in 1982 it was already
unimaginable to produce anything in black and white for television.)

The Outsider is also different from the previous film in that Tarr does not stick to
close-ups. He uses a whole range of framings adapted to the given dramatic situation,
as a 'normal' feature film would do. Yet the dominant shot type is still the close-up in
the dialogue scenes, and dialogue scenes dominate this film too. So the close-up is the
dominant shot in the film, but it does not have such strong stylistic value as in *Family
Nest*. As noted earlier, the average shot length in this film is virtually equal to what we
find in *Family Nest*, with some extremely long takes, the longest being six and a half

minutes long. So the changes in *mise-en-scène* are due to the wider frame rather than to the longer or shorter takes. This will come later, in *Almanac of Fall*. It is the basic narrative situation that requires a wider visual perspective in *The Outsider* as compared with *Family Nest*. In the first film there are at least three protagonists – Irén, Laci and his father – with two or three supporting characters, and the story turns around their intimate personal relationships. In *The Outsider* there is only one protagonist but a lot of supporting characters who come and go and belong to the various locations András spends his life at: his several workplaces, his several homes, the street and more than one pub. He meets different people at these locations, and none of the relationships with these people is as intense and intimate as the relationships represented in *Family Nest*. Tarr concentrates rather on the atmosphere of these places and on the people who are there, which requires him to show more of the environment than was necessary in the other film. Tarr does not use the technique of revealing camerawork and editing in this film, because he does not need it to intensify the dramatic effect of the scenes. In this film neither the relationships nor the situations are filled with as much tension as in *Family Nest*. In fact this story is about a person who is falling out of all of his relationships and misses all of his opportunities to begin a coherent, purposeful life. He is stuck in a human environment that is full of people like him: all kinds of misfits, alcoholic has-been intellectuals, and drug addicts.

Camerawork is rather static in *The Outsider*; there are few panning movements, and no arbitrariness in the camera movements to give it a touch of self-consciousness. There is no trace of the author's intention to make this film feel like a documentary. The overall stylistic texture of this film is much less coherent than that of *Family Nest*. Most of the film is made of static 'talking head' close-ups; there are some more or less static long shots, especially in scenes which feature several people in restaurants and pubs.

Although dialogue scenes are relatively long, all of them have a specific narrative focus, unlike in *Family Nest*, where the only function of most of the dialogue scenes was to raise dramatic tension and to describe the characters' human relationships. There is one scene, however, that stands out in this respect. The style of this scene is so different from the rest that the viewer may find it either very annoying or very interesting, and wonder why Tarr has staged this dialogue in this way while in the rest of the film he does not use disturbing stylistic effects. This is the scene where András and Kata – his new wife – have a passionate argument for the first time in the story, shortly after their marriage. András is a disc jockey in a dance club and he is on a stage when Kata arrives and wants to talk to him. She does not go up to the stage and András will not come down to her, so they talk in a very uncomfortable position, quite far apart from each other. They have to shout, because the music is so loud, and we can barely see them, for the lighting is so poor, and the shot is dominated by the discotheque's coloured lights. The scene lasts nine minutes, and there is only one long take in it, lasting ninety-two seconds, yet all of the shots feel much longer, because of the deliberately poor quality of the sound and the image. In this take, over a minute and a half long, we barely see the characters. Kata's face is in the middle in the darkness, between two lights, which nevertheless do not light her face up, but rather make it even darker (figure 6). The dialogue of the two characters is almost entirely suppressed by the loud

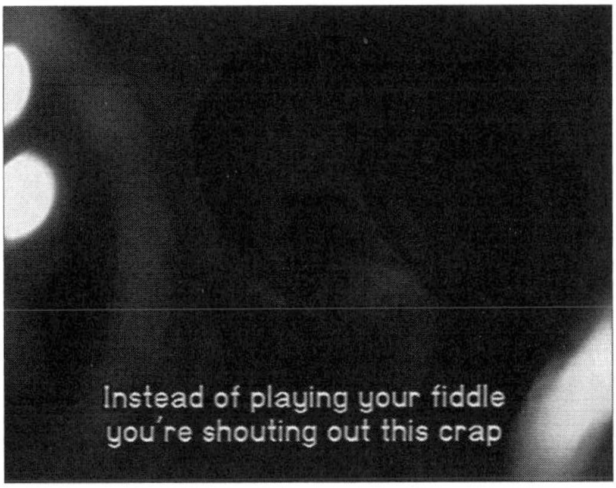

Figure 6

Instead of playing your fiddle
you're shouting out this crap

music, and sometimes their faces are completely in the shade because of the low-key lighting and the coloured lights around them.

This scene differs more from the rest of the film than the card-playing scene in *Family Nest* does from its own environment. The card-playing scene can be regarded as an excessive example of an already introduced stylistic pattern – a frequently panning camera – whereas nowhere else in *The Outsider* can we find effects that make acoustic and visual perception difficult, so this is not a stylistic pattern that characterises the film, but rather a unique stylistic effect relating to the narrative function of this scene. It showed for the first time Tarr's keenness for expressive stylistic solutions, for working with strong visual and acoustic effects, which would be prominent in the second period. Stylistically, *The Outsider* can be viewed as a film in which Tarr tried something slightly different than what he did in *Family Nest* within the same stylistic system. In both films he tried to reach some kind of radical solution. Divergence from the norm was achieved in *Family Nest* through the claustrophobic atmosphere and the excessive shocking surprises, in *The Outsider* through the excessively dedramatised narration.

The Prefab People

This film is about a young couple with two small children living the life of an ordinary lower-middle-class family in a housing project in a provincial small town. The man, Robi, works in a factory, and his wife, Judit, is at home with the children. The film starts with a scene where they break up. In the next scene, which obviously goes back in time, they are together, celebrating their wedding anniversary. We learn that Judit is bored and keeps asking her husband to help her in finding a job at the factory. Robi does not really care about her problem; in fact he is bored of family life and of his wife's depression. He has an opportunity in the factory to go to work abroad, which would allow him to earn more money, and to be away from the family. Judit protests against the idea of remaining alone for two years with the children and no work. In a similar scene to the one we saw at the beginning of the film, Robi packs up and leaves his wife. However, in the last scene we unexpectedly see them together again, buying a washing machine. Their relationship seems to be more depressing then ever before.

In *The Prefab People* Tarr carries out a major change in his style, and applies a narrative device that already represents a distancing from the documentary-fiction norm, even if it does not represent a real break yet. Instead of a strict linear narration, he starts the film with a scene from the end of the story, and repeats the scene at the end of the film in its correct chronological place. This is the scene in which the husband, who has had enough of family life, packs up and leaves the family. But the film does not end there. After a long monologue from the abandoned wife, we see them together again buying a washing machine, suggesting that the whole story starts all over again. This is the first time that the most fundamental narrative pattern of Tarr's second-period films, the idea of circularity, appears clearly in the oeuvre. And the stylistic novelty is that this time he works with professional actors using the same improvisation technique as in the earlier films. These two changes modify considerably the effect this film has on the viewer as compared to the two earlier films. While in *Family Nest* the main effect was the creation of a sense of the film resembling a *cinéma vérité* film – that is, of its seeming to be like a documentary film, whereas it was a complete fiction – in *The Outsider* the creation of a documentary-like impression was not the main purpose. In *The Prefab People*, by contrast, the fictitious character of the story is already emphasised, and the everyday banality of the scenes and the improvisation of the actors serve to make the story elements look as ordinary as possible. One can clearly see to what extent Tarr wanted to get away from the documentary look. Ordinary events in *Family Nest* are extremely intensified and dramatic, and sometimes – primarily in the scenes where the father is present – this has a caricatural effect, and, after all, the scenes become extraordinary. This kind of intensity is entirely missing from *The Outsider*. It comes back in *The Prefab People* but without the caricatural effect. Tarr was careful not to go beyond at any moment the most banal and ordinary communication, and what he tried to do was to make this banality feel unbearably suffocating without intensifying the scenes themselves. Intensity is provided by the condensed, expressive play of the actors, which was the main reason he used professional actors.

This has an effect on staging and style. The expressive power of acting is what allowed Tarr to create longer takes than in his previous films where the average shot length corresponded to the average shot length of documentary-fiction films using non-professional actors. Improvisation from good professional actors makes it possible to follow their play without editing and at the same time keeps the spectator's curiosity alive. That is what allows Tarr to use even longer takes in *Almanac of Fall* and to develop a genuine long-take style, which later would become a stylistic pattern in its own right, independent from acting technique.

Stylistically *The Prefab People* is even more balanced than *The Outsider*, with no excessive scenes like the discotheque scene in the latter film. *The Prefab People* is also based on dialogue scenes, but the predominant shots here are the medium close-up and the medium shot, unlike in *Family Nest*. Just to compare: the rate of close-ups in *Family Nest* is 63 per cent of the total running time. In *The Prefab People* this figure is only 13 per cent, and there is as much versatility in the shots here as in *The Outsider*. One of the longest close-up scenes has the same narrative position as the monologue scenes in *Family Nest*. After the second appearance of the scene in which Robi leaves his family, we have a three-minutes-and-ten-seconds-long close-up scene of Judit, the wife, talking to the camera. However, because of the repetition of the scene, the lack of a documentary look, and the fact that we know that this is a professional actress, this scene does not have the feel of an 'interview'. Although we cannot know whom she is talking to, we suppose with less conviction than in *Family Nest* that this is a documentation of some real-life event. So, a very similar scene in a very similar narrative position in this film has an entirely different effect on the viewer than in the other film, due to the narrative structure and the acting.

Macbeth

Macbeth is a television play produced in the same year as *The Prefab People*. Originally, it was an assignment for the film academy, and later Tarr proposed turning it into a television play. The original version is lost. Surprisingly for those at the time who followed Tarr's works, it contains nothing at the level of style, narration or subject matter similar to what Tarr was known for in his early period. On the other hand, it can be said to contain almost everything Tarr would be known for in his second period. To be more precise, it shows the other side of Tarr's interest in filmmaking, which had little opportunity to manifest itself until that time: his taste for continuous-long-take composition and stylised acting. This 72-minute-long film contains just two shots. The first is five minutes long, and the rest of the film consists of a single shot. In terms of shot length no subsequent Tarr film ever surpassed this early piece. Tarr regards this film mainly as an experiment, and that is what it is in many respects.[5] Technically speaking, this experiment had more than one difficulty to resolve.

One difficulty is that, just as in theatre, actors have to know their text from the beginning to the end, and all the details have to be rehearsed before the performance, because there is no way of repeating any detail individually. But, unlike in theatre, there are only so many opportunities for rehearsal, and for the actors, there is no opportunity to do it better once the take is recorded. Not to mention that there are no intermissions between acts for them to rest either. Regarding *mise-en-scène*, the greatest difficulty is how to signal time and space changes. Even in theatre there are some conventional solutions for that. But Tarr makes the action continuous and there is no empty space in the film, let alone fade-outs and fade-ins to signal time lapses. There is, however, a stylistic pattern developed by Tarr's compatriot, Miklós Jancsó, in the late 1960s for this purpose. The narration compresses several time and space segments into one single long shot by constantly moving from one space segment to another. This way time lapses in the story become changes in space achieved by the movements of the actors and the camera, and sometimes of the light. Changes in space in the story are much easier to achieve, since this is a theatre play that takes place in different parts of a castle. Tarr designed a set that is reminiscent of a dark cave or tunnel for the most part. (In fact the film was shot in an underground tunnel system under Budapest's Castle Hill.) So, when the characters move around in the set there is not much visual change in the film; the whole thing remains in the same highly, almost theatrically, stylised environment. Tarr also included a battle scene with horses, and even this does not break the theatrical stylisation of the film. Tarr doesn't follow Jancsó in two important respects. First, he almost never uses long shots, only medium close-ups, close-ups and some longer shots. And second, related to this, the actors do not move as much as in a Jancsó film. Tarr keeps close on the actors' faces, and focuses on their personal interactions rather than on the choreography of their movements. Most of the time the camera moves when the actors have to move or when there is a change of scene in the story, but it always stays close to the actors. Despite the continuous composition of the single, more than one-hour-long take, camera movements are functional in this film and lack the ornamental effect they have in Jancsó's films and in later films by Tarr, especially his next, *Almanac of Fall*.

The next stylistic element that is new in this film is the highly poetic dialogue of the characters, which replaced the improvised everyday talk Tarr used in his early films, even in those featuring professional actors. Obviously the question is not why Tarr uses Shakespeare's text when adapting *Macbeth*, but why he adapts *Macbeth*. This kind of interest in artificial theatricality and poetic discourse was not really predictable after his first two films. Radical intervention in the linear narrative flow was already present in a way in *Family Nest*, and more clearly in *The Prefab People*, but visual artifice and poetic stylisation were not present in the dialogue. These elements appear one by one in individual films in the early period against the background of the *cinéma vérité* or direct cinema style as additional elements motivated by Tarr's predominant thematic interests: selfishness, treason and manipulation in personal relationships.

Macbeth proves that already in the early 1980s Tarr was looking for something very different to what he was doing earlier in his feature films. He reached his second-period style step by step, always changing one or two stylistic elements, but in *Macbeth* he gathered almost all the elements to see how they worked together in an entirely different environment. He tried out long takes, an artificial set, special lighting effects, and a stylised literary text; he mixed professional and amateur actors; and above all, he chose a story in which power games, conspiracy and moral corruption were in focus rather than poverty and housing problems. In his next film Tarr applied many of the lessons he had learned from this experiment.

Almanac of Fall

This film is an ensemble play about five people living in an apartment. The entire play is about the characters' changing relationships. They make alliances, they betray each other, they fight, even physically, they try to seduce each other, they tell lies, they do whatever is necessary to have more control over one another, but they remain together in the same apartment.

By the early 1980s it was not only the 'documentary look' that lost its interest for Tarr, but also all superficial indicators of realism. *The Prefab People* and especially *Macbeth* were clear indications of that. In these films one can clearly discern a certain effort to get as far as possible from the visual environment of his previous films: the proletarian or lower-middle-class lifestyle so well-known in Hungarian films of the time. These films were no longer a kind of imprint of 'Hungarian life in the early

1980s'; detachment from the concrete social and economic environment appeared in them instead. Thanks to this, the difference between his films and the rest of the documentary-fiction films – the concentration on human rather than social relationships and the political environment – became immediately apparent. However, a distinguishable personal style used to represent the environment of the personal dramas was missing. *Almanac of Fall* was one way to go, and *Damnation*, three years later, was another. And the latter has proven to be the real way for Tarr.

Retrospectively, it is clear that for him the dilemma was not between 'realist' and 'artificial' or 'artistic' representation. It was between a personal and an impersonal representation of reality. What he was aiming for was not a political judgement of the object of representation, which was already present in the documentary-fiction films. It was the expression of a point of view of his own, a state of mind, rather than an objective critique, which unavoidably required an individual style. Most of the important ingredients of this style were already present separately in his films. Apparently, what was missing in order to come to the right solution was a literary background with a specific circular narrative structure and a peculiar artificial language, which Tarr found in László Krasznahorkai's novel *Satantango*, in 1985. In 1987, the stylistic solutions Tarr felt an attraction to came together with this narrative background to form a stylistic universe we could name *the pseudo form of the real*. *Almanac of Fall* is an important step toward this form.

Stylistically, *Almanac of Fall* stands between the two periods of Tarr's oeuvre, making a bridge between them. It brings the subject matter from *Family Nest* – intrigue and conspiracy of the members of a group of people living in a closed environment with each other. Once again, the location is an apartment. Only this time the camera never leaves the apartment. The film adopts the direct cinema approach of *The Prefab People*: the dialogue is improvised but professional actors do the improvisation, which renders acting more expressive and psychologically more nuanced. It adopts the artificial, even theatrical-looking set design from *Macbeth*, only this time visual artifice is emphasised much more. It adopts the long-take camera movement style also from *Macbeth*. As unlikely as it appeared at the time, *Almanac of Fall* was a result of a conscious search for a style where the real can meet the artificial, the personal can meet the social, the subjective authorial gaze can meet the objective social gaze. As in all of his previous films the narrative is based on dialogues, and in this respect *Family Nest* is the closest comparison, since in this film there are absolutely no scenes other than dialogue scenes. However, a quantitative difference shows Tarr's very different stylistic ideas. While the first film was composed mostly of close-ups (63 per cent, as mentioned before), in this film the figure is only 17 per cent, around the same as in *The Prefab People*. It seems that the distance Tarr kept from his characters in the early 1980s remained a constant feature.

At the same time *Almanac of Fall* was also a film of its time. The mid-1980s was a period when the visual artificiality of post-modernism moved from the visual arts to the cinema. Strong, colourful lighting effects; artificial-looking set designs; an expressionist acting style; eclectic mixtures of various visual styles; and direct citations of works of fine art, theatre and opera characterised a series of art films of this period. To name just a few: Jean-Jacques Beineix's *Diva* (1981) and *Betty Blue* (1986), Rainer

Werner Fassbinder's *Querelle* (1982), Peter Greenaway's *The Draughtsman's Contract* (1982) and other of his 1980s films, Francis Ford Coppola's *One From the Heart* (1982) and Derek Jarman's *Caravaggio* (1986). In Hungary the most prominent representa-

tive of this trend was Gábor Bódy, with his monumental *Narcissus and Psyche* (1980) and *Dog's Night Song* (1983), in which Béla Tarr made a brief appearance. Since this was an immediately available and contemporary stylistic method of discon-necting himself from superficial realism without joining the classical narrative and stylistic mode that also came back into fashion (the Hungarian representatives of which condemned him as unprofes-sional and amateur), Tarr chose to follow this new trend of artificial theatricality by asking one of Hungary's most fashionable artists of the time, Gyula Pauer, to be the set designer for his film.

In the beginning of the 1970s, Pauer had invented something he called 'pseudo art'. It started out as a marginal trend in the early 1970s conceptual avant-garde, and ended up as a mainstream concept in the post-modern art of the 1980s. In a nutshell, the essential idea of 'pseudo art' was to create an artificial surface which pretends to hide something and at the same time reveals its own falsity, inasmuch as it shows that in fact it hides nothing. It uncovers the manipulative nature of the artistic look. This is how Pauer explained it in his 'Pseudo Manifesto' in 1970:

'PSEUDO exposes itself as a false image, or at least as a complex object providing a false appearance.'[6] Tarr asked Pauer to design interiors that looked real and arti-ficial at the same time. He wanted the set to evoke a once rich bourgeois lifestyle, already on the way to disintegration, and at the same time he wanted the sets to appear artificial, not corresponding to any part of reality. Pauer designed a series of rich bourgeois interiors and placed artifi-

Figures 7a–d

cial elements in them to alert viewers to the fact that what they were seeing was not something one could encounter in the real world (figures 7a & b). It is art, in the 'pseudo-art' sense: it pretends to represent reality, and at the same time it reveals the falsity of this pretence.

In this scene, and in many others, the wall is covered with drapery mounted in such a way that some creases can be seen; the picture on the wall is also covered by this creased drapery. The viewer gets the impression that the drapery covers the scaffold of a theatrical set rather than the walls of a real apartment. It is not a real room, and the design lays bare the artificiality of the space. In other scenes the composition, the lighting and the carefully scattered objects provide the same effect (figure 7c).

At other times we can identify bizarre shadows too. In figure 7d we not only see the 'pseudo' drapery on the wall and the shadow of a statuette lit from below by a covered light source, so that this portion of the wall becomes a composition of pure shadow and light, but in the middle of the image we can see the shadow of an armchair turned upside down, which clearly cannot be a 'realistic' part of an apartment. It's function is purely ornamental.

Camera angles

Tarr's camerawork intensifies the artificiality effect. The apartment looks like a labyrinth, where the spatial relations remain unclear. We do not know how many rooms there are in this apartment, or which room is next to which, although we constantly move about from one part of the space to another. Very often the camera looks through windows or openings to give both a sense of depth of space and an unusual framing. Framing a composition sometimes seems to become a case of clearly masking something. That is, much of the visual space is covered by a foreground object which has an opening in the middle, and we can see the scene through this opening.

Such framings come in a variety of different forms in *Almanac of Fall*. Tarr uses objects, doors, windows and furniture to frame the scenes in which the characters interact. He often uses very unusual camera positions to create this framing or masking, as in figure 8, where the camera views the scene from under the piano.

Sometimes unusual camera positions become clearly 'impossible', at least from a realist point of view. Both instances are associated with the same couple of characters.

In another scene one of the male characters shaves the other one, and we look at them from above, from the point of view of the ceiling (figure 9).

The other case is the exact opposite of this viewpoint. When the same two characters have a fight, we see it from an even more impossible position: from the point of view of the ground (figure 10).

These extreme camera positions have no function other than to create a feeling of artificiality and particular emotional

Figure 8

Figure 9   Figure 10

effects through their unusual points of view. The unusual camera position reduces the reality effect of the image and pushes its graphic, abstract compositional properties to the foreground. When these abstract elements serve to provoke emotional responses in the viewer, we are close to the expressionist principle of style. In many ways we can see the renaissance of expressionism in the late 1970s/early 1980s post-modern style: strong emotional content is accentuated by visual effects like abstract and distorted compositions, unusual, unrealistic points of view, strong lighting contrasts and unrealistic lighting, and in the case of colour film excessive use of vivid colours. In figure 10 one can notice more of these features: the composition is rather abstract and plain due to the unusual, disturbing point of view, and colours are dominated by an unrealistic and vivid green contrasted by pink lights on the edges of objects and bodies.

Camera movement

The other spectacular stylistic feature of this film, which will undergo considerable development in later Tarr films, is the complicated long-take camerawork. As mentioned earlier, the length of the takes in Tarr's films constantly increased during this period. But the camera movements are not particularly complicated, not even in the excessively long single take of *Macbeth*, due to the narrowness of the space and the fact that most of the time the camera remained close to the actors' faces. It is in *Almanac of Fall* that the movements of the camera are truly detached from narrative functions and gain autonomous stylistic values.

Different kinds of autonomous camera movement can be discerned in this film:

1. Complex form of the revealing camera movement. Tarr did not use much revealing camera movement in his films after *Family Nest*. But in *Almanac of Fall* this device comes back, only in a much more complicated form than in *Family Nest*. While in that film it was basically used to reveal characters also present in a given scene who are not visible at the beginning of the scene, and the technique was in most cases a panning movement, in *Almanac of Fall* entire space segments or scenes are revealed by complicated travelling shots. Some of these movements involve the camera travelling through various spaces and passing by objects or characters to arrive at a final position where a scene starts. This is a technique that is familiar from the films of Andrei Tarkovsky, especially after *Solaris* (1972). It is also noteworthy that both in the Tarkovsky films and in *Almanac of Fall* the space is filled with a variety of objects that have an essentially ornamental function. In *Mirror* (1974) the long travelling shots take place mainly in interiors of large apartments or houses with several rooms, creating the impression of someone invisible traversing these rooms. What one cannot find in Tarkovsky's films, by contrast, is the recurrent pattern of looking through door openings and window openings with window bars in front. This is a stylistic pattern that appears in a spectacular way in some Fassbinder films of the late 1970s and early 1980s.[7] Tarr combined these effects to create his idiosyncratic camerawork in this film.

2. Obstructing camerawork. This type of camera movement is related to the second effect mentioned above. Here the camera passes in front of various openings that reveal or obstruct the view with their shapes. A clear example of this from the beginning of the film is the scene where Hédi and her son János have a fight. The camera moves across a space that is separated from the characters by a wall with different openings such as doors or windows. We can never see the scene in its entirety, only some parts, and even then the action is sometimes covered by different parts of the wall and the door (figures 11a & b).

There can be found combinations of revealing and obstructing movements. In a scene where Tibor and Anna start having sex, the camera first shows the kitchen sink, then moves slowly sideways to reveal through the kitchen door the scene in the next room, then stops for a while, then moves on, meaning that the scene disappears behind the kitchen wall (figures 12a–d).

Figures 11a & b

Figures 12a & b

Figures 12c & d

3. Framing and de-framing. In this film Tarr creates views where he systematically emphasises artificial frames, as is shown in figure 8. He often uses tracking shots to create framings and to dismantle them. The above example (figure 12c) illustrates the framing movement. It not only discloses the scene but also frames it. The opposite case is when the camera movement starts out from a framed image, and ends on an image without frames (figures 13a–c). In this case the scene is shown first in a mirror, together with the frame of the mirror. Then, via a slow movement we discover the placement of the mirror, and as the camera moves away from the mirror we can see the scene itself without the frames.

4. Impossible camera movement. We saw earlier that there are some 'impossible' camera positions in the film. There are also 'impossible' camera movements. At the end of the film, when Hédi calls the police, we see the scene in a medium close-up, so that a considerable amount of the background becomes visible. In fact the background is only a mirrored image of Hédi and the wall with a glass door that normally would not be visible, because it is on the other side of the room. At one point the background starts moving, as if the camera is making a slow tracking movement from right to left and back. Because Hédi's position doesn't change in

Figures 13a–c

Figures 14a & b

the image, the impression is that the camera is slowly turning around Hédi, which is why we see the background moving but not Hédi's position. However, Hédi's mirror image does not change angles, which suggests that in fact the camera is not changing its position relative to Hédi and to the mirror. In fact, what happens is that the mirror image is moving slowly sideways in the frame of the mirror while the scene in front of the camera is stationary relative to the camera. Because the movement is so slow, this is hardly noticeable; the viewer only experiences a strange feeling of instability. The technical setup was such that the mirror, the little table with the telephone in front of the mirror and Hédi in front of the table were moving together with the camera on the same dolly, so that the movement is perceptible only relative to the objects moving by in the mirror. (Note the change in the background in figures 14a & b.) But for the viewer it is impossible to tell whether the background is moving in the mirror or the mirror and Hédi are moving together with the camera.

5. *Choreographed tracking shots.* Sometimes the camera movement is motivated only by a certain choreography following either the characters' movements or a certain track in the space. The clearest example is the last party scene of the film, where the camera moves into the room, turns around the characters in one long shot, closes in on them and moves away again, before moving out of the room.

To summarise, we can say that Tarr's early films were considerably different from the documentary-fiction stylistic norm which they otherwise followed. Although this difference can be grasped in stylistic terms, it concerns in the first instance the thematic focus. Tarr was interested mainly in human relations rather than in socio-logical or political reality, which he considered only as a background for his stories. He wanted to catch the 'real' on the level of human communication, and he tried to adjust the stylistic norms of the documentary current to this level, which already had some stylistic constraints. Additionally, he realised that this was possible only if he accepted a particular authorial position, since what he wanted to provide was not an 'objective' sociological description, but a subjective interpretation of human relations. Step by step, he selected and combined his stylistic and narrative devices so that the authorial aspect became more prominent, while the 'reality effect' remained intact, thanks to improvisational acting. After all this, Tarr reached the stylistic system of John Cassavetes' films made in the 1970s, which he knew well and respected a lot.

At the same time, in *Almanac of Fall* Tarr tried in every possible way to move away from the visual realism and functionality of the documentary-fiction style. He used set design, composition, camerawork and lighting to emphasise the highly stylised character of this film on the visual level, but on the other hand, he kept the reality effect in the characters with the help of improvised dialogue. More than ever before, the two poles of Tarr's artistic ambition, poetic universalism and factual realism, became visible. Meanwhile, he found in *Macbeth* the main vehicle for his own stylistic expression: the long take. At this time the big question for Tarr was whether this mixture was the way to do it or whether there was another kind of structure in which these two poles could be unified. Two problems came into the foreground. Both concern the most essential traits of Tarr's style. First: what should be done with the long tracking shots, and what should be their function? And second: should the 'pseudo look' of the environment be kept in this highly artificial form, or was there another way of creating the pseudo effect? The answer was hidden in a radical change in the poles, and the incorporation of (pseudo-)realism in the environment and poetry in the characters.

Notes

1   See András Bálint Kovács (2008) *Screening Modernism*. Chicago: Chicago University Press.

2   See Thomas Elsaesser (1989) *The New German Cinema*. New Brunswick, NJ: Routledge.

3   Alexander Kluge (1975) *Gelegenheitsarbeit einer Sklavin. Zur realistischen Methode*. Frankfurt: Suhrkamp Verlag, 733.

4   Bálint Kenyeres (1997) 'Interview with Béla Tarr', *Metropolis*, Summer, 118.

5   Personal communication, 2010.

6   http://www.pauergyula.hu/kepzomuveszeti.html

7   See, for example, *Despair* (1978) and *Veronika Voss* (1982).

CHAPTER THREE

The Tarr Style

Tarr was given the manuscript of a young Hungarian writer, László Krasznahorkai, in early 1985 by literary critic Péter Balassa, who thought that this novel could be suitable material for a Tarr film. It was Krasznahorkai's *Satantango*, his first novel to be published. Krasznahorkai was a relatively unknown author at that time (he is only one year older than Tarr), having published only some short stories in literary journals. By the time *Satantango* came out later in the year, Tarr had already agreed with Krasznahorkai to make a film of his book.

To make a literary adaptation, especially of a highly stylised text such as *Satantango*, was already a considerable shift in Tarr's artistic conception. Certainly, *Macbeth* was a literary adaptation, but it was a compulsory exercise assigned by the film school, so it could not be considered a sign of Tarr's keenness for literary material, and judging from all of his films up to *Almanac of Fall*, the strongest invariable of his style was the improvisational work of the actors, especially regarding the dialogue, whether they were professionals or amateurs. The fact that he suddenly changed this particular element had serious consequences for other aspects of his style.

Tarr claims that he was not looking for anything at this time, especially not for some literary background for his films. As a matter of fact, he claims to not have had any particular plans in mind after finishing *Almanac of Fall*. It is also certain that his encounter with this manuscript was serendipitous, even if it is very likely that at some point later in time he would have read *Satantango* anyway, as this book has become a considerable national literary success (which is not to detract from Balassa's perceptiveness in intuiting that Krasznahorkai would be a good author for Tarr). Tarr never returned to improvised dialogue after *Almanac of Fall*. Moreover, for the rest of his filmmaking career he stuck with Krasznahorkai's literary works. This shows two things: first, Tarr was open to any kind of inspiration that would help him find the best combination of the stylistic tools he had been using; and second, Krasznahorkai's literary works and aesthetic approach turned out to be very productive in this respect.

One cannot say that Tarr was consciously preparing for a radical change, especially not that he knew what kind of radical change he wanted to achieve. What is more, even today, he cannot even see a radical change here.[1] In *Almanac of Fall*, however, anyone could see that Tarr was finished with everyday realism, and was trying to construct a form that could include all the stylistic elements he thought were important in his previous films. Tarr knew that one of his strengths was the way he could work with actors, professional or amateur, and have them behave and talk so that lively, real-life characters were born on the screen without any literary elaboration of their dialogue. However, this kind of reality effect was a limitation in that it meant that the everyday banality of life stories and personal relations could never really be eliminated. *Almanac of Fall* showed that even if he went as far as he possibly could in artificial stylisation of the environment, the improvisational method in the dialogue pushed the film back into the everyday reality of the early 1980s. The appropriate literary material would allow Tarr to change his approach and take off from social and historical concreteness. The manuscript of *Satantango* suddenly cleared the path for Tarr towards a stylistic conception, one of the basic elements of which proved to be the exact opposite of what had seemed to be one of the most essential ingredients of previous Tarr films: improvised dialogue. The shift to highly literary, artificial dialogue had very serious consequences regarding the entire stylistic universe of Tarr's films. *Macbeth*, *Almanac of Fall* and *Damnation* can be regarded as three different attempts to find a new aesthetic. He tried highly stylised dialogue with theatrical sets and extremely long takes in *Macbeth*, a theatrical set with a not extreme but still long-take style and improvised dialogue in *Almanac of Fall*, and a stylised but natural set with stylised dialogue and extreme long takes in *Damnation*. And this last aesthetic was the one he chose to adopt.

The novelty of this system was based on a shift in the representation of the environment and the characters. In the early Tarr films the main emphasis was on the representation of the characters' relationships, but the significance of the representation of the environment increased between *Family Nest* and *The Prefab People*. In *Almanac of Fall* the representation of the environment was already just as important as that of the characters. In this film Tarr draws greater attention to the environment through highly unnaturalistic, poetic and artificial visual effects. In the films of the second period, Tarr-style representation of the environment has already an unquestionable predominance. Character movements and positions, and camera movements and positions are mainly functions of the representation of the environment rather than of the characters. But the environment, albeit stylised, is not unnaturalistic any more. Tarr reaches back to reality, but this reality is totally different from what it looked like in the early films. This peculiar emphasis on the representation of the environment becomes one of the cornerstones of the Tarr style.

The other shift in the stylistic system between the earlier and later Tarr films is the way the characters are represented. From *Family Nest* through *Almanac of Fall* the emphasis is clearly on the representation of the characters. Albeit to a decreasing extent, close-ups of characters' faces were dominant in the films, and the overwhelming majority of the scenes were long dialogue scenes. Already between *Almanac of Fall* and *Damnation* we can detect an important decrease in number and length of dialogue scenes. Also, in all of the second-period Tarr films there is a clear contrast between two essential features: the way the characters behave and look and the environment they belong to on the one hand, and the way they speak on the other. Or, to put it in an even more simple way, there is a tension between the characters' exteriority (including their environment) and their interiority. One can say that the shift in the stylistic system of the Tarr films is from one important point of view the shift that occurred in the relationship between the characters and their environment. From *Damnation* the viewer may have a strong feeling that the characters of the stories are in one way or another trapped in an environment they do not belong to.

It is in this respect that we can clearly speak about two periods. While in the first period the characters behaved and talked in ways that are consistent with their environment – even though they were carefully individualised characters, unlike in most documentary-fiction-style films – in the second-period films most of the characters talk as if they do not belong to their environments. This structural shift is illustrated in simplified terms in the following table:

	Environment	Characters
first period	realist	realist
Almanac of Fall	poetic/lyrical	realist
second period	realist	poetic/lyrical

Even though 'realist' and 'poetic/lyrical' can correspond to very different textures and techniques in each case, these categories broadly characterise the main stylistic tendencies in each period. Or, to put it in another way so as to emphasise a little more the continuity between the two periods, we can say that the individual characterisation of the characters distinguishing them from one another became more explicit, concise and poetic in the second period, laying bare the psychic individuality which distinguishes them from their environment (and in both periods, characterisation is constructed in a basically realist way). Later on I will fine-tune this structure by showing the evolution within the Tarr style.

Clearly, not all of the features of the Tarr style can be connected to this structural change. But I believe that the different stylistic influences that can be found in these films, and the various individual solutions, were selected according to their potential to support this basic structure.

Long-take style

The most spectacular stylistic feature of the Tarr style, without any doubt, is the use of extremely long takes. This is something that cannot be viewed as constrained by the above-mentioned stylistic structure. Obviously, both realist and poetic representation can be achieved equally through short and long takes. Jancsó's films in the 1960s powerfully showed that the extreme long-take style can be associated with abstract symbolism too. This is what inspired many second- and third-wave modernists, such as Theo Angelopoulos and Philippe Garrel. Tarkovsky also used long takes in creating a dreamlike, transcendental world. Long takes are not predestined to represent a particular world or subject matter; rather this mode has a specific psychological effect associated with it that can be found in all long-take-style films.

The most basic effect of a long-take shot is the imitation of the continuity of the human gaze, especially when it is associated with a moving camera, which it mostly is. However, this gaze can be an inner gaze or it can be directed to the outside world; it can show all kinds of environments, not only real ones. In consequence, all kinds of long takes create in the viewer some feeling of participating in the space viewed. The participatory effect is enhanced by the movement of the camera during a long take, as it provides the sensation of moving about in the space, the spectator discovering the space together with the camera; and it can be attenuated by static camerawork, which gives the spectator the impression that he or she is staring at a scene, looking at it from an outside point of view, rather than being involved in it. Obviously, the participatory effect can be further enhanced by specific elements of a scene; a suspense effect may be used, for example, as it often is in thrillers. Either way, the long take is always more anthropomorphic than short takes and discontinuous changes of angle.

Basic types of long-take styles

The long take is a stylistic option that can be used for various purposes, and its different utilisations do not form a set of so many options or logical possibilities. However, there are typical variations which became the most successful, the most imitated solutions in film history. It is not always very easy to decide what effect a given long-take shot has in a particular film. Not only because in a single long take there can be many changes of effects, especially when a camera and character movements are involved, but also because the effect produced in the spectators is never exactly the same from person to person.

This is true even when specialists are involved. For example, film critic Scott Foundas feels that with the long takes in *Satantango* Tarr 'is really sort of immersing you in this world… It really is like you're living in these spaces.' David Bordwell on the contrary emphasises the distancing effect of the same long takes: 'I don't really see myself as complicit. I do see that it is about dignity, but it is almost an observation from a rather detached standpoint.'[2] Being immersed and being detached are rather opposite sensations. This contradiction may be the result of a true ambiguity in Tarr's use of long takes, but it might as well be simply due to the fact that the effect of long takes cannot be unambiguously categorised after all. I will argue that in some cases it can be, and in Tarr's case we have to deal with a true ambiguity: providing the sensation of being inside and outside at the same time is one of the specificities of Tarr's long takes, and it is a direct consequence of Tarr's moral attitude regarding his characters, which I will discuss further in chapter six.

In what follows, I will briefly characterise four types of use of long takes, most of them combined with long camera movements, which I think are the most influential in the cinema of the 1960s and 1970s, as well as in Tarr's work: process of de-dramatisation (Antonioni), choreography of continuous change (Jancsó), immersion and psychological participation (Tarkovsky), and distanced observation and self-conscious authorial presence (Godard).

Antonioni

There is no need to go into details of Antonioni's long-take style. This has been discussed at length and in great detail in film historiography.[3] Antonioni himself commented on this several times, and his comments serve best to explain his choice, especially in his early period, to create long-take compositions. This is how he explains the emergence of his long-take style in his first film:

> I felt that I still shouldn't let the characters go when the drama, or at least what we wanted to show of it had already taken place, when we had gotten through the climax, and the character was alone with the consequences of the scenes, shocks, heavy psychological moments which afflicted her, and pushed her toward the next event. I felt that even in these apparently insignificant moments I had to keep following her, when it may have seemed that we shouldn't be interested in the way she behaved, in what expression her face had, in what gesture she made. I tell you that I had my opportunities exactly in these moments when the characters (when I say characters I mean also actors) remained alone, because very often I followed them without them knowing it, or when they thought that the take was cut.[4]

The goal Antonioni wanted to achieve through his long takes was the representation of a psychological process leading from an empty moment through a dramatic climax to another empty moment. He wanted to show the way a dramatic moment is born and the way the same dramatic moment vanishes. Everything in Antonioni's films is about the vanishing of human emotions, and in the beginning of his career the long-take style was the form with which to show that.

Technically speaking Antonioni's long takes join several parts of a scene in one continuous sequence. Where conventional *mise-en-scène* would cut up a scene in several shot/counter-shot pairs, Antonioni moves either the camera or the actors or both in order to create a new setup in which someone who was not in the centre of the scene in the previous part becomes centred or visible. He moves the camera or the actors only in function of the interactions of the characters. He does not change angle while one character speaks. In the case of a three-character conversation, he usually puts two of them facing the camera and the third with his or her back to the camera. When either one of the two characters facing the camera speaks, the camera is stationary. When the third starts to speak, either they change place, with the camera moving around a little, or there is simply a cut, if the scene has already lasted around a minute. Antonioni in his early long-take period never moves the camera independently of the characters.

Antonioni's most famous early long take is the bridge scene in *Chronicle of a Love Affair* (1950). This is a four-minute single shot making more than one entire 360° circle, while the two main characters' exchange develops from neutral conversation into violent animosity, and then calms down again. The actors change place at each stage of the conversation, moving around the camera, which follows their motion. Usually, in the early Antonioni films, while the characters are speaking they remain stationary, as does the camera. Character and camera movement occurs when a new character enters or leaves the conversation or when the conversation takes a turn. Even in a long conversation scene a shot very rarely lasts more than one minute, but rarely too is it shorter than thirty seconds. Antonioni's takes become shorter at the turn of the 1960s, but when they stretch over thirty seconds, the technique remains the same.

With this technique Antonioni creates an atmosphere of smooth continuity between events, where none of the events obtains dramatic accent. When a given event has in fact a strong emotional charge, it evaporates immediately. That is why we can call its main effect 'dedramatisation'.

Jancsó

Jancsó radicalised this technique in two ways. First, he made the sequences longer. In his films made after 1965 we can rarely find shots shorter than one minute, and they most often run five to eight minutes in length, and sometimes are even ten minutes long. Second, the narrative stages merged together in one shot represent not small dramatic changes of a single scene, but entire event sequences eventually embracing a lengthy time span. This had several consequences. First, camera motion became more predominant. Since there are no long dialogues in Jancsó's films, there is no reason why the camera should remain stationary, showing the same characters. Second, camera motion and character motion became choreographed so that the individual compositions represent different events of an event sequence. Third, the movements of the characters became increasingly symbolic, as did the characters themselves and the props too, and became similar to a ritual dance. In fact dance appears in Jancsó's work in 1968 and remains an important element of the character movements until the end of the 1970s. Fourth, the camera motion became somewhat independent from the characters' movements as the different events are linked together by camera movements. Whenever another event follows, the camera turns away from the previous scene, or the characters walk out of the frame and others come in while the camera moves to another segment of the space. In these instances the camera sometimes does not follow any character; it makes a 'connecting' movement.

Tarkovsky

The typical Tarkovsky long take is different in many respects from the Antonioni-Jancsó conception. That said, Tarkovsky also uses his long takes to follow a given event sequence, but his novelty in the long take style lies somewhere else. Tarkovsky's goal is not to represent an event sequence in one segment to show how one thing is born from another, but rather to give the viewer enough time to be able to 'see through' the physical aspect of the images. This is why, unlike Antonioni's and Jancsó's, Tarkovsky's long takes most of the time show not characters or character interactions but objects or natural landscapes. Long takes in Tarkovsky's films are often not associated with events. Watching scenery becomes an event in itself thanks to the time dedicated to showing it. Tarkovsky very often does not integrate different stages of a dramatic event in a single long take. The most typical Tarkovsky long takes do not contain events at all. They contain a view of something or a motion going forward in a given space without a narrative subject. For example in *Mirror* the long tracking shot in which the camera slowly moves forward in the author's apartment for more than two and a half minutes represents a point of view of nobody in the narrative. During this shot we can hear an off-screen conversation between the author and his mother, but since we know that he is ill and in bed, this movement cannot be his perspective. Also, we can hear his voice at the same volume as we are moving forward, so we can suppose that he is not even present in this space. The long tracking shot's function is not to represent an event sequence, since depicting the conversation would require the visualisation of at least one of the parties. The function of this long tracking shot is to make the viewer wander around slowly in this apartment to get a feeling of what it is like being there. The typical Tarkovsky long take is always participatory: it makes the viewer participate in the scene. The gaze it represents is always that of someone intimately involved in the environment. This gaze does not represent anyone actually present in the space. It rather represents someone becoming invisibly part of the scene.

This is why the most important stylistic element in Tarkovsky's camerawork is the camera movement rather than the long take. He uses camera movements more consistently than long takes. In the Antonioni-Jancsó style camera movement is a consequence of long takes; with Tarkovsky it is rather the other way around. Tracking shots or panning movements most of the time make it necessary to make a given shot long, but many times we encounter relatively short takes following each other where the second continues the first's movement. The above example is a case in point in this respect too. The first shot is a two-minute shot, with the camera travelling forward, followed by a twenty-second shot continuing the previous shot's movement. In order to create a feeling of how a memory is evoked in a given physical environment, he joins two camera movements, which together provide the feeling, regardless of the length of the individual shots.

Because Tarkovsky's long takes are very rarely (if ever) motivated by dramatic events, and because the camera movement plays the most important role in them, the long-take camera movements have a considerable independence from the narrative. We can characterise the typical Tarkovsky long take as a tool for providing the viewer with the time to experience immersion in the image.

Godard

Tarr often cites Godard, saying, 'a real director makes the editing in the camera'. He used to add also: 'I do it more consistently than him.' This is naturally true. Godard is usually not counted among the long-take-style directors; on the contrary, he made his name with extensive use of jump-cuts and fragmentation of scenes, and he has remained faithful to his peculiar 'patchwork' style ever since. Yet, since in Godard's style one can find an example of virtually everything, long takes are not missing from his ouevre either. What is more, very often one has the impression that his takes could run forever, and that he just cuts them at a certain point, arbitrarily. David Bordwell characterises Godard's shots as seeming to 'run too long or to be curtailed before they have finished'.[5] Just like Tarkovsky, Godard is not a consistent user of long takes, but his long takes are as idiosyncratic as those of the Russian director, and are as intimately associated with camera movements as those of the above-mentioned filmmakers.

Take the often cited and well-known scene of the traffic jam in *Weekend* (1967). It consists of four shots and three intertitles. The length of the individual shots is very uneven. The first lasts two and a half minutes, the second only one and a half seconds, the third two and a half seconds, and the fourth more than five minutes. However, each of these shots makes the same movement, a rightward tracking shot the same distance from the object of the image. It is as if it were a single eight-minute continuous long take parsed later, as if randomly. Since the event it describes is monotonous and repetitive (the main character's car trying to advance, passing by those trapped and waiting patiently in the line), actually nothing changes during the whole time. The camera in this scene does not follow an action, does not link different actions together, and does not represent a participatory gaze within the fictional space. It depicts a monotonous movement that could last forever from a distanced exterior angle. Unlike in the long takes of all of the above-mentioned filmmakers, Godard never changes his distance from the object represented; he always remains alienated from the space, and his camera movement becomes as mechanical as the movement it depicts. This camera movement is not only detached from the subject matter, but is clearly arbitrary, and this arbitrariness is its main message. It calls the viewer's attention to the person behind the camera, the author who does this, and invites the viewer to wonder why he does it. Just like Tarkovsky, Godard uses length of take to provoke a certain emotion in the viewer, only in his case it is not immersion and participation, but rather, on the contrary, alienation and disturbance.

Sometimes the mechanical character of the camera movement becomes even more explicit. In *Vivre sa vie* (1962) Godard stages a conversation scene recorded in a two-and-a-half-minute-long take. In this case the camera moves, but makes a completely mechanical movement. It travels back and forth behind the back of the person facing Nana, as a result of which he never faces the camera. It shifts between three positions where it stops for a few seconds. We see Nana from either the front right or the front left, or we cannot see her at all, as the man's head obstructs her. The movement of the camera is segmented by these stops, and it has a mechanical feeling simply because it also makes a stop in a position from which nothing can be seen, and because the movement becomes repetitive. Instead of following some action or immersing the viewer in the fictional space, the camera movement becomes a self-conscious play, partly thanks to its duration, which gives the viewer time to realise and understand this effect.

Godard also makes static long takes with no camera movement whatsoever. In these cases the feeling of the arbitrariness and of the disturbance comes from the staging. When he does this in his earlier films we can be sure that we will have to watch a scene from an angle where we can see almost nothing, and the static long take is there to frustrate the viewer. *Vivre sa vie* starts with a one-and-a-half-minute close-up of Nana, the main character, but we can only see the back of her head (her face appears only in a mirror in the background). In his later period he often stages static frontal shots, as if it were a documentary interview. In *Tout va bien* (1972) there is a five-minute static frontal shot of three union activists. One of them gives a speech about the state of the food industry in France. He pretends to be answering the questions of a supposed interviewer behind the camera, whose questions are not heard. But since he is talking to the camera this is not a conventional interview situation where the interviewer stands next to the camera, meaning the interviewee directs his speech to a point near the camera. This shot creates the impression that the union activist is answering directly the unspoken questions of the viewer. This is the most obvious case of the main effect Godard wants to create, which is to make it explicit that someone is behind the camera.

Tarr's long-take style has something of each of these effects. His long takes, especially at the end of the second period, are as long as Jancsó's; he mainly uses them to connect events as Antonioni does, but because in most of them there is very little narrative content, he uses long takes alternatively to create the sensation of immersion or, on the contrary, to alienate the viewer through mechanistic movements or static compositions or by making the camera independent of the character's movement.

In what follows, I will discuss the Tarr style as it appears in *Damnation*. The following chapter will discuss the process through which this style further developed in the subsequent films.

Damnation

When Tarr claims that he cannot see a shift in *Damnation*, he is right from a certain point of view. Again, there is in fact a great deal of continuity and gradual evolution leading to *Damnation* from his earlier works. Taken into account individually, there are no dramatically new elements in this film that had not appeared in one or more earlier works; only their combination and the proportions changed considerably. Using these elements together in a particular combination and proportion had the effect of dramatic novelty.

In *Damnation* the characters originating from a similar petit bourgeois or poor proletarian background as those in the earlier Tarr films suddenly started to talk in an unlikely poetic and abstract way, expressing thoughts and feelings one would not expect to hear often in this social milieu, certainly not in the earlier Tarr films. Very strange sounds and noises, certainly not coming from real-life sources, can be heard constantly during the film, and often it is difficult to tell if a given sound is diegetic or just a non-diegetic effect. The landscape is recognisable and unrecognisable at the same time. Even for someone not familiar with the average Hungarian small-town scenery, the carefully designed character of the exterior views is striking.[6] It is no longer 'Hungary in the 1970s or 1980s', but an unspecific degraded, deserted semi-urban, semi-rural landscape on the way to slow, gradual disintegration displayed in a careful visual composition, fitted with meticulously chosen objects and architectural elements, and lit in a strong chiaroscuro style. Yet the elements are recognisably East European, bearing the signs of a destroyed tradition and an unfinished modernisation blocked halfway to completion. This is a landscape that could be found anywhere from

Montenegro to Poland or from the Czech Republic to Russia. The technological level of the objects seen in the film as well as the clothes worn by the characters evoke the period of the 1970s to the 1980s.

The long take and *mise-en-scène*

With *Damnation* the average shot length of a Tarr film did not just become somewhat longer, as was the case during the first period, but suddenly doubled as compared to *Almanac of Fall*, tripled as compared to *The Prefab People*, and almost quadrupled as compared to *The Outsider* and *Family Nest*. The general feeling one has about the camerawork and the *mise-en-scène* in *Damnation* is that, typically, the camera makes simple horizontal or in-depth movements in spaces in which the characters typically don't move, or make only small movements. The two most characteristic, even emblematic shots of the film in this respect are the first shot, an in-depth tracking shot (figures 22a–j), and the introduction of the ball scene, a lateral tracking shot (figures 20a–c). A very complicated combination of the two basic types is the scene at the Titanik Bar, where the camera travels on the perimeter of the circular part of a space in the shape of a half-circle, at the other end of which there is a band playing. The camera passes by clients of the bar sitting or standing immobilised on both sides of the track

of the camera. The movement of this six-minute-long shot is rather complicated, since it has to turn to both sides to show the people in close-ups before it arrives at the main character's close-up. The camera lingers for a while on Karrer's face, then slowly turns around him to reveal the singer who was during all this time hidden behind a pillar. This revelation comes as a surprise, since we have seen already this pillar on Karrer's right and we could not see the singer from his point of view. In figure 15a we can clearly see the pillar on Karrer's right, behind which the hand of the singer holding a cigarette appears.[7] Yet when we move around him and look to his right from his back we can see the singer, who, from his own point of view, we couldn't see (figure 15b). And as we get closer to her, the pillar disappears too (figure 15c). This is the kind of revelation effect Tarr already used in his earlier films, yet here the source of the surprise is the 'magic' of an appearance rather than the fact that the camera previously did not show a particular segment of the space.

Figures 15a–c

The way Tarr combines his *mise-en-scène* with his tracking shots is definitely not the Jancsó-style combined choreography of character and camera movements. In most parts of this film the characters are stationary; it is the camera that moves among them. More than before Tarr uses depth of space in staging, which is a rather natural consequence of the long tracking shots. However, this film cannot be characterised solely by depth-of-space staging. There are many instances of it (figures 18b & c), but there are many instances of the contrary too. Especially when Tarr makes a lateral tracking shot, most of the time what we can see are different flat surfaces following one another (figures 21a & c and 22a–j). Whether or not the image has a depth of space, the most typical effect of the *mise-en-scène* is the contrast of the slowly moving camera and the immobile characters. This contrast creates the feeling of someone walking slowly through a space where the people are frozen or stuck in their positions and cannot move away.

The camera almost never follows the characters. It is consistently independent from the characters' movements. Either the characters walk out of the frame or the camera moves away from them. When there is, however, some sort of following movement, it is very short and compensated for by other independent movements. The scene where Karrer watches his lover hidden behind a fence is a case in point. The camera first shows the shop, then slowly moves to the right, discovering Karrer hiding and watching behind the fence, then slowly moves back to the left. This is when the woman leaves the shop and comes towards the camera. Karrer steps forward, and both of them start walking to the right. The camera follows them until they reach a road leading away from the camera position. Then the camera stops and we watch them walking away towards the background of the image, and finally they disappear in a curve. But the take is not over. That is when the camera resumes its tracking to the right, but there are no characters in the frame any more. The first tracking movement of the scene, which does not follow any characters, lasts 84 seconds, the second camera movement, which follows the characters, lasts 5 seconds, and the third camera movement, which again does not follow the characters, lasts 30 seconds, and the whole scene lasts two minutes and fifty seconds. So, even in a scene in which the camera is linked for some time to the movement of the characters, 95 per cent of the time it moves independently of them. This is just as in the film's last scene, where for a short while the camera seems to follow Karrer. In fact what happens is that the camera starts a lateral movement to the left, and after a couple of seconds Karrer walks into the picture from the right, but since he is moving faster than the camera, he leaves the frame on the left. The camera continues its movement to the left at the same pace as in the beginning. Even in this case the camera's movement is independent from the character's movement. Comparing the film to *Almanac of Fall*, one can remark that of all the varieties of camerawork Tarr used there, he consistently kept the independent camera movement as his main stylistic device.

In this respect Tarr's staging style reminds one most of Fassbinder's highly static theatrical staging, especially in his early period, complemented by Tarkovsky's constantly and independently moving camerawork. The characters do not move about much in a given scene. They have a certain position relative to the space and to each other, and when they move, mostly, they move a little, for instance, out of the frame, but they very rarely run through long, complicated trajectories like in a Jancsó film. Sometimes they even seem unnaturally frozen. The first love scene is a spectacular example of this. The camera starts backing up from the window, discovering first the woman silently sitting in the bed, staring into the distance. Her body is entirely motionless; not a muscle stirs on her face or body. The camera pans down her body, disclosing Karrer lying on the bed, motionless himself. The most spectacular aspect of the performance by the actress, Vali Kerekes, is that during all the time her face can be seen, which is 45 seconds, she does not blink once. Considering that the average blink rate of a normal relaxed person is 15 to 30 blinks per minute, and that a shooting situation is not exactly relaxing, we can imagine the extraordinary effort the actress must have had to make to follow the director's instruction not to make a single movement with her body. The only sign of life is the movement of Karrer's belly slightly rising and sinking in the rhythm of his breathing, the sound of which becomes increasing loud by the end of the scene, mixing with the strange noise of the cable carts.

The static *mise-en-scène* results sometimes in character postures that are clearly artificial or theatrical. One scene starts with the image of a young woman breastfeeding a baby. This image has no narrative significance, as they do not appear again in the film, and the camera pans away from them after a couple of seconds. They contribute to creating the atmosphere of the following scene, and this narrative disfunctionality is emphasised in the first place by the posture of the young woman, who is not looking down at her baby but rather staring upwards with an inexpressive or rather bored look. Next to her there is a television set broadcasting a soccer game. All the elements of this picture create a feeling of inadequacy and astonishing unnaturalness (figure 16). The other example is in the ball scene, where a man recites a poem to a woman in a strangely distorted posture (figure 23).

Figure 16

The general motionlessness of the characters is contrasted in several scenes by mechanical movements of objects or humans. Two shots after the love scene we can see Karrer at home, staring out the window. He does not move, and the camera does not move either for the entire 27 seconds this shot lasts, but in the left-hand portion of the frame we see the carts passing by, and in the right-hand portion we can see Karrer mechanically chewing something (figure 17). Here the static character of the image is in contrast with the mechanical movements on both sides of the picture.

Figure 17

Other instances of mechanical motion include the first and the last shot of the ball scene, in both of which a man performs a lonely dance without the sound of music, stepping in puddles on a dirty floor. The same feeling of repeated mechanical movement is provided by several musical numbers in the film, especially in those that are played on-screen, like the accordion music, which repeats endlessly the same couple of simple chords.

The world is rather static in this film; motions are repetitive, circular and have no direction. The camera moves about in this world of objects and almost frozen people sometimes in strange postures, revealing them one after the other, as if it were wandering around aimlessly in a dead landscape. In the long takes, camera movements and staging a feeling of both immersion and distanced self-consciousness are present.

A tracking shot experiment: *The Last Boat*

After the international success of *Damnation* Tarr was invited to create a segment for a collective film by thirteen filmmakers, *City Life*, produced in the Netherlands. This short film is based on a Krasznahorkai short story, *Az Utolsó hajó*, from his book *Kegyelmi viszonyok* (1986). This film is also an experiment in long-take tracking shot style. It contains eleven shots in thirty minutes, which equals an average shot length of 163 seconds. This represents a 37 per cent increase in shot length compared to *Damnation*. Each shot is a tracking shot most of the time, the camera travelling slowly from right to left, which makes the camerawork of this film even more mechanical than we see in *Damnation*.

It is difficult to call the content of this film a 'story'. It is rather a narrative segment with no beginning and no end. The film starts with a scene in which someone is probably beating someone else to death, but we see only his movements, not the other person. Then follows a scene in an empty hangar where military or police vehicles cruise up and down. This scene is conspicuously reminiscent of a corresponding scene in Tarkovsky's *Stalker* (1979). In the next, a man sitting on the edge of a bed in an room seemingly in an empty hospital recites a medical text about how to recognise death. Later we see a line of people waiting to board a ship. They are watched over by military personnel and their luggage is screened by x-ray machines. After they all board the ship, one of them gets frantic and screams. Then a barber shaves the man we saw at the beginning of the film. He speaks to him about law and order, the guardians of which are the barbers. Finally we have a long tracking shot sequence of faces of people on the boat drinking, sleeping, playing the violin, and just staring at the water. As the camera turns to show the water in the dawn, the last sentence of Krasznahorkai's short story appears as a title: 'We still lay there, dazed with exhaustion when another night fell, greeted only by muted grunts. Then one of us suddenly raised his head, struggled to his feet, went astern, pointed to the pitch-dark, forever disappearing countryside, and called out in bitter relief: "People, that there was Hungary."'

In this film the long-take tracking shot directly represents a narrative content, which is the slow process of degradation and abandonment of a territory the last inhabitants of which are just leaving. This short film is a clear example of the importance of the environment and the landscape in the second-period Tarr style, and also of Tarr's method of representation in this period, the long-take tracking shot.

Landscape

The shift that took place with *Damnation* in Tarr's career after *Almanac of Fall* was not related to the fact that the environment became an important element of the representation, or that the representation of the environment became highly stylised. All that change took place *with Almanac of Fall*, not after it. The important change was that in *Damnation* Tarr in fact brought back the environment of his earliest films – a run-down Hungarian provincial small-town environment, *and* kept the main principles of the stylisation of *Almanac of Fall* – the 'pseudo-style' – using black-and-white film stock again. Tarr asserted several times in interviews with regard to *Damnation* that the real protagonist of his film was the landscape and that the characters were part of the landscape. We saw how this translates in terms of camera movement and staging.

To integrate human protagonists into the landscape was not a new idea; one only has to think of Antonioni, Jancsó and, in some cases, Tarkovsky. But the way Tarr did this was rather unique. What Jancsó inherited, continued and even radicalised from the great Antonioni films was not only the dispassionate, inexpressive acting style, but also the technique of using character movements in order to explore the space around them. We can find elements of this technique in several Tarkovsky films too, especially

Figures 18a–c

Mirror and *Stalker*. Characters in their films are instrumental in the exploration of the human and physical environment. Static and dynamic compositions in these filmmakers' films emphasise the environment in which characters are rather like other design elements.

Tarr, unlike his modernist predecessors, did not integrate his characters into the landscape as dispassionate, inexpressive objects. Their faces and postures always carry certain expressions, which are also articulated in the composition of the landscape. Those expressions are not psychological or emotional though. They are expressions of a given fate or destiny. Tarr's characters become rather 'models' of life stories very much in a Bressonian way.[8] Later we will see how the Bressonian character is manifested in his last two films. One of the functions of the length of the time he dedicated to showing certain sceneries is precisely to let the viewer discover the close cohesion between the characters and the landscape, or their textural similarity. The more the visual analogy is tangible, the more striking is the characters' invisible, interior desire to be detached from this environment. This is what produces tension in the characters, and it is this ambiguity which underlies the ambiguous effect of Tarr's long takes referred to earlier. Tarr's camera is inside and outside this world at the same time, just as the characters are.

The appearance of the landscape is also unique in the Tarr style, as compared to his modernist predecessors. Jancsó and Tarkovsky have a very consistent and characteristic approach to the landscape. Both prefer natural sceneries. For Jancsó nature is an absolute priority: one can find very few constructed elements in his early films. For Tarkovsky, nature is predominant, but its presence is not as exclusive as in Jancsó's films. The way they represent nature is, however, very different. Jancsó's nature is empty and abstract, most of the time consisting of plains and deserts with very few objects in it. Tarkovsky's nature, by contrast, is saturated and varied, full of plants, water, and artificial and natural forms. This is true all through his films until the last, *Sacrifice* (1986), which is rather Bergmanian, that is, much closer to the Jancsóian empty nature variation. At the other end of the spectrum of the modernist landscape directors is Antonioni, who constructs landscapes of urban rather than natural sceneries. Especially characteristic in this respect are *La notte* (1960), *L'eclisse* (1962) and *Il deserto rosso* (1964). Antonioni's urban views are characteristically empty and inexpressive, most of the time geometrical, and lack expression of human feelings, other than emptiness maybe. In the Tarr style, constructed urban landscape becomes saturated and expressive. In film history, saturated expressive urban landscape was characteristic of expressionism in the early 1920s and in a less abstract way of American film noir of the 1940s and 1950s. In both cases the sentiment expressed by the urban environment was angst and instability. To locate Tarr's use of landscapes within the above-mentioned stylistic variations found in film history we can use a schematic categorisation, as follows (in some cases only the most characteristic works of the mentioned authors qualify):

Antonioni	urban	inexpressive/empty
Jancsó	rural	inexpressive/empty
Tarkovsky	rural	expressive/saturated
Film noir/Tarr	urban	expressive/saturated

However, it is not the film noir kind of expressionism which we find in *Damnation*, even though Tarr applies more than one visual effect characteristic of expressionism or film noir: strong lighting contrasts in black and white (figure 15b), dark and wet street surfaces (figure 18a), deep focus compositions with large contrasts between the foreground and the background (figures 18b & c).

The particularity of Tarr's urban landscapes is that they contain more than one aspect of expressivity. This landscape evokes a strong social milieu without being specific to any particular city, nation or smaller region. Poverty, desolation and rundown shabbiness can be felt in every segment of these spaces (figure 19a). Some general feeling of East Europeanness is detectable all over the landscape, in signs of the abandoned process of industrialisation. And finally, the texture and posture of the

objects, buildings, walls and streets evoke a general feeling of desolation, depression and a sense of things going to ruin, to the extent that at the end of the film we are shown a world that is literally in ruins (figures 19b–d).

This is a particularly intensive and condensed representation of an environment where every little detail contributes to the same feeling. Other than the above-mentioned elements, we find constant rain, and fog, mud and wet surfaces everywhere. Because the natural elements are so intensively present in the landscape, the depressing atmosphere of the environment is not due to the social element of poverty, as it is in Tarr's first two films. Poverty and the shabbiness of the environment are just other aspects of a general depressing atmosphere. That is why Tarr did not simply look for an appropriate location in which to shoot his film, but drew the film's environmental image together from different fragments. The set designer (who is also an actor in the film), Gyula Pauer, talks about the work they did:

We wandered through all the miners' villages and towns in the country. We were looking for an industrial environment that bore the clear and irrefutable imprint of slow destruction and decomposition. What was once meant for dynamic growth and multiplication, what still bore the sign of a nicer

Figures 19a–d

and richer future, but was now in an infinitely run-down state, showed only the death of such old illusions. We found numerous such places all over the country. Decades-old dreams of triumphant industrialisation are now slums, where people can barely survive. We have been to miners' villages where only pensioners live now – 40- or 50-year-old people – who were pensioned off, since the mine was closed down and there was no other work. These people just sit around in the pub all day. We have been to places where the tubs only brought coal-dust, out of which they built a huge spoil-bank. A couple of hundred people are building a mountain just to have something to do. One can see in the architecture of these places that they were meant for a certain way of life, and now they are utterly unsuited for any other. In booths made of bulking paper, fibre and tin plates we found townspeople raising pigs and poultry in such incredibly worn-down houses, where seeing the gate and the staircase one would think life had ceased long ago, and people had moved out. We have also been to restaurants, where now only beer is served, since the National Health Organisation closed down the kitchen and forbade drinks to be served, and where there are no glasses for the beer; people drink from the bottle at three-legged tables covered with appallingly dirty tablecloths. This restaurant was once probably a place of which people were proud. Above the entrance, built in the now memorial 'Stalin baroque' with a classicist portal and a fake-marble row of pillars, decorated with stucco on the ceiling, an illuminated small model cart that moved around on the ceiling. The wall may have once been decorated with fantastic mirrors, brackets and chandeliers. Of all this we now see only broken remains, as if we had trusted naughty children with a nice flat only to find it wrecked on our return. Our most stunning experience everywhere was that this was the result of lives spent in back-breaking toil and not in idleness. At the same time, our purpose in finding these places was not to present a diagnosis of certain devastated areas of the country. The film does not allude specifically to time and place. We deliberately avoided showing any signs of actual politics and economics in regard to this environment. We created the locations in such a way that they reflected the endgame of a world-era, the state of the last moment before final disappearance. The sites are real, but we shot the film in very different locations. Sometimes we only recorded a street scene; sometimes only a house-wall; and we even have a house in the film with an exterior that is in Budapest, an interior in Ajka, and a next-door shop in Pécs. So the film's world consists of real elements, which, however, do not create a real space.[9]

Pauer clearly explains that what they were looking for was not some sociological, historical or political depiction of a concrete social milieu, although every aspect of the environment carries signs of history, politics and social situation. What they wanted to achieve was the forming of this mixture of historical, social and political signs into a vision that shows neither national characteristics nor particular signs of a period of time any more specific than the end of the twentieth century.

Another aspect of the representation of the environment was that Tarr wanted to treat the bodies and the faces of the characters as part of the material environment. There is no obvious traditional form with which to do that. Tarr had to invent something he hoped would achieve this effect. His solution was a sort of tracking shot which slowly pans through a certain space at a monotonously slow pace, not stopping or slowing down when it reaches a human body or face, just passing it by as if it were another object in the environment. This is one of the most important types of shot in the film. And these are the most elaborate and memorable shots of *Damnation* too.

The first two shots of the film are of this kind. The opening image is a three-and-a-half-minute shot in which the camera slowly backs up from the window through

Figures 20a–c   Figures 21a–c

which we can see the mining carts coming and going on the cable. Then we slowly discover that we were looking through a window from inside a room, and after this we discover that this was in fact the point of view of someone sitting in front of the window and staring at the carts (figures 20a–c). The second shot is a lateral tracking shot from left to right, starting from a close-up of the texture of a wall and sliding over to a close-up of the face of a man shaving in a mirror, with the face slowly disappearing behind the head of the man in the dark (figures 21a–c). These shots can be considered as special variations of the revealing camerawork that we found in *Family Nest*. However, three important technical factors ensure that their effect is considerably different in this film, and surprise is not the primary effect of these shots. First, the shots start from objects with no dialogue and no events, just some strange sounds, so they eliminate the expectation that something significant is happening here. Second, the camera movement is so slow that it attributes more importance to the scenery than to the human body hidden in the room. Third, the human figure is either completely immobile or makes very little gestures, like shaving and smoking. The primary effect is the revelation that the person who turns out to be in this space is part of that space. We can call this a *metonymical* use of the tracking shot, and it is especially known from the films of Tarkovsky.

a

b

c

d

e

f

g

h

i

j

Figures 22a–j

Not much later in the film this effect returns more strikingly in an almost six-minute-long take, which starts as a tracking shot through a nightclub, showing individual clients one after the other, each sitting or standing immobile in a given posture as if they were stuck to their tables, chairs or the wall. But the most spectacular instance of this effect is the beginning of the ball scene in the second part of the film. Here, the objective of the shot is unambiguous. This is not a representation, not even a stylised one, of any real-life event. It is a tableau of a group of people with different miserable faces. They are stuffed into a big dance hall, staring at the rain outside. They are distributed in several groups, each group standing in an opening of the hall, and the camera tracks before them in medium close-up. The shot starts on the exterior wall of the dance hall, and between each group of people we can see a part of the wall separating the groups over and over again until the camera passes by all the openings, but continues nevertheless, showing the wall again, passing by some windows, and finally stopping on the same wall texture on which it started (figures 22a–j). Here the faces are clearly composed as part of the texture of the background, and there is no more emphasis on the human characters than on the texture of the wall. Not only are they part of that location, but the way they look and the expression on their faces correspond exactly to the atmosphere evoked by the texture of the surrounding building.

In sum, the novelty of the landscapes in *Damnation* is that although they are created as artificially as in *Almanac of Fall*, the elements in them evoke strong social and historical associations, which make them seem real, although they do not exist as a continuous space in reality. In a way it is the same conception of the pseudo surface as in *Almanac of Fall*: creating an illusion that the surface hides something, in this case a consistent social reality, when in fact it is nothing more than the expression of a strong feeling of abandonment, and slow physical, mental and moral decay.

A landscape film: *Journey on the Plain*

During the shooting of *Satantango* Tarr learned that Mihály Víg knew a lot of poems by heart by the great nineteenth-century Hungarian poet Sándor Petőfi. Petőfi is well-known for his close attachment to his native region, the Hungarian Great Plain, the Puszta. That is where *Satantango* is located, and where all the great Jancsó films are set, as well as a great deal of Hungarian literary fiction. Tarr liked the way Víg recited Petőfi's poems and especially the ones Víg chose to learn. He decided to make a film about Víg reciting Petőfi's poems at the locations of the Plain, some of which he also used in *Satantango*. This way his vision of this Hungarian cultural icon would be created at the same time as his – and Víg's – image of another Hungarian cultural icon, Petőfi. This is a very particular film, since not only do the locations fit with all the Tarr films of the second period – abandoned and run-down buildings, ruins, cheap local pubs – but Víg's choice of Petőfi's poems supports in a particular way this representation. He recites those poems that are the most melancholic and depressed, and that are about alcohol, loneliness and death. The film instils in this iconic landscape a very particular atmosphere through reference to a genuine inspiration for this atmosphere, Petőfi's poems. Tarr's choice to make *Satantango* in this landscape is given some cultural background in this film. This is no longer Tarr's vision of this landscape, but a vision of this landscape as it is expressed in the poems of its greatest admirer.

Sound and dialogue

Almanac of Fall was the first Tarr film where music played a role beyond illustrating the atmosphere of a given location. Tarr was looking for a composer in the alternative rock community of the early 1980s. He found Mihály Víg's music appealing, as it is minimalist, slow, sad and sentimental. It is also very simply orchestrated, mainly based on piano and accordion, and so is a mixture of cheap traditional pub music and sophisticated contemporary repetitive music.

In *Damnation* the music is very often diegetic; that is, it has a source in the image, most of the time a pub, a nightclub or a dance hall. However, in the dance hall scene there are different effects that slightly detach the music from the image and render the diegetic status of the music uncertain. In the introductory part of the scene we can see a man dancing alone in the rain outside the building, but we cannot hear any music, just the sound of his steps in the water. After a while the camera slowly backs up into the dance hall, and only as this happens can we start to hear the increasing sound of the music. In a real-life space this loud music would definitely be heard outside, just a couple of metres away from the open window. So if *Damnation* was a 'realist' film, this music should have been heard while only the lonely dancer was in the picture. But this is not the only strange thing in this scene. When the music becomes audible it is clear right away that the man does not dance to the rhythm of the music coming from the building. Through the mismatch of sound and image, the two segments of the space give the impression of being slightly disconnected. This mismatch is continued later on all through the scene. Sometimes there is a slight discordance between the rhythm of the music and the movement of the dancers or the musicians. It is minimal, yet noticeable enough to provide a feeling of disturbance. The movements are not entirely different from the rhythm of the music, but do not follow it entirely either. Thus diegetic music becomes a somewhat disturbing sound accompanying the images. This leads us to the other important element of the soundtrack: the noises.

Damnation is the first Tarr film in which noises have a very important role, and where they become part of the composition of the atmosphere by being detached from the image. Other than using 'normal' sound effects connected to character movements and objects, Tarr proceeds in two ways. One is what we could call 'alienating sound'. This happens when the natural sound of an object or a conversation is heard, and the sound very slowly becomes unnatural, and sometimes takes on a musical character. The first scene of the film is an example of that. During the three and a half minutes of the shot the natural sound of the carts passing by is enriched by other noises and effects. By the time the camera arrives in the room, it is not the sound of the cart that we hear any more, but rather a very loud and frightening mixture of noises based on the sound of the carts.

The other device consists of creating 'non-natural' noises. In more than one scene one can hear noises that do not come from visible or non-visible natural objects, and they are not recognisable as such. These are 'musical' compositions of noises with the only function of creating an atmosphere for the image. The most shocking example is the second love scene. Karrer and his lover are making love in bed, not exactly passionately, and while we are watching them and the room around them we can hear the unbearably loud noise of the mine carts we see outside the window in the distance. There is no way this noise could be heard this loud in the apartment, so this cannot be a 'natural' noise. It has been made louder to render the atmosphere of the scene even more alienating.

The most spectacular effect of the soundtrack of this film is the use of dialogue. As mentioned earlier this is the first Tarr film – discounting *Macbeth*, which was an adaptation and an assignment from the film school – where the actors did not improvise their dialogue. In itself this fact would not be much worth noting. What is worth noting is that the dialogue is highly poetic, and most of the time appears as inappropriate in the given circumstances.

The biblical speeches of the checkroom attendant woman are not very surprising, as she is a mysterious character providing general moral advice to the protagonist, sometimes in a very cryptic manner. The moral lessons the bartender gives to the protagonists might be surprising, but supposing that they are friends, they are not entirely unlikely. There are spoken passages, however, which are truly unexpected. Two examples are especially striking. The first is when Karrer, the protagonist, offers a job of smuggling something into the country to the husband of his lover, hoping that he will accept it, so that he can remain alone with the lover, who, he hopes, will 'honour' this favour. After he briefly describes his proposition in practical terms, he suddenly starts a speech, which is quite inappropriate in this situation:

> This way it's a nice family story. But it finishes like any other story. And all stories end badly, because they are always stories of disintegration. The heroes always disintegrate and they disintegrate in exactly the same way. Because if they didn't disintegrate it would be resurrection not disintegration. And I'm talking about disintegration not resurrection. Eternal and irrevocable disintegration by the way. Since what is about to happen here is just one of the million forms of ruin, and a rather petty form at that. So if they put you in jail because of your debts, you can't count on temporary ruin, because this kind of ruin is final, as ruin generally is. At the same time there might be just a way to arrest this inevitable ruin. Mainly with money and not by playing the hero. Needless to say it doesn't help the inevitability of this breakdown. It can merely cover over a crack for a moment.

Considering that he is speaking to his lover and to the husband of his lover, who shortly before that threatened to beat him up if he did not keep away from his wife, this philosophical speech comes as a surprise, especially because the two other characters keep listening to him without reacting at all to the inappropriateness of his words. At the penultimate sentence of this speech the camera moves away from them. The last sentence is heard, but they are already covered by a dark wall, and although the speech continues, Karrer's voice slowly fades into the sound of the rain, which will be the background sound of the next shot, in which Karrer walks away. Here Tarr does the same thing with the dialogue as he does in other scenes with the music and with natural sounds: he detaches it from the narrative situation, and makes of it an independent sound effect in which what counts is not so much the information the dialogue conveys regarding the narrative flow or the characters or the specific situation as the atmosphere the sound creates. In this particular case the atmosphere is mainly informed by the radical inadequacy of the ideas and the philosophical way these ideas are put into words in juxtaposition with the absolute banality of the situation and the meanness of all of the characters.

It is interesting that Tarr felt it necessary to make an introduction to this scene so that the viewer would be prepared for the inaptness of the dialogue in a given situation. The scene in which Karrer makes this speech is in fact a long tracking shot that starts in another room, where a man is talking to two half-naked women. The presence of the two half-nudes is not really surprising, as we are in a nightclub, but the fact that the man makes an absolutely incoherent speech about twentieth-century history and about morality and honour is. This man's speech fades into Karrer's just as in the end Karrer's speech fades into the sound of the rain. Thus the whole shot consists of different transitions of space and sound in which the main feeling evoked is inaptness. We can see people in a certain space, but at the same time we feel that they do not belong there.

The next example is even more striking. In the second half of the long ball scene suddenly comes a shot of a man and a woman facing each other. The woman leans against the wall in a quite distorted position with her eyes closed, and the man talks to her (figure 23). The first thing one notices about this image is that the woman fits very well into this environment – a dirty, run-down small-town community hall, introduced by tableaus of the people of this (essentially) mining community in cheap-looking clothing and with rather weary faces – but the man does not. His face, his overcoat, his voice suggest an artist-intellectual figure rather than an impoverished unemployed miner. This is confirmed when we realise that he is reciting a poem to this woman, who does not even seem to hear what he says. On the one hand this scene reiterates the idea of the inaptness of dialogue and situations; on the other it reinforces it by emphasising the inaptness of character and environment.

This character appears one more time, at the very end of the ball scene, performing a similar step dance to the man's at the beginning of the scene. This step dance is a motivical closure of the scene, since it started with one, although it is quite different from that one. The first can be interpreted within the narrative frame of the scene, which is a public dance party; admittedly, the man's lonely dance is a little off the beat, but this should not surprise us if we suppose that he is drunk, for example. At the end of the scene this interpretation is impossible. The ball is over, everybody has left including the musicians, and therefore

Figure 23

this step dance has no narrative meaning. The appearance of this dance has to do with the alien nature of this character. This person does not belong to the environment and does not do what the people belonging to this environment would do. It has to do with the mechanical meaninglessness and aimless repetitive or circular movements mentioned earlier. This is an overt authorial commentary about this world.

But as an authorial commentary, there is more to it. This step dance is in fact a direct citation of a 1975 film, *A császár üzenete* (*The Message of the Emperor*) by László Najmányi. In this film the same actor, Péter Breznyik, performed the same step dance. Tarr asked Breznyik to appear in his film and to dance the same dance he did twelve years before, in Najmányi's film. Obviously, this fact remains hidden in the film, since very few Hungarian viewers, and probably no foreign viewers at all, are likely to know the source of this dance. And consequently almost nobody understands the sense of this gesture. In Najmányi's film the protagonist starts to smooth down a freshly covered grave by stepping on it. Slowly, his tapping on the ground with his feet becomes a sort of dance on the grave. Probably no viewer will have the meanings associated with a dance on a grave in mind, since to have these meanings in mind it would be necessary to know the reference. But if we know this reference, we realise that this makes sense also in this film. Even if virtually nobody knows this, Breznyik's character is so conspicuously alien to this environment, and his two acts – reciting a poem for a woman not of his kind, and tapping the muddy wet floor of the dance hall alone – are so inappropriate in the situation that his presence creates a sense of an avant-garde, self-reflective, probably even ironic, gesture.

Creating tension between soundtrack and image is a well-known practice of modernist and avant-garde cinema. The particular utilisation of this device in this film, which creates a contrast between the social milieu and the characters' philosophical or poetic utterances, however, has a concrete antecedent in Hungarian cinema. In the same year that Najmányi made his film, in 1975, another avant-garde artist, Tamás Szent-Jóby, made a short film called *Kentaur*. This was shot in a documentary style, as if it were a reportage about working people in various workplaces, for example women working in a textile factory. Szent-Jóby made the workers speak like philosophers and political ideologists. While working and talking to each other they say sentences no textile factory worker, or even engineer, would say in real life in an everyday situation in a workplace. The film was quite well-known in avant-garde circles, although it was banned and confiscated by the political authorities, as they believed (with some reason) that the film was mocking communist ideology. In 1983 another Hungarian filmmaker, András Jeles, used the same idea in his film *Álombrigád* (*The Dream Brigade*), which was also banned. So, we could say that in 1987 this solution was already a tradition of a certain current of politically inspired Hungarian underground cinema. The fact that Tarr used this idea as well as the hidden reference to the 1970s Hungarian avant-garde cinema in *Damnation* says a lot about what he feels is the tradition he belongs to.

Notes

1 'I don't think that one could draw a line at *Damnation*. ... I don't see a turning
   point there...' http://www.origo.hu/filmklub/blog/interju/exkluziv/21080130-
   tarr-bela-hat-megjott-a-hajo-interju-a-londoni.html. On the other hand, this is
   what Tarr said in 2001 to French film critic Émile Breton about *Damnation*: 'This
   was when I started to have a different approach to cinema. To me this is a landscape film. ... Fundamentally, the question is how you can bring life into the
   picture independently of narration. It is due to this film that I came to realise
   that the narrative has no importance whatsoever. I was able to film a wall just like
   a painter would have painted it. What interested me in a scene was the falling
   rain, the awaiting for the most banal event to happen. I think the story in this
   film could be told in twenty minutes. For me, the important things are the time,
   the sky, the cranes, the machines in a factory, the gaze.' Émile Breton (2001)
   'Quelques jalons dans une oeuvre vouée au noir', *Vertigo*, 41, 100.
2 'Talking about Tarr: A Symposium at Facets', booklet for the Facets edition of
   Satantango, 2008, 11–12.
3 See, for example, Noël Burch (1969) *Praxis du cinéma*. Paris: Gallimard; Seymour
   Chatman (1985) *Antonioni, or the Surface of the World*. Los Angeles: University of
   California Press; Kristin Thompson & David Bordwell (1994) *Film History: An
   Introduction.* New York: McGraw-Hill, 423–30.
4 Michelangelo Antonioni (1999) *Michelangelo Antonioni*. Budapest: Osiris, 94.
5 David Bordwell (1985) *Narration in the Fiction Film.* Madison: University of
   Wisconsin Press, 328.
6 'It's very easy to identify where those early films are taking place. They have a
   kind of fixed urban, contemporary reality to them, and these later films, starting
   with *Damnation*, really seem to be taking place in some kind of suspended reality.
   You can't really identify the time period or the location: it is going into this more
   cosmic or macrocosmic or allegorical realm...' 'Talking about Tarr', 9.
7 As far as Tarr is concerned the hand of the actress revealed behind the pillar is a
   mistake in the picture, but this mistake is fortunate for us, as we can clearly see
   that someone is hiding there.
8 For Bresson's conception of the 'model', see his *Notes sur le cinématographe*. Paris:
   Gallimard, 1998.
9 András Bálint Kovács (ed.) (1988) 'Monológok a Kárhozatról', *Filmvilág*, 2, 19.

CHAPTER FOUR

The Tarr Style in Evolution

In the films subsequent to *Damnation* the basics of the Tarr style do not change, but a certain evolution can be detected in several details. This chapter will discuss this evolutionary process.

The constants are rather obvious. All the films are black and white. Average shot length (ASL) does not go under two minutes, for any of the films, but in two cases it increases by 84 per cent as compared to *Damnation*. The environment is characterised always by some combination of desolation and poverty (in *Satantango* and *Werckmeister Harmonies* the same East European environment as in *Damnation*; in *The Man from London* and in *The Turin Horse* a contemporary Mediterranean and nineteenth-century rural environment, respectively). Expressionist lighting, strong black-and-white contrasts and deep-focus staging – in short, film noir visual style – is the dominant visual effect in all of the films. Sounds, noises and music are almost equally important factors of the aesthetic composition of the visual style. On this basis certain aspects become more emphasised in individual films, while others are less salient or even eliminated.

There is even less change in the themes represented. All the stories continue to be based on the situation of entrapment, but from *Damnation* on these stories will strictly and consistently adhere to a circular structure and be detached from all historical and geographical concreteness. It appears then that stylistic elements change and develop independently of the thematic layer of the films. As shown in this chapter, a certain internal evolution can be traced in the films of this period which, I claim, results in an increasing degree of emotional expressivity in the films. Tarr seems to seek an ever more powerful way to express a feeling of general desperation over the impossibility of changing the situation of human helplessness.

Satantango

The tendency of increasing average shot length continues with *Satantango*, but there is not such a dramatic leap between *Damnation* and *Satantango* as there is between *Almanac of Fall* and *Damnation*. While the increase in the latter case was 108 per cent, between *Damnation* and *Satantango* it is only 22 per cent. What is interesting, however, is that within the film itself there is a constant increase in average shot length too. Given that this is a seven-hour-long film broken into three parts, it may be interesting to see how this important stylistic parameter behaves across the parts. What we find is that the first part has slightly shorter shots on average (133) than the second part (137), and the third part has considerably longer shots (166) on average than the second part. This increase in shot length cannot be attributed to dramaturgical factors, since there are no more actions in the first part than in the third part. It is a purely stylistic process, which correlates with a narrative process in the film. As I will show in the next chapter, the narrative structure of *Satantango* becomes increasingly linear toward the end. Increased continuity and increased linearity together emphasise an unstoppable movement towards an unavoidable collapse.

Camerawork and staging

What we can see on the other hand is that the increase in the shot length did not go together with the same camera style as in *Damnation*. Rather than intensifying camera movements, Tarr used some extreme long shots that are conspicuously static. The static character of many of these long shots is emphasised through the use of off-screen sound. Characters in these shots talk to other characters off-screen, the camera not letting the off-screen person on-screen during the conversation. In the second shot of the film the on-screen person even turns his back to the camera, so that the viewer cannot really see either one of the two characters having a conversation. At other instances the camera shows characters disappearing in the distance from a stationary position. This is a stylistic solution that does not occur in earlier Tarr films, and especially not in *Damnation*, where the camera was almost always in motion. However, the idea behind it is the same as that behind the solution so characteristic of *Damnation*: the movement of the camera is independent from the action that takes place on-screen. Whether the camera is constantly moving or stationary, it is not the movements of the characters that determine its behaviour. In *Damnation* Tarr used only the dynamic version of this pattern; in *Satantango* he used both the dynamic and the static versions.

The introduction of static camerawork laid bare the modernist, even avant-garde, stylistic inspirations of this film. The origins of this stylistic pattern can be traced back to the early Bresson films, which inspired Godard, but especially Fassbinder, whose early films abound in long static camera shots and the use of off-screen space. We can also think of the experimental/underground films of Michael Snow. Although both versions of the independent style were widely used during the modernist era – Godard, for example, used both equally – after modernism's decline the static version became scarce. Only a few directors, such as Abbas Kiarostami and Kitano Takeshi, as well as some other East Asian art filmmakers, continued to use it consistently. However, the other version of this pattern became mainstream during the 1980s, mainly due to its suspense effect. A moving camera that does not follow a character always suggests some unexpected event or scene to be disclosed. Even if no unexpected event occurs, the suspense is always there. That is the reason thrillers and horror films often use this tool. And it became increasingly fashionable as the use of Steadicam and CGI became widespread, since both can produce movements and trajectories that were unimaginable before. Furthermore, the ever-moving camera became a Hollywood mainstream device in the 1990s, although in this case, of course, most of the time it remains close to the characters. Considering all this, one can say that a freely and constantly moving camera has become a widespread stylistic device in a wide range of cinema, from mainstream Hollywood to sophisticated European art films. So, while with *Almanac of Fall* in 1985 Tarr adopted the artistic version of an increasingly popular mainstream device of world cinema, and in 1987 he spectacularly enriched it with the long-take style, in *Satantango*, with the long-take static shots, he complemented his stylistic arsenal with the non-mainstream, modernist solution of independent camerawork.

Along with a large number of long tracking and long static shots, there can be found some very traditional devices too, such as quick shot/reverse-shot exchanges in dialogue scenes (such as in the first conversation scene with Futaki and Schmidt, and the interrogation scene at the police station), simple action-following camera movements in many scenes, Jancsóian camera movement and character movement choreographies (such as in the last police station scene). Hence the more balanced stylistic texture in *Satantango* as compared to *Damnation*. It even can be said that Tarr uses the same principle of variation regarding different long-take solutions in this film as he does with other solutions across his oeuvre. We can find a large variety of tracking shots and static shots, in all of which the predominant effect is the Godardian and Tarkovskian independence of the camera movements.

A good example is the scene when Futaki packs his belongings to leave the settlement forever. This is a shot that lasts 4 minutes and 32 seconds. It starts by showing Futaki's empty room. After a while (8 seconds) Futaki comes into the picture without the camera moving. We see him packing, and several times when he leaves the frame the camera does not follow him, just as in the previous example. After 3 minutes and 35 seconds the camera suddenly starts a slow lateral tracking movement to the right, independent of Futaki's movements, almost leaving him entirely out of the frame. Then Futaki also starts his move to the right, and leaves the room through a back door on the right-hand side. However, the camera does not stop its tracking movement; it keeps on moving to the right for another 49 seconds, showing the empty room again. This is a combined variation of static and moving camerawork, but no matter what, the camerawork is relatively independent from the character's movement and action.

Another version can be found in the last police station scene. This is a fifteen-minute scene consisting of two shots, each seven and a half minutes long. Both shots consist of two main parts: a static and a circular tracking portion. The distribution of the static and dynamic portions is almost symmetrical. The scene starts with the static portion of the first shot in a given position, which is also where the scene ends in the second shot in the same static position. Between the two static portions both shots contain a circular movement, clockwise in the first shot and counterclockwise in the second. Both circular movements are introduced by a short panning sequence, which seems to follow the characters' movements, but shortly after this the camera starts a monotonous circular movement unrelated to what the characters do. The only thing that breaks this symmetry is a 1-minute-23-second-long static portion at the end of the first shot. In this scene one can clearly observe to what extent Tarr's camerawork is structured by systematic variation of stylistic options. This is more visible in *Damnation*, because there Tarr uses fewer options, but it is still present in *Satantango*, only with a larger variety of options.

The same can be said with regard to shots in which characters make straight movements, like walking on roads. We have four main methods of representing such movements in this film, and examples abound of all of them. The camera may follow characters from behind (as in the two street-walking scenes featuring Irimiás and Petrina), it may accompany them from the front (as in the scene where the villagers leave their settlement), it may remain stationary, letting the characters disappear into the distance (as in the scene when Irimiás, Petrina and Sanyi walk away on a dirt road, or when Futaki walks away from the train station) or it may show characters approaching its stationary position (as in the scene where Irimiás, Petrina and Sanyika walk in the woods). At one point, one type of shot is even followed by another type. At the end of the first chapter, Futaki and Schmidt are walking away from the stationary camera, and in the first shot of the second chapter the camera follows Irimiás and Petrina walking toward the police station. A fifth version of this shot will be introduced in *Werckmeister Harmonies*.

This variety of stylistic solutions results in a different sort of *mise-en-scène*, partly because Tarr makes less use of the immobile-character-frozen-in-his-environment style he experimented with in *Damnation*. Not that characters do not sometimes remain sitting or standing in one place for a long time, but in most of these cases the camera is stationary too, and does not make movements which would treat characters like objects of the environment. (The main exception is the scene with the characters sleeping and the camera panning around them.) The main examples are the waiting scene at the police station with Irimiás and Petrina, and the first pub scene with Halics.

The latter example is particularly interesting. This is a three-and-a-half-minute scene, a very nice long shot composition, in which the human character is part of the symmetrical structure of the graphical composition of the image (figure 24).

Although it may seem that this character has been and will be sitting in this nice picture forever, after three minutes he suddenly leaves the frame for some thirty seconds, during which time we hear him talking off-screen, and then comes back to sit down in the same place for another minute. The camera does not follow him, just shows his empty place for thirty seconds. Although the composition would suggest something like the character's being 'rooted' into the environment, finally it is the character who moves out of the frame, rather than the camera passing by the character and leaving

Figure 24

him where he is. This is just the opposite of *Damnation*'s often used and conspicuous *mise-en-scène* technique. But this solution is sometimes combined with camera movements in such a way that both the immobility and movement of the camera remain independent from the action on-screen.

As concerns depth of field, *Satantango*'s staging style is very similar to that of *Damnation*. There are even fewer flat surface pictures or passages than in the previous film. Two shots of this kind are, however, taken over from *Damnation*, in a much shorter form: one is the tracking sequence in close-up of the stack of glasses in the pub, and the other is *Damnation*'s emblematic tracking shot of the wall with openings in which different people stand. There is, however, a great difference between these two tracking shots. In the case of *Damnation*, the shot does not have any action represented in it, nor is it very specifically embedded in the narrative. In *Satantango* it represents a particular episode of the plot. Therefore, in the openings in front of which the camera passes along, the action is placed in the background, so there is a rhythmic alteration of the focus between the foreground (the texture of the wall) and the action inside the room. In *Damnation* everything is composed in the foreground. The tracking starts on a flat surface and ends on a similar flat surface. In *Satantango* the camera comes out of the room where the action takes place to the exterior of the building, and at the end it re-enters the building, into the space where the action will continue after the camera has moved along the exterior wall. So, this camera movement is less self-contained and isolated from the rest of the narrative than the preceding one in *Damnation*, and is more motivated by the narrative content of the scene, but, at the same time, with that little modification, it fits into a consistent pattern of the Tarr style. Here again, Tarr starts exploiting the possibilities hidden in a given pattern by making little changes to this pattern.

Environment

The environment represented in *Satantango* is similar to that of *Damnation*, except that it is mainly rural. In this case Tarr did not have to draw together the location of the plot from a dozen pieces found all over the country. He found most of the locations of the settlement as they were in the Hungarian Plain. The extreme poverty and desolation of the apartments, the houses and the yards is very much in line with *Damnation*'s conception, only everything is in a much worse condition than in *Damnation*. When we see Futaki's apartment it is almost impossible to believe that someone is actually living there (figures 25a & b).

Just as in *Damnation* the settlement that is the main location for the plot does not have any well-known structures. While in *Damnation* the houses and the streets have a look somewhere between a small town and a village, in *Satantango* we have a cross between a village and a totally unstructured habitat. There are no roads, only paths, within the settlement, the buildings do not suggest from the outside that people are living there, and there are no community spaces – no church, no shops, no official buildings – in the settlement except for the pub, which in turn has no connection to other buildings; rather it stands alone at some unspecified location.

Just like in *Damnation*, it is almost always raining outside, and when it is not raining, there is a very strong wind. These will remain the meteorological constants

Figures 25a–b

of the Tarr style for the rest of Tarr's film-making career. All of his films in this period are set in the most desolate and unpleasant period of the year, lasting from late autumn to early spring, with bare trees, grey skies and no snow, just wind and cold rain.[1] The rain has no symbolic or allegorical meaning in Tarr's films. It is an expressive element that contributes to the feeling of hopeless misery. Rain is what creates dirt and mud and makes everything disintegrate. And mud is what traps someone where he or she is. Strong wind takes the place of the rain in the last two Tarr films, but in the case of *The Turin Horse* the wind is not entirely without symbolic meaning, a point to which I will return later on.

Characters

The social place of the characters in *Satantango* is at least one class lower than that of the characters in *Damnation*. The social milieu in this film is one of absolute hopeless misery. *Damnation*'s most spectacular new stylistic device of contrasting moral, psycho-logical, physical and social degradation with poetic and philosophical dialogue, which is also present in this film, could be even more striking than in *Damnation*, but this is not the case. Tarr uses this tool in a very focused manner, rather than as a general, overall method. While in *Damnation* all of the main characters at some point had some very abstract, philosophical or poetic lines, in *Satantango* these kind of lines are spoken mainly by two characters: Irimiás and the captain at the police station. Even though the passages are most of the time surprisingly abstract and poetic, in both cases they are almost completely motivated by the narrative. The same device still has its original stylistic value, but it fits more into the narrative world, which is why the tension between the environment and the dialogue of this kind is, after all, not as striking as in *Damnation*. There is one important exception to this rule. Around the end of the film Irimiás dictates a letter to the police captain, which we expect to be part of his mission as an undercover agent. When he starts the letter with 'Dear Mr. Captain…' the viewer expects to hear some concrete information or report. Instead, the letter continues as follows:

> Eternity lasts forever because it doesn't compare to the ephemeral, the change-able, the temporary. The intensity of light penetrating darkness seems to weaken. There is discontinuance, interruptions, holes, then finally the black nothing. Then there are myriads of stars in an unreachable distance with a tiny spark in the middle, the Ego. Our deeds can be rewarded or punished in eternity, and only there, because everything has a place, far away from reality,

where it fits into its place, where it has always been, where it is going to be, where it is now. At its only authentic place.[2]

This text is totally outside the narrative context, even if one supposes that it is the introduction to Irimiás's report on the settlers the clerks read and re-edit in a later scene. This text is as radical as the checkroom attendant's monologues or Karrer's monologue. All of these texts come from someplace else, a place very different to the place where the speakers are. While in *Damnation* the main role of these texts is to poke a hole, as it were, in the desolation of the physical universe in order to let some sublime spirituality get through, if only for a second, in *Satantango* these kind of texts serve also to disgrace this spirituality. The person who says them is a demonic conman who uses his intellectual power only to dupe and abuse everyone.

There is another feature of character representation that is novel in *Satantango*. Except for one character (the bartender), *Damnation*'s roles were all played by professional actors, some of whom are well-known stars in Hungarian cinema, some of them less known. In *Satantango*, out of the nineteen roles of the film ten are played by non-professional actors, and the narrator's voice is also that of a non-actor. We have to deal here with a new variation. While in the earliest Tarr films non-professional actors improvised their own dialogue, in *The Prefab People* and in *Almanac of Fall* professional actors improvised their dialogue, and in *Damnation* professional actors spoke written literary dialogue, in *Satantango* mainly non-professional actors speak written, literary dialogue. In this regard also we can note a certain permutation of specific technical elements. In Tarr's works one can find all the possible variations as regards the professional/non-professional actor and improvisation/literary dialogue elements. All of the variations occur at least twice throughout his oeuvre, which means that Tarr considered all of them valid and viable solutions. This can be summarised in the following table:

	non-prof. improv.	prof. improv.	non-prof. no improv.	prof. no improv.
Family Nest	X			
The Outsider	X			
Macbeth			(X)	X
The Prefab People		X		
Almanac of Fall		X		
Damnation				X
Satantango			X	X
Werckmeister H.				X
The Man fr. London			X	X
The Turin Horse				X

One can clearly note the tendency towards the second half of Tarr's oeuvre to apply the classical combination of professional actors and written dialogues. Improvised dialogues always have some reality effect, even if the dialogue is spoken by professional actors. With *Damnation*, Tarr went to the opposite extreme: he increased the artificial, poetic, unnatural effect in dialogue. In fact, what happens in *Satantango* is that Tarr introduces yet another way of maintaining the unnatural, artificial effect of the dialogue. On the one hand, in some scenes, just like in *Damnation*, Tarr adds abstract content and poetic style to the dialogue. On the other, he makes even the most banal dialogue sound unnatural simply by having non-professional actors speak it. This solution is not without antecedents, even in Tarr's career. In the beginning of *Macbeth* the three witches are played by non-professional actors, three well-known theatre and film directors. Since this is not a dominant part of the film, it does not have a salient effect on the style – not to mention that for non-native speakers this fact probably remains imperceptible. (That is why I added parentheses in the above table.) But it is important to note that Tarr, already in 1982, gave this solution a little try.

The most important antecedent of this device is in a Hungarian film from the same year, 1983, made by a friend of Tarr, Gábor Bódy, who tragically passed away in 1985. In his film *Dog's Night Song*, Bódy not only cast some of the roles with non-professional actors, but he played the main role himself. The reason why this case was particularly memorable is that Bódy had a way of speaking that was clearly disturbing. His diction was so far away from anything that was permitted by the norms of professional acting that critiques did not even tackle this question, and implicitly attributed this choice to Bódy's well-known avant-garde inclinations, and to the act of authorial self-reflexivity.[3] Bódy, however, had a very precise agenda with that choice. The role he plays is that of a *fake* priest who deceives people with his charismatic personality. In fact he is an agent of an international secret sect. The question is why he insisted on using his own voice, in spite of his clearly unprofessional diction, which had some speech defects, and risking making his film an object of ridicule. He could have easily dubbed his own voice with a professional actor's, and his personal appearance would still have had the authorial self-reflection effect. The answer to this is that the strangeness and 'unprofessionalism' of his voice calls attention to the fact that someone is *awkwardly acting* here in a role that was not meant to be played by him. The tone of his voice alone simply says: something stinks here. Using his own voice is a disturbing provocation that prompts everybody to ask why he would do this, for which question obviously nobody could have the correct answer.[4]

In *Satantango* the most conspicuous non-professional intonation is that of Irimiás, played by Mihály Víg. Not only has he no formal training in acting, but he has a clearly audible and distinguishable speech defect. Irimiás's is a similar character to Bódy's fake priest. He deceives people by playing the role of the saviour, but he is only an undercover police agent. His awkward intonation, together with his speech defect, draws the viewer's attention to the fact that something is wrong here: he is *acting* badly, still the others believe him. Everything he says sounds incredibly fake, just because of his intonation, and that is what is the most telling with regard to the other characters' relation to him.

Tarr denies any conscious allusion to Bódy's film in his choice of Víg for that role.[5] Nor do we have any explicit written or recorded document supporting the hypothesis of a conscious connection. The parallel remains striking, nonetheless. This is the sort of artistic impact that is hard to give a clear and unambiguous explanation for. This solution is clearly not a 'norm', not a 'tradition', not even a 'convention', not least because of the ten years that passed between the two films. A psychoanalytic explanation could quickly come to our rescue, and would easily explain the relationship between the two films; alas, it would hardly rest on historical facts, and will have to remain a light hypothesis forever, as it is very unlikely that we would ever have access to Tarr's unconscious thoughts of 1991. We can also choose not to bother too much with this fact, since technical solutions or even meanings in culture just spread a bit like diseases, and for an artist it is not necessary to be aware of their origins to be able to use them creatively. But in this particular case we do not even need some kind of contagion theory to explain an impact where direct causal connection cannot be established, because some connection in fact can be established, and the thing to be explained should be the process by which this connection led Tarr to use this solution. We have to find a more fact-based hypothesis than a psychoanalytical one as to why Tarr did this. We need a hypothesis that not only rests on the striking similarity, but fits into the evolutionary pattern of Tarr's career too, and goes beyond Tarr's own explanation, which is that this similarity is due to pure coincidence. There are too many cinematographic and biographical links to accept this as a coincidence. My claim is that Tarr made an avant-garde gesture that was in currency ten years earlier, and the reason why he did it was that he considered his films as in a way continuing this avant-garde movement.

Tarr's taste for Hungarian avant-garde art can be clearly detected in some traces in his films and biographical data. For many years in the early 1970s, Tarr was close to Hungary's most virulent underground or avant-garde theatre groups, the Orfeo theatre and the Halász theatre. These groups not only covered theatrical activities, but represented a whole way of life and attracted all kinds of avant-garde artists, and many young people like Tarr, who just wanted to be around them. Tarr was immersed in that culture without actively taking part in their creative activities. *Damnation* and *Satantango* abound in hidden and direct references to Hungarian avant-garde art of the 1970s and 1980s. I mentioned the most salient example that can be found in *Damnation* (direct citation of an avant-garde film of the 1970s) in the previous chapter. In *Satantango,* avant-garde references are even more hidden but unmistakable for someone who knows this subculture. More than one-third, precisely seven, of the main characters of *Satantango* come from this particular subculture, only one of whom is a professional actor, Miklós Székely B., playing Futaki. Other than Mihály Víg, we find the following avant-garde artists in the film: Schmidt is played by a well-known avant-garde painter and musician of the 1970s and 1980s, László feLugossy; Halics is played by someone close to this circle at this time, Alfréd Járai; Petrina is played by an avant-garde filmmaker of the early 1980s, Dr Putyi Horváth; Gyula Pauer, well known for his 'pseudo art' of the 1970s and 1980s, also has a supporting role in *Satantango*; and finally, the captain of the police is played by a famous writer, close friend and collaborator of Gábor Bódy, Péter Dobay. This is more than coincidence. As for the concrete similarity between *Satantango* and Bódy's film, we should note that Tarr knew Bódy and his film well, and they respected each other's work in spite of the fact that at that time they did not belong to the same artistic current: Bódy was a sort of avant-garde icon at the beginning of the 1980s, while Tarr was slowly moving away from the opposite camp to where he was considered to belong, the semi-documentary practice. However, Tarr was the one in this camp whom Bódy respected the most, and he called the early version of *The Outsider* an 'experimental film', which certainly counted as a compliment from Bódy at that time.[6] In these films (*Damnation* and *Satantango*) Tarr consistently pays tribute to the avant-garde spirit of a historical period which he himself did not play a role in forming; yet its influence is detectable in his films ten years later. And because this influence is really detectable, the references are more than just paying tribute. Tarr shares the impulse with the avant-garde of the 1970s and early 1980s to consciously corrupt a professional filmmaking practice by moving stylistic elements out of their usual contexts and using extreme or absurd effects to make the work more expressive. This is the same avant-garde spirit that ten or fifteen years earlier informed Gábor Bódy's films, as well as the artistic creations of the artists who appear in his films. The idea to make a professional film look non-professional was an avant-garde idea of the early 1980s in Hungarian cinema practised most consistently by Bódy. Tarr used this conspicuously amateurish acting as one stylistic element among others, but it was an important ingredient of his film, given his intention to demarcate it from the rest of Hungarian cinema, much as the same solution was important to Bódy's intentions ten years before. So, even if it might be true that Tarr did not specifically have Bódy in mind when making that choice, the fact that his attitude and way of thinking was informed by the avant-garde make this choice more than a coincidence. To explain it, it is enough to know that this solution had an avant-garde currency ten years earlier, and that Tarr consistently wanted to make explicit his relationship to this period. In his own way Tarr kept alive (or revived) this avant-garde. Finally one must remark that Bódy's film and Krasznahorkai's novel were born in the same historical period, in the first couple of years of the 1980s, which makes both works' main character – the ideological, quasi-religious conman, who is in reality the agent of a secret organisation, and whose fakeness is nevertheless apparent and ridiculous – a topical character of the period.

Werckmeister Harmonies

This film also represents some less conspicuous stylistic changes as compared to Tarr's previous works, which are important nevertheless. The first change to remark on is a quantitative one. As mentioned earlier, the average shot length of this film is longer by 51 per cent than that of *Satantango*. This is the second biggest increase of average shot length in Tarr's career. The longest take in the film is the first one, which is 9 minutes and 36 seconds long, and no take is shorter than 45 seconds. This quantitative increase of shot length alone, however, would not entail any significant stylistic change. What it means is that after the success of *Satantango* Tarr has become more self-confident in exploring more possibilities of the stylistic patterns of the long take.

What is remarkable in this film is a change in the historical model of long-take style. Instead of further developing the Godard-Tarkovsky kind of independent

camerawork, Tarr shifted to the Antonioni-Jancsó model of accompanying complicated character movements. In this film we find no long camera movements travelling
around spaces or among characters independently of the characters' movements. Nor
do we find long static shots in which the characters just walk in and out without the
camera turning to follow their movements. Every movement of the camera is motivated by character motion, and even if sometimes a character goes out of sight for a
moment, the camera catches up quickly with his or her trajectory.

Extended long takes that follow characters result in even more complicated camera
movement choreography than that found in *Satantango* or in *Damnation*. This is especially true when the characters move through different spaces. In the film's third shot
we follow Valuska's movement for seven minutes as he enters Mr. Eszter's house, helps
him to bed, and then makes some arrangements in the apartment before leaving. Topo-
graphically this is a simple circle, as the apartment's arrangement is such that proceeding
from one room to another finally makes a circle. But the different closing ins and
backing ups, stops, turns and pans needed to follow Valuska make this choreography
very complex. This complexity, however, is quite easy to follow. This is due to the fact
that the shot is composed as if it were a sequence of seven static shots (figures 26a–g).

Figures 26a–f

Figure 26g

Whenever Valuska has to do something in the apartment the camera stops on a well-composed image. These stops can last as long as a minute. During these stops the camera does not move, or moves just a very small amount when Valuska moves away from the camera or even leaves the frame. Between these stops the transitions include turns, back ups and closing ins. All this provides the camera movement with a certain rhythmic 'breathing' that prevents a too-mechanical following technique that would pass unnoticed and could have been easily replaced by simple editing. The camera movement is fundamentally subordinated to the character's movement, yet it is autonomous enough to provide through its own tempo and micro-movements an emotional accent to the scene.

Two more scenes are composed in this manner. One is the hospital scene, and the other is the night scene at the main square. In both of them we can find relatively autonomous camerawork, which is nevertheless fundamentally motivated by character movements. This hospital scene is a single eight-minute-long take with a constant forward movement. In it, the mob proceeds from ward to ward, systematically destroying the whole institution. The characters run in and out of the picture and the camera moves forward down the corridor much slower than them, following them into the wards and the corridor. The camera movement is entirely motivated by the characters' movements, only it follows them at a different speed. Interestingly, in the last part of the shot, where the mob stops the destruction and starts leaving the hospital, they do it at the same speed as the camera has moved all along. So, one could say that the speed of the camera movement in the first part of the scene is anticipatory, as it were, as regards the characters' movement in the second part of the scene – as if the camera just 'knew' that finally they would slow down. The other example is the second main square scene, where Valuska is wandering around among the mob. The camera follows his trajectory in such a way that it 'loses' him from time to time, moving forward, and 'meets' him again. The basic movement pattern is motivated by Valuska's movement, but the camera still has a considerable autonomy.

This latter scene is interesting from yet another point of view. As mentioned earlier, in *Satantango* Tarr did not use camera movements travelling around in spaces among or in front of 'frozen' characters, which was the characteristic camera movement in *Damnation*. This kind of camera movement returns in *Werckmeister Harmonies* with an important variation, inasmuch as this pattern is not combined with the total independence of the camera. There are two scenes in which the camera moves around at length among immobile characters. Both take place in the main square of the small town where the whale is on display. The mob gathers in that square, doing nothing but just standing in little groups. The first is a five-minute shot; the second is a three-minute shot. In both, the camera wanders around among the characters, who barely move and sometimes even seem frozen. The big difference between these two shots on the one hand and *Damnation*'s similar shots on the other is that here the camera does not move independently but follows Valuska walking around among the people in the square. The two shots can even each be considered further variations in their own right. In the first shot the camera remains strictly attached to Valuska's movements all the way. In the second, which is in the night scene, the camera is periodically detached from Valuska's track, losing and joining him several times.

Figure 27

Once again, we can detect in this the variation principle, by which a stylistic solution from one film returns in another in a slightly different context and combination. Some combinations remain ephemeral; some become so successful as to crystallise into a pattern. This is what happened in this film with a special variation of camera movement that follows moving characters. In *Satantango* different variations of this movement can be found, but the main solution is that the camera proceeds either in front of the characters or follows them from behind. These are not particularly innovative solutions; they may become memorable owing to their other characteristics, such as their length or their other visual or acoustic elements, for example the strong wind blowing waste from behind in the scene where Irimiás and Petrina are walking toward the police station. In *Werckmeister Harmonies* Tarr introduced another variation on following walking characters at length. In a scene we can see Mr. Eszter and Valuska walking on the street side by side, and the camera follows them, showing their profiles in medium close-up (figure 27).

This scene lasts two minutes and thirty seconds, within the shot. During this two and a half minutes the two characters talk only for thirty seconds; during the rest of the time they remain silent. All we can hear for two minutes is the rhythmic sound of their coordinated steps on the pavement. This solution – in this shot, of that length, with this rhythmic design – was made emblematic by another director, Gus Van Sant, who replicated the same combination of stylistic parameters in his film *Gerry*, in which he pays tribute to Béla Tarr.

Deep-focus compositions have been an important characteristic of the Tarr style ever since *Damnation*. Contrast, even tension, between foreground and background was systematically used by Tarr to increase the dramatic power of the images. This can be detected also in staging style. One can discern a clear shift in Tarr's films from horizontal staging toward in-depth staging. We need only compare ensemble pictures typical for almost all Tarr films from *Almanac of Fall* (figure 28) and *Satantango* (figure 29).

In this picture the characters are lined up in a row around Hédi in the middle.

Figure 28

Figure 29

Figure 30

Figures 31a–c

Even though two characters stand behind Hédi, they are close to her and there is no background anyway, so basically, the composition is horizontal, as if the five characters were standing in a straight line. This composition is radicalised in *Damnation* by a lateral tracking shot passing along the lined-up characters (see previous chapter, figures 22a–g). A similar ensemble picture in *Satantango* by contrast looks like figure 29. The characters line up in a curve. This picture is made with a wide-angle lens – which can be seen in the distortion of the two front most characters – so as to provide a great depth of field. In *Werckmeister Harmonies* extreme deep space compositions occur very often, and are emphasised by lighting effects (figure 30).

Sometimes Tarr not only stages deep-focus compositions which are static with characters moving in and out of the frame, but he enhances the dramatic tension through the revealing camera movement. A good example is the scene in which Valuska brings Aunt Tünde's luggage to Mr. Eszter's home. Not only is there a tension between the foreground with the luggage, but the camera makes a revealing movement to increase this tension (figures 31a–c). In fact this is a three-stage movement. In the first stage we can see Mr. Eszter in the background. After a while the camera makes a slight movement to the right to reveal Valuska's presence in the room. But this movement is just an indication; Tarr does not show Valuska's entire figure – it is just enough for the viewer to see that he is still there, and did not leave the room when he left the frame. The main camera movement is the last one, as the camera is suddenly lowered to reveal the presence of the luggage, thus creating a high tension between the object in the foreground and stunned Mr. Eszter in the

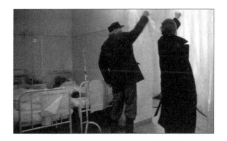

Figures 32a & b

background. This is not really a revealing movement, since we know that the luggage is there, although we have not seen it before this change of camera position. This is a very classical visual emphasis to increase dramatic tension.

The second example can be found at the end of the hospital ravaging scene. In this case the camera movement truly reveals something stunning: an old man's naked body in the background. The revealing gesture is closely related to the above-mentioned characteristic of the camera movement of this scene. As already described, the camera moves slower than the mob. Most of the time the camera enters a ward only when the destruction of the furniture and beating up of the patients are already underway or are finished in that particular ward and are to be continued in the next one. Arriving in the last ward, the camera slowly moves around in it; meanwhile two characters cross the scene, and stop at an opening covered with a shower curtain. With a coordinated brutal gesture they strip down the curtain and freeze. That is when the camera arrives there slowly and turns to reveal what they see in the background (figures 32a & b). The dramatic tension is not carried solely by the depth-of-space composition; the revealing gesture of the camera movement increases this effect considerably.

Werckmeister Harmonies represents a classical turn in the evolution of the Tarr style. A lot of effects relating this style to modernism or even to the avant-garde disappear: juxtaposition or mixing contrasting elements, independent camera movement, references to or citations from avant-garde art, sharp contrast between the characters' social position and their poetic or philosophical dialogue. After *Satantango* the linear chronology of the narrative returns, and the narration is focused on one character.

The Man from London

This film is based stylistically on the changes carried out in *Werckmeister Harmonies*. There is no return to the modernist solutions of *Satantango* or *Damnation*. On the contrary, if there is any stylistic development in this film, it is toward a more purist, crystallised form of the Tarr style.

In *Werckmeister Harmonies* strong black-and-white contrast compositions were dominant, but in *The Man from London*, with geometric minimalism added, these compositions become really classical, having strong film historical associations. Even if Tarr is reluctant to admit conscious references to film history, Bresson, Fassbinder, Carné and some film noir directors obviously come to mind. There are also shots in which the mini-

Figures 33 & 34

malist aesthetic of the composition dominates any other effect of the image (figures 33 & 34). There are even compositions where the complicated structure of mirrored images of *Almanac of Fall* returns in a more minimalist form (figure 35).

Strong lighting effects all over the film evoke the expressionist and film noir visual aesthetic in its most elaborate form (figure 36). More than in any previous film, black-and-white contrast creates a strong graphical effect, rendering some compositions painterly rather than realistic (figure 37).

Figures 35 & 36

The Man from London is Tarr's first film in which the environment carries no traces of contemporary East European landscape. This is immediately clear for an East European viewer, maybe less obvious for a West European viewer, and probably unnoticeable for a non-European viewer. Differences are very small between this film's constructed environment and that of *Werckmeister Harmonies*. Both are located in a traditional half-urban, rather old-fashioned small-town world of

Figures 37 & 38

deserted streets with houses with run-down exteriors and poorly furnished interiors. Furniture items are rather eclectic, ranging from cheap shabby articles to items of modern technology. For example in *The Man from London* most of the props date from the early to mid-twentieth century, but the cashier machine in the fur shop and the freezer in the shop where Henriette works indicate the late 1990s or even the early 2000s. Compared to these items the rest look to indicate poverty rather than a different historical period.

This is the first film in Tarr's career where the representation of the environment conveys positive feelings, at least to some extent. There are long shots of the town where the beauty of the location overshadows the general shabbiness of the individual buildings (figure 38).

One can even find direct reference to the history of photography. In the scene where Maloin and his daughter have a drink before they go out to the fur shop we can see two dancing characters, one of whom holds a chair in his hands above his head, the other of whom balances a snooker ball on his forehead (figure 39). This scene was inspired by a photograph

Figure 39

by the French photographer Robert Doisneau, while the idea of the woman playing the accordion came from another Doisneau picture.

All of this suggests that in *The Man from London* Tarr, while maintaining the main aspects of the Tarr style, connects it to various cinematic or extra-cinematic historical visual models. This is what we might call the *classicisation* of the Tarr style. While *Damnation* is full of aesthetic distance and avant-garde references, *Satantango* is full of irony, *Werckmeister Harmonies* lacks aesthetic distance in the avant-garde sense almost entirely and includes minimal irony (basically limited to the scene of the hotel porter's lunch and the police commander's drunken babble), cultural references in *The Man from London* are changed from avant-garde to classical modernism (Bresson, Fassbinder, film noir), and the only scene in which there is some aesthetic distance is the bar dance with the snooker ball and the chair.

There are some other minor but important stylistic changes too. The most spectacular change is the radical reduction of dialogue. Not only is there no tension any more between the characters' low social status and the poetic text they recite, but most characters do not even say a word in the film. Most importantly, the protagonist, Maloin, has very few dialogue scenes, and even in dialogue situations he prefers to keep silent. Verbal communication is extremely reduced in this film as compared to the previous Tarr films. This is even more striking if one takes into account that in more than one scene personal conflicts could be normally resolved if Maloin explained his situation or gave some more information. Lack of communication becomes in several instances the cause of conflicts and even of tragedies. When Maloin visits Brown in the shack, to bring him food, the result of this visit is a tragedy, as Brown thinks that Maloin came to give him up to the police. This is explicit in the novel, and implicit in the film. Tarr arranged this scene so that nobody would really know what happened until later, when Maloin tells the investigator that he killed Brown. Only when the investigator specifies that this was in self-defence can we construct the most likely chain of events. It is only then that the viewer may conclude that if the two of them had talked, Brown would not have had to die. In no other Tarr film is lack of communication the cause of a tragedy. Misunderstanding and violent and deceptive communication can often be found in the earlier Tarr films. Silence and a communication gap are something new.

The Turin Horse

The fact that this film was announced by its author as the last Béla Tarr film must turn the critic's attention to, among other things, the question of whether or not this film is different from the previous ones, whether it is a conclusion in any way, or a repetition or closure. In other words, since it stands out as an intended closure of a series of works, does this fact show in one way or another?

In different aspects of the style we can see different characteristics. As for the spatial aspect, this film goes back to the first-period Tarr films: a strictly circumscribed narrow space that the characters almost never leave. Apartments became psychological traps for characters in at least three early films: *Family Nest*, *The Prefab People* and *Almanac of Fall*. In *The Turin Horse* the characters are physically trapped in a house, which they can leave only for short periods, and even then they cannot go further than a few hundred metres. The conflict in this film is due not to communication problems, as in the early Tarr films, but to the mere fact that they cannot leave the property because of the weather conditions and the illness of the horse. So, for the first time, the physical situation is not an occasion to develop the main theme of the trap of personal conflicts, but becomes the main issue as a result of natural forces.

The trap situation known from the early Tarr films is coupled in this film with a new expression of an important element of every Tarr film: the dialogue. Until *The Man from London* Tarr moved between two extreme approaches: entirely improvised dialogue and abstract or poetic written dialogue. In *The Man from London* Tarr does not take either approach; instead, he incorporates a hitherto unusual value: a radical reduction in dialogue. This is the film in which the characters say only very short and concise sentences, and much of the dramatic tension and conflict of the film is a result of what they do not say, or of the fact that they do not say anything.

This value is developed to an extreme in *The Turin Horse*. The characters' verbal exchanges are reduced to simple words or short sentences that they utter very seldom, and which refer to the immediate context, such as orders to do this or that, or are simple remarks about the immediate environment. With one exception there are no long tirades, no discussions, no verbal developments of states of mind, no reactions to what others do.[7] The two last films brought a new phenomenon into the series of Tarr films, which were hitherto rather talkative. The gradual suppression of dialogue contributes to a certain dramatic tension created by the increased visual expressivity of the images.

Not unrelated to this effect is the considerable increase in the importance of music and other noises in this film. Repetitive music, the constant roar of the wind and several other sounds accompany the images, creating a more lugubrious atmosphere than in any preceding Tarr film. Clearly, this music/noise 'symphony' takes the place of dialogue in *The Turin Horse*, which is a very different effect to the verbal minimalism we find in the late Bresson films or in early Jancsó films. Far from being a minimalist reduction, the lack of dialogue is a means of increasing emotional expressivity, ceding space to musical compositions. In fact, that is the form the evolution of expressivity took in the Tarr style. Visually, we find no more expressionist compositions than in *The Man from London*; on the contrary, lighting is most of the time rather balanced, especially in outdoor takes. Also, there are only a very few abstract compositions, and the black-and-white contrast does not shape the space as in *Werckmeister Harmonies* or in *The Man from London*. Lighting becomes a central effect only in the last couple of minutes of the film, when, according to the story, all light is gone, and the scenes take place in almost complete darkness. This is where the viewer can experience the incredible sophistication of Tarr's lighting technique. There is no complete darkness preventing us from seeing anything; there is just enough light to make the characters look like light-grey shadows in the grey darkness.

In this film Tarr, remarkably, returned to static camerawork and reached the longest average shot length of his career. He almost entirely got rid of independent camera movements, the camera mostly following the characters' trajectories, many times turning around them. Most of the time the characters stay in a small indoor space, which is the only room of a house. There are no complex structures as in *Werckmeister Harmonies*, no long distances between multiple locations as in *Satantango*, not even multiple rooms as in *Almanac of Fall*. This is why increasing shot length was a real technical challenge in this film. This explains the extended use of Steadicam, which allows small and fine movements even in narrow spaces, and over short distances.

Evolutionary processes in the Tarr style

Length of take

One can rarely find consistent stylistic tendencies overarching the whole active period of a filmmaker's career. Usually we can distinguish between different 'periods' having constant features, which either disappear or reappear or alternate. Very often different periods have no relationship to one another at all, making the career stylistically eclectic. Very few directors work in such a way that they chisel some stylistic parameters throughout a whole career, experimenting with them by trying them out in different combinations. Ozu, Dreyer and probably Eisenstein come to mind in this respect. There are a certain number of preeminent stylistic parameters that each Tarr film is based upon, using different values and in different combinations. Examples include the long take, mobile camerawork, unconventional use of dialogue, and depth of space. These parameters determine considerably all of Tarr's films, obviously

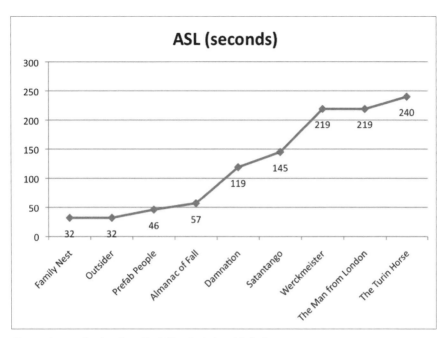

Chart 1. Average shot lengths in Tarr's films (excluding *Macbeth*)

together with other changing parameters, like visual expressivity, sound design and acting style, the changes in which are not always preeminent in all the films.

One of the parameters, the length of take, shows a remarkable pattern in Tarr's career. As shown in chart 1 opposite, we can identify a constant and almost monotonous increase in shot lengths in Tarr's films. Discounting *Macbeth*, which is a film made of two takes, but was not a movie release, each film has a higher ASL than the previous one. Only in two cases do we find an ASL equal to that of the previous film: *The Outsider* has basically the same rate as *Family Nest*, and *The Man from London* has the same rate as *Werckmeister Harmonies*. But there are no drop-offs: the constant increase in length of take is the rule in Béla Tarr's career. It is also remarkable that the same tendency can be discovered within *Satantango*, which is a film made over two years and with a length of five normal-length feature films. The takes in part three are 30 per cent longer than in part one, on average.

The nature of this increase tells us that Tarr is not simply a director who likes long takes and does not vary the length of his takes according to the needs of a particular narrative. If this were the case, either ASL would be about the same everywhere or there would be an irregular variation in the curve. What we see instead is a constant and considerable increase over 34 years. And not a slight increase either: the shots in *The Turin Horse* are almost eight times longer on average than those in *Family Nest*. The only question is to what extent ASL increases from one film to another, not whether it does.

This chart does not visualise well the incredible shift between *Almanac of Fall* and *Damnation* with respect to shot length. Analysis of the rate at which average shot length changed from one film to another provides an interesting perspective on the problem

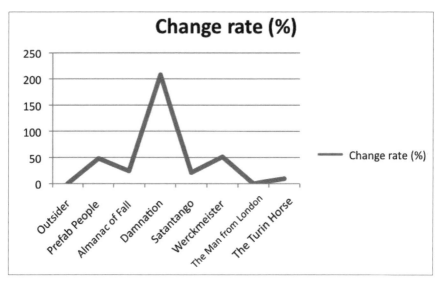

Chart 2. Rate of increase of ASL

of the periods in Tarr's career. The change rate of average shot length from one film to another spectacularly demonstrates a huge jump after *Almanac of Fall* (chart 2).

The first thing that we can say is that there are no negative values; that is, there is no decrease in ASL in consecutive films. The other thing to remark on is the spectacular change with *Damnation*. In this film the increase in ASL surpassed 200 per cent as compared to the previous film, after which the increase continued at about the same rate as before, only at a much higher level.

This steady tendency of increasing shot length looks like a conscious and independent factor of Tarr's films in the sense that it does not depend on any other feature of the film. Whatever other parameters change or remain the same from one film to another, ASL will be bigger than in the previous films, and *Damnation* was with no doubt a turning point.

Tarr definitely did not have a plan according to which, in each subsequent film, takes should be longer than in the previous one, nor has he been aware that this pattern exists. But increasing shot length is what he has been doing, with remarkable consistency. In a way this was a conscious process, in the sense that throughout his filmmaking career the problem of shot length has remained prevalent, and each film was in a way a new experiment in exploiting the possibilities of the length of takes. This is the most important medium for Tarr for communicating an atmosphere or a feeling in his films, and its constant increase shows that it is this communication process that Tarr wants to make more effective in each subsequent film.

To understand what is communicated through this process, it is essential to see whether there is any other stylistic process that changes together with the increase of the length of the takes. This is how we can get closer to the unique combination of stylistic features which supports a unique artistic expression on the one hand, and explains the trajectory of the evolution of the Tarr oeuvre on the other.

Indeed, we can find two other important features that change together with the length of takes throughout Tarr's career. One is the rate of moving camera in the films, and the other is the expressiveness of the visual compositions.

Moving camera

As discussed earlier, long-take styles may come with either predominantly static or predominantly dynamic camerawork. In the Tarr style one can find all the four basic models of the long-take style. We find static long-take compositions especially in *Almanac of Fall*, *Satantango* and *The Turin Horse*. In the other films extreme static long takes are not typical. Camera movements are mostly of the complicated character-following Jancsó type, but especially in the films preceding *The Man from London*, independent camera movements are very frequent. Both the alienating Godard kind and the immersing Tarkovsky kind occur in Tarr's films. This flexibility is made possible by the use of the Steadicam in the 1990s, starting from *Satantango*. The Steadicam makes it possible to follow a character's movements through different height levels and different spaces, to turn around the character, to change angles without the limitations of the traditional dolly. Movements can be less geometrical, and the distance between the camera and the characters can be very flexible. The liberty of Jancsó's camerawork was made possible mainly by the minimalism of the set: bare and empty spaces with very few physical limitations. This is why the scenes in a Jancsó film very rarely take place in closed places like a room. With the help of the Steadicam Tarr could achieve the same flexibility in his camerawork, even in small, closed spaces.

Moving camera has been a natural element in Tarr's films from all periods. Extended camera movements appeared with the spectacular increase in length of takes. One can observe a similar tendency in the use of moving camera to that in the use of long takes, as illustrated by chart 3. On the vertical axis we find the percentage of moving camera in a given film. One thing we can say is that in the beginning of Tarr's career the rate of moving camera did not exceed 30 per cent. It was even around 2 per cent in *Family Nest*. In other words in the case of this film the camera is static 98 per cent of the time,

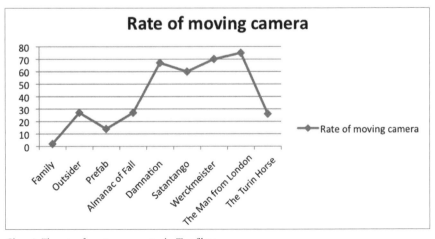

Chart 3. The rate of moving camera in the Tarr films

and in the case of *The Outsider*, 70 per cent of the time. This rate is exactly the inverse 28 years later: in *The Man from London*, the camera is moving more than 70 per cent of the time, a rate that no Tarr film had reached before. Another thing we can say is that the use of a moving camera constantly increases, a pattern broken only by a marginally higher percentage of static camerawork in *Satantango*, which led to this result. And in this respect too, we can note a jump between *Almanac of Fall* and *Damnation*.

One could say that long takes and moving camera go together, so the longer the takes, the more mobile the camera in general. In fact, there is a clear tendency for long-take-style films to also use more camera motion, but this is not a rule. We find many examples to the contrary, and we do not even have to cite well-known underground films like those of Andy Warhol. For example, Taiwanese director Edward Yang's almost three-hour-long *Yi Yi* (2000) abounds in seventy- to ninety-second-long, absolutely static shots. On the other hand, we find very many films with excessively short takes, and, at the same time, with a high moving-camera rate. For example, in a mainstream Hollywood movie, made approximately at the same time as *The Man from London*, Spike Lee's *The Inside Man* (2006), we find an average shot length of around five seconds, that is, forty times shorter than in Tarr's film, but the film still has exactly the same rate (70 per cent) of moving camera. Moving camera is clearly not linked to long takes. And even if the opposite is true less frequently, long takes may well be coupled with static camerawork. And Tarr's career is the best proof of this. In his last film, which has the highest average shot length in his career, the rate of moving camera, which has increased constantly during the past thirty years, suddenly drops back to the level of 1980, that is, to around 30 per cent. This film is as static in its camerawork as films made at the very beginning of his career and consists of longer takes on average than any of the previous Tarr films. We will see that Tarr returns in his last film to the beginning of his career in other respects too. Long takes and moving camera are clearly independent stylistic patterns. And we see that both parameters have a tendency to increase over the years in Tarr's films, and both of them increase suddenly a great deal between *Almanac of Fall* and *Damnation*.

Expressivity

The third relatively consistent tendency in Tarr's films is the growth of expressivity of the visual compositions, which obviously cannot be linked to the increase in ASL or the rate of moving camera. Expressivity is not something that can be quantified, but it is not a merely subjective aesthetic effect either. Expressivity in film history has been a recognisable stylistic norm since the 1920s. German expressionism, Eisenstein, Orson Welles and finally film noir have shaped the basic forms films have used ever since to create a fearful, emotionally saturated, grim, mysterious or dangerously unrealistic atmosphere. We can detect a tendency in Tarr's work not only towards the increased use of expressive visual effects but also towards incorporating compositions reminiscent of historical examples of visual expressivity.

Expressive visual stylisation appeared for the first time in Tarr's oeuvre in *Almanac of Fall*. Unnatural, colourful lighting and extreme camera angles carry this effect in this film (see chapter 2, figures 7c & d, and figures 8–10). As mentioned earlier, this kind

Figure 40

of excessive expressivity was fashionable for a certain period at the turn of the 1980s, but not so much by the end of the decade. Tarr retained the expressive quality of his images but returned to a more traditional form of cinematic expressionism: the strong black-and-white contrast compositions, and strong lighting effects. Many of the more memorable shots of *Damnation* are composed this way (see chapter 3, figures 15a–c, 18a–c and 21c). Deep-focus compositions were not more prevalent in *Damnation* than in *Almanac of Fall* or even than in *The Outsider*. In *Satantango*, by contrast, deep-focus staging is much more prevalent (figure 40), and at some instances it is coupled with strong black-and-white contrast and wet surfaces, which moved the Tarr style toward classical film noir stylisation.

It is, however, in *Werckmeister Harmonies* where this combination becomes the main stylistic effect of the form. This film abounds in sharp black-and-white contrast, high-tension deep-focus compositions (figures 30 and 31c). In many images in this film, lighting becomes the most important compositional tool. In *The Man from London* this tendency is maintained and complemented by some utterly abstract or painterly images (figures 33 & 37) or by compositions reminiscent of film historical references (figure 36). Not only does the expressivity of the visual aspect of Tarr films increase, but together with this increase the self-conscious film historical positioning of this visual world appears.

Conclusion

The longitudinal comparative and quantitative analysis of the formal aspects of Béla Tarr's films provides us with some interesting insights regarding the course these films have traced during the past thirty-five years. We can safely assert that in many respects there are two stylistic periods in Tarr's career. However, the main elements of the 'second period' Tarr style are present in the early films with different prevalence, in different combinations and with different values. The only feature that was missing from the first three films and was added by *Almanac of Fall* was visual expressivity. This feature is combined with the most characteristic feature of the early films: improvised acting style and dialogue. This latter disappeared entirely from the later films, and visual expressivity became prominent. We found two quantifiable parallel tendencies of increasing devices: average shot length and camera mobility. These tendencies are remarkably consistent throughout the whole corpus. Together with visual expressivity we have three dominant features of constantly growing prominence in Béla Tarr's films until the last film, where two of them suddenly drop back to the level of the early films. This fact can only be seen as the manifestation of some wish by the author to create a kind of stylistic synthesis in his last film. But until this last film these factors increased together. As argued earlier, none of these characteristics could be viewed as a necessary consequence of any other, which is clearly shown by the fact that in the last film they are separated. This means that not only do we have a particular stylistic combination of three important visual and temporal elements, but all of the three elements become increasingly important in Tarr's career, a fact that needs to be explained. Why has Tarr continuously increased the values of these parameters in his films, until *The Man from London*, while freely applying or abandoning others, like independent camera movement, improvised and poetic dialogues, and colour film stock?

This question cannot be answered on a stylistic level. If there are no strict rules or conventions for a given form, there are no stylistic reasons for a given stylistic combination either. Justification of a given set of stylistic features can be provided either through a historical explanation or through reference to the aesthetic or psychological effect it has on viewers. Historical explanations consist of listing the cultural traditions an author can be associated with, the explanation being that a given author uses a set of solutions because those solutions are like cultural traditions for him or her. But this kind of explanation is relevant only inasmuch as one can show that not knowing the given cultural tradition, one could not enjoy a film the same way a 'native speaker' could. But if, on the contrary, the style can have the same effect on an alien to the given tradition, the historical explanation loses its aesthetic relevance (which does not mean that it is irrelevant biographically, historically or otherwise). For example, the time Tarkovsky dedicates to showing natural sceneries can be explained with reference to the relationship the Russian Orthodox tradition has to the icons, which, according to this tradition, are the sacred manifestations of the holy universe.[8] This is doubtless correct, but anyone enjoying a Tarkovsky film would come to the conclusion that the beauty of the images, and the camera's unusually long contemplation of them, provides the sensation of 'seeing through' the physical aspect of the objects or the natural scene toward some transcendental existence. On the other hand, if someone does not enjoy these long, slow, actionless, meditative images, knowing about their traditional background will not help a bit. Conversely, in other cases, it is necessary to learn about a cultural tradition in order to be able to appreciate its products. For example, much of Indian cinema is very difficult for a Western viewer to approach and to appreciate because of the vast differences between the way those films express the same human situations and feelings. Even theorists inspired by cognitive science, such as Patrick Hogan, admit that knowledge of 'rasa theory, the theory of aesthetic emotion initially developed in ancient Sanskrit texts' is necessary to understand and to tune ourselves in to the wavelength of Indian cinema.[9] In these cases aesthetic and even some psychological effects are dependent on the knowledge and conceptual understanding of a cultural tradition. This is why culturalist and cognitivist explanations of works of art should treat each other as complementary rather than mutually exclusive.

As noted earlier, there is nothing 'Hungarian' in Béla Tarr, and no Hungarian cultural or cinematic tradition would help in appreciating or understanding his particular stylistic universe. (Complete ignorance of historical and geographical facts may obviously lead to serious misunderstandings, but misunderstanding will not influence appreciation, as some commentaries of foreign critics, academics and everyday viewers show.) The fact that in Hungarian post-war cinema Miklós Jancsó created a powerful long-take abstract cinematic style tells us nothing about why Tarr developed his own long-take abstract cinematic style. It tells us nothing because, firstly, many other international directors also developed some kind of long-take abstract cinematic style in the period Jancsó did; and secondly, in the cinema of Béla Tarr one can find many other influences too. So, tradition doesn't explain anything; on the contrary, Hungarian art-film tradition had been anything but like the Tarr style when the latter appeared. On the other hand, as mentioned in the introduction, the combination of the main ingredients of the Tarr style has become itself an initiator of a fashion in 1990s Hungarian cinema (black and white, grim atmosphere, long takes). Consequently, the only way the Tarr style can be explained is through the effect is has on the viewer. To this end, we have to enter into the narrative universe of the Tarr films.

Notes

1   This fact makes the issue of the production of Tarr's films rather complicated. He has shot his films, starting from 1987, exclusively in the period between November and March. Exteriors for his films could be shot only on a day with no sunshine and no snow. In the event that, for some reason, Tarr could not finish shooting before the weather turned pleasant and leaves appeared on the trees, he had to wait another eight months to continue shooting. The production of *The Turin Horse*, for example, should have started in November 2008, and should not have lasted more than two months, which would have meant that the whole film could have been ready by the summer of 2009. But the construction of the set was finished only in February 2009; shooting could start in March, but the weather was already 'too good', so real takes started only seven months later, in November 2009. Because of the heavy snowfall in December, production of the film had to stop and could resume only in March 2010. This factor alone is responsible for some extensive delays in the production of Tarr's films.

2   I have slightly altered the film subtitles so as to make the passage more faithful to the original Hungarian.

3   See Ákos Szilágyi (1983) 'Morbiditás és burleszk', *Filmvilág*, 12, pp. 5–8.

4   Ten years after his suicide it turned out that Bódy was an informant of the Hungarian secret police. Putting himself in the role of a fake priest is without any doubt was a secret confession.

5   Personal communication, 2010.

6   See András Bálint Kovács (1983) 'Ipari rituálé és nyelvi mítosz (an interview with Gábor Bódy)', *Filmvilág*, 6, pp. 13–16.

7   Originally there were two long tirades in the film, but after some deliberation Tarr decided to cut out the second one, and for a long time he considered also cutting out the first, which would have left the film with less than a dozen sentences in it over two and a half hours.

8   See András Bálint Kovács & Ákos Szilágyi (1987) *Les mondes d'Andrej Tarkovsky*. Lausanne: Éditions l'Age d'Homme.

9   Patrick Holm Hogan (2008) *Understanding Indian Movies*. Austin: University of Texas Press.

CHAPTER FIVE

Narration in the Tarr Films

The narrative features of the Tarr films can be assessed really only in relation to the themes they are utilised to express. The stories of the Tarr films are focused on only one basic theme, and each film's story offers a variation on this theme. The basic theme of all of Tarr's films is *entrapment*. Each film shows a situation which the characters are incapable of getting out of, however hard they try. They remain hopeless captives in their miserable situation, whether or not they are responsible for their own suffering. Different types of situations can be discerned in different groups of Tarr films.

The most frequent topic of the early-period films is what I will call 'everyday hell'. This theme is about how people make each other's lives a living hell, thinking that the people close to them are the only obstacles to their happiness. They torture each other psychologically and sometimes even physically; they have no respect for each other and have no plans of how to get over their problems together with the other person. This is the main topic of three early films, *Family Nest*, *The Prefab People* and *Almanac of Fall*, but one can also find this motif in other Tarr films, such as *Damnation* and *The Man from London*.

The other topic, mainly typical of the second-period films, is *betrayal and conspiracy*. *Damnation*, *Satantango* and *Werckmeister Harmonies* in particular are based on this theme, but just as in the case of the first topic, it is a frequent and important element of many other films too, such as *Almanac of Fall*, with the topic first appearing consistently in *Macbeth*. Whereas in the 'everyday hell' type of film entrapment is an existential situation which forces the characters to live together, in the 'betrayal and conspiracy' story type the characters are in principle free to go, but they choose to stay, thinking that cheating the other will help them to move forward.

Two films cannot be categorised as focusing on these topics, and they are similar in many respects. Both *The Outsider* and *The Turin Horse* tell the story of people who are totally lost and incapable of finding a way of coping with their environment, but not because they are betrayed or because other people make their lives difficult. In *The Outsider* it is the protagonist's personality that makes it impossible for him to move forward in his own life; in the case of *The Turin Horse* it is the physical environment. However, these films are also powerful stories about the situation of entrapment. The narrative features of the Tarr films are all direct consequences of this basic topic.

There is one narrative feature that probably anybody who has seen at least one Béla Tarr film from the second period would immediately mention: that they are extremely slow and relatively long. The length of a film is relative but quantifiable. The slowness of the narration is also relative but not quantifiable. The general impression of viewers that Tarr's films are long is due to a single film, *Satantango*, which is not only 420 minutes long, but is meant to be screened in a single session, unlike its famous predecessor, Fassbinder's *Berlin, Alexanderplatz*, which was released as a television mini-series. This is what made *Satantango* not only a long film, but also a screening event. But *Satantango* is also an exception in Tarr's own career. The length of Tarr's released feature films excluding *Satantango* is about average for their film historical context, and does not change much. It varies between 100 and 146 minutes. It is not the objective and quantifiable length of the Tarr films that makes the viewers feel that they are long; it is rather their other, non-quantifiable feature, their extreme slowness.

The questions regarding narrative slowness are these: what may be the reason for it, and what makes it acceptable (for a certain art-film audience)? To answer these questions we have to map all the important features of Tarr's narratives, and try to find the relationship between them. We have to find their specific function in the overall effect of the Tarr style. I will argue that what the dramaturgical form of Tarr's films succeeds in doing is making the viewer believe the same illusion as the characters, which is that the story is going somewhere, even if slowly, while in fact it is only making a circle, and arrives at a situation as hopeless as the one it started out from. The main problem Tarr resolves in different ways in different films is *how to create the deceptive sense that the characters' situation is evolving toward some solution and, at the same time, to make one feel the hopelessness of this situation right from the beginning; the art of Béla Tarr is thus to make believe without hiding anything.* To reach this paradoxical sensation is the main function of the Tarr style as well as of Tarr's narrative devices and character representation. The aesthetic and emotional effects resulting from this are very complex, but the main driving force of these effects is the dialectics of hope and hopelessness.

The technical realisation of this dialectics and the most important manifestation of entrapment in the narrative structure is the fundamental *circular dramatic form* of the Tarr films. This means essentially that the dramatic conflict developed at the beginning of the story is not resolved in the end. On the surface, circularity appears in different forms, discussed later in some detail. I will explore four aspects of Tarr's narration that are more or less constant in the oeuvre, and that are the main cornerstones of the complex effect of his narratives: *banality of narrative events*; *slowness of narration and suspense*; *static situations* and *circular narrative form*.

Banality of narrative events

The basic building block of the early Tarr films' static stories and of later films' circularity is the banality, or the unexceptional, everyday character, of the events. Even though some events may result in small changes, none of these are of the sort one would call exceptional, which would undo the initial situation of the characters. At his best, Tarr is able to render even the most excessive or exceptional event an everyday banality that has no effect on the characters' way of life.

Family Nest's radicalism is also due to this effect of rendering the shocking or exceptional banal. The main example is the most shocking scene of *Family Nest*, and probably of the whole Tarr oeuvre: the rape story. Every element of this story is shocking or surprising. Accompanied by his elder brother, Irén's husband, Laci unexpectedly arrives home from two years of military service. His father makes a remark regarding the fact that they were not informed about the son's arrival, but after all everybody is glad to have him back again. This is surprising, but as the family members get over it very quickly, the viewer also takes it as normal. Shortly after their arrival the family and Irén's friend visiting her sit down to have dinner. After dinner Irén and her friend go to the next room to take Irén's little daughter to bed, while the rest of the family remains in the main room playing cards. After a while Irén's friend announces her intention to leave. Surprisingly, the two brothers also stand up and announce that they will go to the pub for a beer. Irén is absent in this scene, and nobody among the rest of the family members remarks on the fact that the son, who has just arrived, is going to the pub instead of spending time with his wife and daughter. Again, they take it as normal, so the viewer is also obliged to accept it as something that is part of the normal course of events. The next scene is clearly shocking, because instead of going to the pub the two brothers rape Irén's friend on the street. The whole story comes to a point where the viewer can no longer consider it an 'anthropological' description of the way of life of a certain subculture that may be surprising, but after all has to be accepted as normal. The woman tries to resist, struggles, and wants to escape, which makes this scene not an ethnographic curiosity but a clear-cut case of a sexual crime. And then comes an even more shocking surprise. After the rape, the three of them go to the pub together and drink peacefully. Tarr's procedure is the same here as it was before. Whatever happens, if the characters cope with it, the viewers have to cope with it too. If the young woman instead of going to the police goes to the pub, and accepts a drink from her two rapists, and no violence is involved any more, the viewer has no other option than to take it as 'the way things usually go around here', however unusual and shocking all of it may seem. And that is what makes the whole story after all an impassive 'ethnographic' description of a certain cultural milieu. The film forces us to accept that even though we know rape is a crime, and even though the young woman protests, at the end all this becomes a part of everyday life.

Originally the script had this story without the shocking twist at the end. The two brothers were to bring the young woman to a pub, get her drunk, and rape her afterwards. This version seems more 'logical', or closer to the way things are likely to happen in real life,[1] but dramaturgically this solution has two important weaknesses. First, if we see the young woman drinking with the two brothers first, we already know that the two brothers have left because of the woman, and thus we have a certain expectation of things getting worse, so the rape would not really come as a surprise, even if it is shocking. Second, if the woman gets raped after getting drunk, she would become a simple victim, which would provoke the viewer to make a conventional moral judgement on the brothers alone. The way the events proceed in the film makes the viewer make a moral judgement against the young woman too, or drop any moral judgement at all. Part of the shocking effect comes from the fact that what we see is a legal crime according to the law but apparently it is not a big crime on their terms, and not even on the woman's terms. That is the way they live; this act, and probably other kinds of crime too, are just ordinary parts of their lives, and they do not ever reflect on this fact. And that is what is shocking for the viewer. This is where the film becomes ethnographic: the viewer feels that this moral universe cannot be part of his or her world, and if it is, if this really happens in our world, then it seems even more scandalous.

Clearly, this series of events does not constitute an average 'everyday' rape case. Every element is at the borderline of the 'normal' (if there is such a thing as a 'normal rape'). But nothing in it seems totally impossible either. And once the viewer accepts the course of events as possible, the aesthetic effect of the film starts to work. We find ourselves in the middle of a world that looks familiar and predictable, but which turns out to be entirely unpredictable and full of surprises. The viewer believes that anything can happen in this world. And that is Tarr's great achievement: he makes the viewer believe something can change in this world, whereas in fact nothing really happens to effect any real lasting change. At the end, what we get is what we see. It is just like what we expect at the beginning of the film, but in the meantime we are made to believe that we were wrong. In fact we know this world from afar, and we expect nothing good from it. But Tarr shows us that, in fact, we don't know this world in detail, and we don't have much idea as to how much more horrible it is than we think, although, in the end, the result is in fact what we expected.

However, Tarr's purpose is not simply to show something that is more horrible than we think it is. The illusion through which he leads us to the expected result is an illusion inasmuch as it deceivingly suggests that something in this world can in fact change. But as long as the characters and the viewer are captives of this illusion, there is some positive element in it. This is the human capacity for the desire for a better life and for real values, in whatever ugly or ridiculous way the characters may express it. This illusion is the most essential part of Tarr's characters, the part which gives them dignity. I will discuss this later, in the section dealing with character representation.

Topic 1: Everyday hell

Three of the four early Tarr films, *Family Nest*, *The Prefab People* and *Almanac of Fall*, have the same topic, which is how ordinary people make one another's life a living hell. This topic itself requires banality as the main characteristic element of the story. Not only do no extraordinary things happen in the stories, but they have no outcome whatsoever. If we consider the ending of *The Prefab People* as the outcome of the series of events resulting from the leaving of the husband, we can say that an important narrative feature of the early Tarr films is that their narratives have neither start nor ending. We step into the middle of an everyday event that seems to go on unchanged for some time, and step out of it without reaching any solution or substantial change. However, in order to give the stories a certain linear narrative development, Tarr incorporates in each of the stories one linear plotline that starts after the beginning and ends before the end. This way the basically circular narratives have a linear supporting element.

Family Nest

The film starts with the day that has the potential to change Irén's life: in the evening of an ordinary day her husband, Laci, unexpectedly arrives home from his military service. It may seem that her humiliating situation in the apartment of her father-in-law might now end, because her husband is back, and will protect her from the constant mean and violent verbal attacks of her mother-in-law and father-in-law. The rape scene at the beginning of the film suggests to the viewer that nothing of that sort is likely to happen, and that is what Irén will realise at the end of the story too, when she is ousted from the apartment by her father-in-law, with Laci's passive assistance.

The hopelessness of Irén's situation has two sources. One is the housing conditions of 1970s Hungary, which were the result of massive urban immigration without appropriate housing development by the government. Whole families lived in a single space or in one-bedroom apartments, without even a proper bathroom; two or more families lived in larger apartments, obliged to share bathroom and kitchen facilities with strangers. Generations grew up in these conditions without any hope for improvement of their housing situation. The other has nothing to do with the housing conditions, but rather with the aggressive and amoral attitude of the family members Irén has to live with. It is not possible for her to cope with the parents of her husband, but there is no escape; she has nowhere to go. Most of the scenes illustrate the human condition of this family rather than their housing situation. Tarr dedicates only one scene to the latter: when Irén goes to the city council to apply for an apartment. In the rest of the film he shows everyday scenes depicting the relationships between and attitudes of family members. These scenes are dialogue situations not associated with actions or stories. Most of these dialogues have as their only function the characterisation of the players. The more banal and empty the dialogues, the better, for this purpose. These people do not have any extraordinary problems in their lives other than the living conditions which they share with a million other people. It is not these conditions that make them the way they are; this situation only makes the way they are even more unbearable. Any extraordinary story event would suggest to the viewer that their behaviour is due to material problems. This is why it is essential for Tarr to make the story out of scenes as insignificant as possible.

This doesn't mean, however, that nothing is building up from these situations during the film. The challenge of *Family Nest*'s narration is that in spite of the banality of the events, the scenes coming one after another have to contribute to motivating Irén's leaving the house. This is the only important narrative change in the film, whereby Irén finds herself in an even more desperate situation than that in which she was before. Tarr achieves this by two means. One is a linear plotline starting around forty minutes into the film and ending after around one hour and ten minutes, representing Laci's father manipulating his son to get rid of Irén. Although the film starts with a violent argument from which it becomes clear that the parents want Irén out, this is the first thing the father actually does to reach this goal. This plotline has the function of providing a supporting element to the otherwise circular or static structure. It does not even fill the whole thirty minutes; it takes only two scenes. The first is when Laci's father tries to convince Laci of Irén's infidelity; the second is when in an argument over money he brings this issue up again, and Laci starts to question Irén. This is what leads to the break-up; it is at this point that it becomes clear that Laci's parents not only verbally abuse Irén, but are ready to try anything to get rid of her. But this alone wouldn't be enough for Irén to leave the house or Laci to let Irén go.

The other means of motivating Irén's departure is the description of the emotional bonds between the family members as being weak and unreliable. To demonstrate this, the narrative uses a contrasting method. The characters' behaviour in individual scenes is in strong contrast to the way the given character behaves in a subsequent scene. The rape scene is the most telling example of this. This is how the sequence goes: a) a peaceful family card game; the young woman and the two brothers leave; b) the two brothers rape the young woman; c) the three of them drink relaxed in a pub; d) Laci goes to bed and tenderly embraces his wife, whispering nice comforting words in her ears.

The characters' behaviour in each of the scenes is in contrast to the way they behave in the previous or next scenes. We don't expect the two brothers to rape the girl, and we don't expect her to drink with the brothers afterwards, and we don't expect Laci to be so tender with his wife following all this. Sometimes the contrast is in a single scene. When Laci, Irén and their little daughter go to the amusement park, the whole scene has an atmosphere of peace, happiness and cheerful relaxation. That is also the only scene where there is light music all the way through. However, in the last sequence Laci is not with his family any more; he drinks alone while his wife and daughter are on the merry-go-round, and the scene ends with him vomiting, having drunk too much.

The situation is the same with Laci's father. Until the end of the film it seems as though the father is consistent in his behaviour. Although he is very arrogant and rather stupid, he seems to consistently defend very conservative family values and a working ethic. That is why it is shocking when at the end of the film we see him a little drunk, courting a woman, Irén's friend by the way, which both makes him ridiculous and discredits everything he has said before and every moral lesson he has given to all of the members of his family. Even this scene is not unambiguous. The father's behaviour is repulsive and ridiculous during the time the woman sits next to him and he tries to approach her. When she finally has had enough and leaves the table, the scene does not end. We see him alone at the table drinking and singing a sad folk song about how lonely he is. Although he does not win our sympathy with that, we no longer see him as harmful and violent as before, as he shows some desperation, even though we know that he is the victim of himself alone. The last contrast is the fake interview scene with Laci, who is far from being cynical or unsympathetic to Irén, where he winds up crying over this situation, and the viewer cannot help feeling a little sorry for him too.

The film's most audacious narrative turn is when it apparently shifts genre, and ends as a (fake) documentary. The last two scenes are arranged as if they were interviews with the characters who act, as if the film's story were about their real life, and they played their own roles in it. I elaborated on this in chapter two from a stylistic point of view; from a narrative point of view this part is a reflection on and thereby a closure of the director's statement at the beginning of the film: 'This is a true story, it didn't happen to the people in the film, but it could have.' The fake interview sequence at the end of the film confirms this statement stylistically, but also brings this extradiegetic element into the diegesis. Through this narrative device Tarr turns the initial director's statement into an aesthetic experience of the film, whereby the viewer forgets about the fictional character of the story and accepts it as a literal part of reality. That aesthetic experience is what makes the director's statement really credible.[2]

The Prefab People and *Diplomafilm*
The Prefab People is Tarr's second 'living hell' film. The narrative process and the basic situation are similar to *Family Nest*'s, but there are some changes. Around half of the film plays out in an apartment, and a little bit less than half in different exterior locations. This provides a less 'claustrophobic' effect than the *mise-en-scène* does in *Family Nest*. After all, the family conflict here is not related to the housing situation. However, allusion to the Hungarian housing situation is not missing from the film entirely. Its title refers to the housing projects that were built extensively at the end of the 1970s and early 1980s around Budapest, with the help of the low-quality Soviet technology of prefabricated concrete panels. The word 'panel' in the Hungarian usage of the time evoked for everyone those very low-quality buildings on the outskirts of Budapest, occupying huge territories with their monotonous geometrical planning and without any green areas around them. For most working- and lower-middle-class people this was the only housing solution, for which they longed during many years, like Irén did in *Family Nest*. It appears as though Tarr followed Irén and Laci after they reunited and finally had an apartment of their own. Both films represent a situation which leads to a couple's break-up. And both proceed through banal, everyday scenes. This film is based on a contrasting structure similar to that of *Family Nest*, only the contrasts here are not as shocking. The contrasting structure concerns the circular frame of the story: at the beginning and at the end of the film we find the same event sequence: a) Robi unexpectedly packs up and leaves his family; b) the couple is reunited.

It is not simply the scene of Robi's leaving that makes this narrative circular. It is this larger event sequence that suggests that this life goes on the same tracks forever with different variations, without any way for the characters to step out of their vicious circle. That is what this circular form suggests, but it is not what it explicitly articulates. The first break-up scene looks like a flash-forward to the end of the story, and it seems as if afterwards the narrative goes back to an earlier stage to show what led to this outcome. The two break-up scenes are very similar but not identical. Firstly, they are different in length. The first scene is a 140-second single shot, while the second scene is a 240-second single shot, so the second is almost two minutes longer than the first. They differ also in small gestures, in little bits of dialogues, and some camerawork, which is due to the characters' different movements. The scene we see at the end of the story is thus not *exactly* the same as the one we see at the beginning. This little difference is important, otherwise the last scene coming after the second break-up scene, where the two of them are together again buying a washing machine, wouldn't make much sense. Even though it can be interpreted as a flashback – just as in the beginning where the scene could be interpreted as a flash-forward – this doesn't make much sense, as we have already seen enough of their relationship. Why show another banal scene from their life together *after* their break-up? This scene makes sense only if this is not a flashback but a chronological continuation of the preceding events, suggesting that Robi came back, but nothing is resolved.

Having said that, it is very unlikely that any spectator would notice these differences in the movie theatre, because the narrative content is the same, the starting and ending situation is the same, and basically the two characters behave the same way. Most viewers would interpret the two scenes as identical, and the repetition as just a narrative frame.[3] But, again, on this interpretation the last scene does not really fit. Still, precisely because no other interpretation is possible, most viewers would come to the conclusion that probably it is the film that starts again rather than their life together, which may have the same interpretative effect as would the other possibility, that this is a story that repeats itself over and over again. Thus, in spite of the ambiguity and lack of explicitness of this ending, its circular effect is very strong, and that was Tarr's main intention here. From this film on circularity will become the most important structural element of Tarr's narratives.

Just as in the previous films, banality of life is what each scene suggests to the viewer. Tarr doesn't use the method seen in *Family Nest* whereby a scene, even if it is shocking or extraordinary, becomes ordinary, because in this film nothing is really shocking or extraordinary. On the other hand, he uses the contrasting method within one scene exactly the way he used it in *Family Nest*, especially in the amusement park scene. In this film there are three such scenes, and these are longer and more elaborate than the amusement park scene in the first film. But the idea is the same: to take an event that is supposed to be pleasant and cheerful, and that could bring family members closer to one another, and spoil it gradually so that at the end it becomes clearly embarrassing and unpleasant, possibly engendering conflicts rather than agreement. We can even say that these three scenes make the backbone of the narrative: together they occupy one-third of the film's running time.

That is how the chronological narrative starts after the flash-forward. Robi and Judit have their nine-year wedding anniversary, which they celebrate at home. Robi buys a bottle of cheap brandy and some hairspray for his wife, which doesn't make her particularly happy. Right after they have their first drink, Judit brings up a subject that will be the source of the conflict (she had asked Robi to arrange a job for her in the factory, but he didn't attend to his wife's request); she winds up crying, and finally the whole celebration of their wedding anniversary turns into a bitter fight, making them more unhappy than they were before. The second scene of this kind is when the family goes to the local beach, and Robi stays behind to say hello to a friend. This visit lasts only twenty minutes according to Robi, but an hour and a half according to his wife, and when he finally arrives by the pool she starts a fight again, which makes him leave the scene and the rest of the family alone at the beach. The third is the longest. It is a company party for which Judit excitedly prepares, having her hair done and dressing nicely. She speaks at length to the women at the hairdresser's about how much she loves dancing. At the party Robi dances only with other women; he winds up drunk, and his wife is totally depressed. All of these occasions could have been special and constructive for their marriage, but all these events just contribute to its decay.

Just like *Family Nest*, this film represents very little tenderness in the couple's relationship. The only two scenes in which they show some tenderness for each other are the anniversary scene, where this emotion dissipates very quickly within the scene itself, and the love-making scene after Judit opposes his going to work abroad. But right after this Robi leaves his family. In the rest of the film he either ignores her or has the necessary minimum everyday conversation with her. There is one exception, where Robi tries to explain to his wife that it would be a good thing if he accepted a job abroad for two years. Other than that there is no substantial communication between the two of them, even in the two break-up scenes, in which Robi just leaves without any explanation. The emotional bonds represented here are as weak as in *Family Nest*, and even though communication is not as violent and aggressive as in the first film, it is no less void of human understanding. Because of the lack of explicit social content in their conflict (comparable to the housing problems in *Family Nest*), nothing outside their personal relationship can be realistically blamed for it. That is why Tarr felt it was important this time to use professional actors, who are more experienced than amateurs in expressing different and nuanced psychological states. There are no scenes in this film which could shift the viewer's perspective out of this family context. The only scene which shows that Robi is interested in anything in the world is when he explains the difference between socialism and capitalism to his son in an extremely primitive way, which is not primitive because he wants his son to understand but rather because that is the only way he is able to talk about these things. They are watching a television programme where some scholar is speaking about the nature of world capitalism in very abstract ideological terms. As they listen, Robi sort of translates what he hears, as much as he can understand it, into the primitive terms of dialectical materialism such as he remembers from school. A complicated and sophisticated ideology coming from the television and its simplified mirror image sunk into the brains of ordinary people are juxtaposed in this scene to show that emotional and psychological emptiness is coupled with an effective ideological brainwash in the lives of these people. The social milieu around them does not offer any more possibility for them than their own family life, which provides in turn very restricted prospects in financial terms. It is not a particular meanness or moral decay that works in this film, as was the case in *Family Nest*, but a simple lack of personal and social awareness of a whole social milieu that is translated into a personal relationship.

In this film the characters' lives are a living hell not because they torture one another actively, which sometimes they do too, but because the things they expect from one another are unavailable to them. Both feel that they are prisoners of their own family and they do not have control over their own lives, and because of that they cannot make the other's life happier either. They both think in their own ways that leaving home is the solution, while there is nowhere to go for them.

The Prefab People has an antecedent, which is Tarr's forty-minute-long diploma work, submitted a year before at the film school under the title of *Diplomafilm*. This film contains all the important elements of *The Prefab People* except the circular structure. The characters and the actors are the same, the conflict is the same, and the outcome is the same; even the interview scene at the end is there. In this film one can trace back the original idea of the story. In the interview scene Judit tells the original story Tarr heard about a man leaving his family and moving into a house across the street, just opposite his former home. From that point on, he was living in separation from his family, but they could see each other every day from a distance. This narrative motif is missing from *The Prefab People*. In *Diplomafilm* the wedding anniversary scene is preceded by several other scenes which either come later in *The Prefab People* or are simply missing from it. The most important scene missing from the longer version is the first shot in *Diplomafilm*. Here, Robi is talking to the camera about his work, emphasising the powerful position he has at the power plant. Robi says that he is at the top of everything, and everything depends on him. With the push of a button, he can turn whole neighbourhoods black, he can kill a patient on the operating table, he can make the streetcars stop. This scene is meant to be very ironic, and the actor's way of talking is exaggerated in such a way that the viewer can see the absurdity of a petty person's self-image as someone very important. However, this scene does not contribute to the development of the real conflict with his wife, since there is no plotline dealing with his work or with his psychological complex of being the master of the world. Other than that, this scene ridicules Robi in a way no other Tarr character is ridiculed; Tarr omitted this scene from *The Prefab People*.

Diplomafilm's narrative structure is linear and not constructed upon surprises. As the viewer is prepared for the wedding anniversary by other scenes where the couple's imperfect relationship is exposed, the fact that the anniversary turns out bad is not really surprising. It is immediately followed by the scene where they buy a washing machine, which is more logical dramaturgically, but not at all surprising. The scene where Robi packs up and leaves the family is, again, logically at the end of the story, but by that token, it is not surprising either.

What Tarr accomplished in *The Prefab People* was the creation of the surprise effect with the help of the circular structure.

Almanac of Fall

The next film dealing with this topic is Tarr's last film of his first period (or the intermediary film between the two periods). In this film, Tarr returns to the narrative framework of his first film: an ensemble play in a closed environment, which is again a single apartment. This time Tarr develops the claustrophobic effect of this situation to an extreme: no scenes occur outside the apartment. The characters' situation is also similar to that in *Family Nest*: most of them live there because they have nowhere else to go, or because this is the simplest way to solve their housing problems. However, they are not forced to be together as in *Family Nest*. The apartment is owned by an elderly lady, Hédi, who lives there with her son, János. Hédi's nurse, Anna, has moved in, because it is simpler for Hédi, and she brings her boyfriend, Miklós. The last person to move in is Tibor, János's friend. There is enough room for everyone here, narrow space is not a problem, and seemingly Hédi is rich enough to sponsor this little community. The characters have no goals that would make the story progress, such as having an apartment of their own, or having a decent occupation, or making more money. This story is about a power game for the control of a territory. It is an abstract closed-situation drama where the story moves forward through different shifts in the positions of the characters relative to each other. This is the first time that the permutation principle appears in Tarr's oeuvre explicitly in a dramatic construct. And it is associated with a similarly explicit circular dramatic structure, which, as already mentioned, after *The Prefab People* will be the main structure of Tarr's narratives. All of the first-period Tarr films' narratives are based on the representation of personal communication in rather everyday situations. The narrative structure of *Almanac of Fall* is based on dialogues between pairs of characters, with the relationships within the pairs changing each time. In this film there is no linear plotline, and the only movement in the film is the changing relationships of the characters. The difference between the initial and the concluding situation is that Anna, instead of being Miklós's girlfriend, is now János's fiancée or wife, although she is dancing with Miklós in the last scene while János sits by the table with tears in his eyes. These shifts go through violent, sometimes even physical fights, betrayals, rapes, lies and mean manipulation. But the initial set of characters remains stable. The catalyst of the series of changes is Tibor, who moves in about fifteen minutes into the film and is taken away by the police in the last scene. His presence brings some hidden conflicts to light, and accelerates slow processes. But when he is gone the initial power relations are restored, and only slight changes take effect in the relationships of the characters.

It is very easy to outline the structure of the drama. The characters can be placed in different categories: 'primary', 'secondary' and 'tertiary' tenants. Primary tenants are those who are within their rights to stay in the apartment: Hédi and her son, János. Secondary tenants are those who are invited by a primary tenant: Anna (invited by Hédi) and Tibor (invited by János). Miklós is the only tertiary tenant (invited by a secondary tenant, Anna). As Miklós has the weakest status among the initial characters, it is in his interest to make a move forward and become a protégé of a primary tenant, which is why he is the only one who must not have a conflict with the primary tenants. There are two ways of accomplishing this: either he could always stay beside them, or he could not communicate with them. Miklós goes both ways. The couple we see communicate the most are Miklós and Hédi (they have five scenes together), and the couple we see communicating the least are Miklós and János (they have only one scene together). All the other pairs get into conflict with each other at some point. Hédi and Miklós are stable allies, informing each other about everything that happens with the others and manipulating them. On the other hand, Miklós avoids interfering with Hédi's and János's conflict. Anna is a secondary tenant, and as she is losing Hédi's confidence, she recognises her interest in Hédi's and János's conflict. This is the reason why she becomes János's fiancée in spite of the fact that János brutally raped her in the kitchen previously (the '*Family Nest* pattern'). Tibor is the catalyst of the story because he stirs up the relationships, but he cannot stabilise his own situation because, in the meantime, he makes all the wrong moves. He loses his protector's confidence, but fails to gain his other possible protector's (Hédi's) confidence because he steals her golden bracelet and has sex with her new protégé's girlfriend (Anna). This way, he helps the others gain their new and better status (Anna becoming János's wife, i.e. a stronger secondary tenant status, and Miklós becoming Hédi's personal confidante, i.e. a secondary tenant status), but propels himself out of this setup.

More than in any previous Tarr film, there is no problem to resolve for the characters. Although, obviously, each of the secondary and the tertiary tenants has some kind of housing problem, otherwise they would not be living there, this is not a topic of conversation between them. We suppose that if they wanted they could arrange their lives in other ways too. Staying here is only the simplest solution for them for the moment. But once they are there, their goal is merely to keep their status in the hierarchy by any possible means. Every kind of human contact is an instrument to this end, and they use the whole array of possible relations to reach their goals, from intimacy and sex to physical violence. There are no moral or physical taboos: betrayal, rape and physical aggression towards the elderly are as common here as tenderness, confidentiality and sincere confession. No manifestation of any human relationship can be trusted because all such manifestations are just weapons in the power game. More than in any previous Tarr films the amoral nature of human relations is laid bare in *Almanac of Fall*, as there are no exterior circumstances involved in the story to be blamed at least in part for the miserable lives of the characters. There are no financial or moral issues at stake, yet, instead of cooperation the characters without exception resort to ruse, aggression, manipulation and betrayal, by which they make it impossible for the others and for themselves to base their relationships on trust.

The 'living hell' topic in *Almanac of Fall* does not come in the form of a story of banal everydayness. This situation is not typical in any of its details, but what is more important, the narrative does not reveal the most basic everyday details about the characters, such as for example their profession, their history or their goals for the future. The previous Tarr films abounded in such details; in *Almanac of Fall* it seems as if the power game fills the characters' entire lives. From this film on, the banality of everyday life will not be the medium of Tarr's stories. Everything will be exceptional, and if all we can see in these films is cruelty, misery, suffering and human baseness, then all of these qualities will be exceptional in their extent too.

Topic 2: Being lost in one's life (1)

The banality of everyday life was a medium for yet another topic in the first-period Tarr films: how someone can be totally lost in his or her life with no perspectives and no opportunities. In a way, all the other films touch upon this theme too, but the one in which this is the central topic is Tarr's second film, *The Outsider*.

This is Tarr's only single-protagonist story in the early period. The reason why this is relevant is that the film shows that multiple-protagonist or ensemble plays are more appropriate for Tarr's themes and narrative methods in this period. A story that does not have a conflict, which would provide it with a goal-oriented trajectory, makes it very difficult to distinguish a single protagonist. The only exception is when the distinctive feature of the protagonist is that he or she does not have a goal, and doesn't want to accomplish anything. This protagonist type was actually quite fashionable in 1960s and 1970s European art films and even in certain American films at the turn of these decades. This kind of protagonist was mostly associated with the general idea of alienation, loneliness and deficiencies of human relationships. Characters like Guido in Fellini's *8½* (1962), Guiliana in Antonioni's *Red Desert* (1964), Joseph Block in Wim Wenders' *The Goalkeeper's Anxiety at the Penalty Kick* (1972), Robert Lander in another Wenders film, *Kings of the Road* (1976), and Travis from Scorsese's *Taxi Driver* (1976) are just a few of many aimless, depressed or alienated characters from this period who contributed to the formation of this art-film archetype. The character of András is an example of this archetype placed in a Hungarian small-town environment of the late 1970s.

Banality of story means in this case that the protagonist is not challenged in any important way, and he himself does not have any goals that would disrupt his environment either. Yet a series of important changes take place in his life which would normally perturb anybody else, but not him: he loses his job and his place to live, a woman gives birth to his child but he does not want to take care of it, he gets a new job and a new place to stay, his brother comes home after three years of absence, he meets a woman who he marries, and finally he is drafted into the army. Each one of these changes would be enough for a drama of deep psychological crisis. András just gets over them quickly with no emotional shock. Tarr's procedure is the same as in *Family Nest*: if the character takes it easy the viewer has no other choice than to get over it as quickly as the character does, and to accept the event as unimportant. András's reactions to these events make them, after all, irrelevant. Tarr's challenge in this film was to show a series of otherwise important life events that happen to a character for whom none of them makes any difference. The film works only if the viewer sympathises with András and finds that none of these changes really represent opportunities for him. For the viewer who feels that András is just a lost alcoholic who is simply too weak to grab the opportunities that he is given in life, this film does not work. The danger of the single-protagonist structure within the framework of Tarr's topics is that there is too much weight on the protagonist, who does not really control the narrative. Outside of melodrama, a multiple-protagonist structure is much less ambiguous with regard to stories that represent helplessness and inability to control one's life, because individual personality traits are less exposed than the external factors. Multiple protagonists are caught in a web of constraining forces from the outset, and the viewer does not expect them to act entirely on their own. A single protagonist either strives to reach something or must have very good reasons not to do so. If those reasons are not unambiguously exposed in the film, the viewer can be easily lost in assessing the relevance of the given protagonist.

Accordingly, this is the only Tarr film of the early period where it looks as if the protagonist proceeds in some direction. However, András is not the driving force of these events; they only happen to him, and most do so without his active participation. All he does is back out of situations which would need his engagement. The only time he does not is when he marries Kata, giving some hope for a change, but very soon it turns out that this marriage will not influence his way of life. At the end, when she proposes to have children, which would engage András more in this marriage during his military service, he backs out again. As they leave, there is no doubt in the viewer's mind that it will not be long before this relationship breaks up. After all, the apparent trajectory of the events brings András back to the point where he started: alone, poor, with a job which does not get him anywhere, and which provides him with just a basic living. This is where circular form appears implicitly within a static narrative. Whenever András is pushed by an 'opportunity', he soon falls back to his initial position.

This position is also embodied by a physical place which is the ultimate 'attractor' in András's life, the place where everything and everybody converges: the pub. In all of Tarr's films until *Satantango*, the pub is a key location, and alcoholism is a natural condition for the characters. Nowhere it this as true as in *The Outsider*. No less than seven scenes are located in a pub, and these scenes last 57 minutes altogether, almost exactly half of the film's running time. Many times in pub scenes the protagonist is not András, but someone who talks to him, and who he is listening to. Characters so far unseen just pop up in the pub talking for a few minutes, only to then disappear again from the film. That is how the film ends too. András and Kata walk out of the restaurant-pub, but we do not follow them; rather, we stay in the pub watching a company of local politicians drinking and having fun for another eight and a half minutes. Their cultural level is not much higher than that of the rest of the characters in the film (and in the pubs), but they have a higher social status. Tarr suggests by this gesture that wherever we may go in this society we find the same routines, a little lower or a little higher maybe, but mentalities are not that different, only the sets and the financial background are.

Thus Tarr makes his principal point, which is that the lack of perspective of his characters is not due to the fact that they are unable to resolve their problems (which is also true), but because there is nothing in the larger social environment to provide them with goals. The reason why this seems to be Tarr's most fundamental idea in his early films is that we can detect a clear tendency in the first three films to emphasise this idea by gradually purging any concrete social or moral factors that could be blamed for the characters' misery, such as housing problems in *Family Nest* and alcoholism in *The Outsider*. In *The Outsider* there is already no identifiable concrete social conflict between the protagonist and his environment. However, his and other characters' heavy alcoholism (one of them even dies from drugs and alcohol in the film) appears as a generalised 'bad solution' in the society that can be blamed. In *The Prefab People* nothing other than the general idea of a lack of perspective in life, which the characters cannot escape, is to be blamed for their unhappiness. And in *Almanac of Fall* the social environment disappears entirely.

But this is exactly why *The Outsider* is a step forward in Tarr's career. It is no longer a network story in a precise social situation (as *Family Nest* is), but it is not yet a personal relationship drama with nuanced character depiction either (as *The Prefab People* and especially *Almanac of Fall* are). It was certainly *The Outsider* that convinced Tarr that for his particular approach he had to mix sophisticated character formation, which needs professional acting, with the reality effects needed for his particular topics. That is how he found the solution known already from the 1970s Cassavetes films: improvised acting and improvised dialogues delivered by professional actors rather than amateurs. This was a novelty in Hungarian cinema, and became Tarr's method for his two subsequent films.

Banality of everyday life such as we can see in the early-period Tarr films is not the main characteristic of the second-period films. For one thing, psychological and social misery is so condensed in these films that this condensation alone makes the story worlds of these films exceptional. Secondly, due to the circular trajectories these stories are built upon, the narratives need events that are out of the ordinary, if not exceptional, whereas in the early period, where the static nature of the stories was more emphasised than their circularity, extraordinary events were unnecessary; on the contrary, as we have seen, even extraordinary events were represented as ordinary parts of everyday life.

Slowness of narration and suspense

This is one of the most spectacular qualities of the Tarr style, but it somewhat characterises Tarr's early films too. Paradoxically, even though slowness of narration is not a quantifiable feature of narration, it is one of the least ambiguous non-quantifiable qualities. I seriously doubt that there is anyone in the world who would say about *The Man from London* that it is a film of a fast and sweeping tempo. It could be an interesting project for spectator research to determine why we find a narration slow or fast, but there is one sure thing: when we do, it is with surprising unanimity. Another, much more controversial, question is whether we find a slow narrative also boring. But in this book I will not judge Tarr's films in this respect. I will try to account for the means by which Tarr (and other slow-tempo filmmakers for that matter) makes his films enjoyable for an audience that is willing and able to accept slow narration.

In music, tempo is quantifiable. It is marked by a number, which is called 'beats per minute' and which is given by the composer. In cinema the equivalent of 'beats per minute' could be 'events per minute', which would show how many events the viewer has to process in order to follow the narrative. The problem with this is that events are not distinct units, whereas a 'beat' could be given a very clear definition. Because spectators unanimously would describe a narrative tempo as slow or fast we can say that they have a common sense of what an event is, even though it would be hard to give it a general definition. As long as this is the case we do not need a better working definition than the one that says that we classify a narrative as slow when the events in it last much longer than the understanding of their narrative meaning would require for most audiences. The implication of this is that in a slow film there are fewer events than in a fast-paced movie. This definition is easy to use when a film shows a repetitive action like shaving or a simple movement like walking. Ambiguity begins to arise when a film represents a series of different actions, all of which are parts of a goal-oriented action. In this case we feel slowness if little actions are shown to take as long as they take in real time, regardless of the fact that we know what the character's goal is. Usually, when we can guess the end result of a series of actions, detailed description of steps that are not decisive or are clearly redundant makes the narrative slow. Such slow narratives are also boring for most viewers, who prefer many spectacular actions, and who are not interested in watching everyday activities in movies. The question is how is it possible that this kind of slow narrative is not boring for everyone? And we are not talking about some idiosyncratic spectatorial mindset here, but about an audience for a widespread narrative form that has been around in art cinema at least since Italian neorealism of the 1940s.

There are basically four ways of slowing down a narrative. The first is showing monotonous movements for a long time. The second is showing insignificant or everyday details of a process. The third is representing extended periods of time between two events, called *temps mort*. And the fourth is repetition of the same event.

We find memorable moments of *temps mort* especially in *Satantango*, like the beginning of the first police station scene, when Irimiás and Petrina are sitting and waiting in the corridor of the police station. However, this method is relatively rare in the Tarr films. His characters are always busy doing something, however insignificant it may be. They very rarely just sit and wait, meditate or stare into nothingness (we find such scenes especially in *Damnation* and *The Turin Horse*).

By far the most frequent technique to slow down the narrative in the Tarr films is the following of an action sequence in all of its most insignificant details. This creates a sense of *radical continuity*, meaning that virtually no element of an action sequence is omitted through the continuous representation of the given action sequence. *Satantango* abounds with scenes of this kind. The most spectacular of them is the doctor's episode, in the first part. This episode lasts exactly one hour. It recounts the doctor's everyday activities, consisting mainly of reading, spying on the neighbours, taking notes of their activities and commenting on them, drinking and satisfying his biological needs. As he is very fat and ill, he does everything very slowly and with great effort. In the first part of the episode, which lasts 37 minutes, almost exactly half of the whole episode, we are in his house, and he barely moves. In the second part he leaves his house to buy alcohol, and meets different people. Each of his acts is followed by the camera in almost real time. For example, the first shot of the scene is a point-of-view shot of the doctor's peeping through binoculars. It is a five-minute take, a real-time rendering of the doctor's action. There are very few time compressions in the episode. Usually, when there is a cut, there is no jump forward in time, just a shift of camera angle. Even when the doctor dozes off, it is not certain that when in the next shot he is awoken by Mrs. Kraner his sleep lasts more than the time elapsed while we were watching him sleeping, which is almost a whole minute. When the camera changes angle the doctor is not in the picture, so we don't see if he is still sleeping or awake when Mrs. Kraner enters the house. And a sound effect suggests that in fact we see the doctor's sleep in real time: we hear the sound of the door opener during the last three seconds of the first shot, while we can see the doctor still sleeping, which means there is an exact time continuity between the two shots, and consequently there can be no time elapsed between them. The first real-time jump occurs after the doctor's fall in his room. It is uncertain how much time this jump spans, but certainly not much action is omitted. The first shot ends with the doctor lying on the floor motionless, and the next starts with him crawling toward his bed, so the only phase that is missing from the continuous series of actions is when he starts moving and gets on all fours. The second time jump takes place shortly after this one, omitting the end of the last phase of his recovery, standing up from his bed and getting himself together. From an action sequence which lasts 37 minutes only two short phases are missing; the rest is rendered in real time.

The third technique of slowing down action is a variation of the previous one. It consists of following a single monotonous or repetitive movement over a long time. The second part of this episode consists almost entirely of this kind of representation of actions. There are various ways Tarr makes these scenes suspenseful or interesting to watch, even (sometimes) over several minutes. When such a movement series is clearly painful or uncomfortable, following it at length always involves some tension stemming from the expectation that at some point this movement will no longer be possible to carry on. This is how we follow the doctor walking in the mud in the heavy rain, almost slipping several times, while it is not clear where he is headed, and the viewer expects him to find some shelter, which he does after a couple of minutes. When he finally does, a five-minute long shot follows in which we see him in the hangar. Here the suspense is created by voices that can be heard at the beginning of the shot, and the doctor starting to look for the source of the voices. Suspense is increased in the second half of the shot when he climbs up the stairs and becomes aware of the two women sitting in the depths of the hangar. From this point on the camera does not follow him; rather we see him walking away from the camera for the last thirty seconds of the shot, clearly increasing the viewer's curiosity.

The fourth technique of slowing down narration is repetition of the same action sequence. This technique is used mainly in Tarr's last film, *The Turin Horse*. This consists of a series of repeated events. Each of these events is an insignificant routine everyday act, like getting dressed and getting undressed, making a fire, cooking potatoes, pulling up water from the well, and so on. The narrative is divided into six days, and each of these events is repeated several times. The overwhelming majority of the narrative events in the film belong to this repetitive series. For example, the events of the man changing clothes, the two characters eating potatoes, and one of them sitting in front of the window are repeated five times each. This unambiguously gives the impression to the viewer that the story does not move forward very much.

The dramaturgical key to making slow narration acceptable is *suspense*. If the narrative suggests that something important is about to happen any time, no matter how slowly it goes, no matter how insignificant the events taking place in it are, it will be able to hold the viewer's attention. The classical example here is Hitchcock's *Vertigo* (1958). Even the most impatient viewers are willing to accept the slow development of the action when they are informed that *something* will happen soon. To this end it is very important that the story gives the impression that it is 'going somewhere', even if it does not. That is the case in Antonioni's *L'Avventura* (1960), where the viewer finds out only at the very end that there will be no solution to the characters' problem. Until then, however, most audiences are willing to sit through all the meanders of the story.

Likewise, the Tarr films started to become really slow at the same time the illusion of a linear development of the narrative became explicit in them. The best way of characterising the early period's narrative strategy is to say that these films use a *cumulative* method. They expose a situation and they accumulate events and changes, which all contribute to the viewer's understanding of this situation, but accumulating these events does not resolve the problems involved. These narratives can be characterised as *static* rather than *circular*, although circularity plays a role in each of them in one way or another. From *Damnation*, by contrast, narrative suspense becomes an important element, together with the single-protagonist structure and an explicitly circular narrative. These elements together provide the illusion to the viewer that at any moment things may take an important turn. Through the use of this structure Tarr slows down the narrative tempo as much as he possibly can.

All of these procedures are complemented by acoustic and visual elements in the films that raise suspense. Visual elements of suspense include almost exclusively the expressionist features of the composition. Strong black-and-white contrast always carries some degree of anxiety, especially if the dark part of the picture is big enough and suggestive of something hidden. Slow camera motion in such a composition always raises some expectation of something popping up from the dark. Tarr amplifies this expectation by the use of acoustic effects. For example, the opening scene of *The Man from London* is a slow vertical camera movement showing the front of a ship. The shot lasts 3 minutes and 20 seconds. In fact it contains two different camera movements. The first movement is an upward panning movement from a fixed vertical position (figures 41 & 42).

When this movement reaches a certain tilting angle, the camera starts to change its vertical position too. This way, moving from the bottom to the top takes twice as long as it would if it were only one type of movement of the same tempo. While we are going upwards, the black-and-white contrast between the two sides of the ship gradually becomes sharper, which amplifies the tension in the picture. The slow elevating movement in itself raises expectation (what are we going to see when we arrive at the top?), but when we arrive at the first peak point from the initial camera position it is clear that from this position we will not see anything of what is on the front deck of the ship. That is when the camera starts changing its vertical position and amplifying the expectation, because at this second position there is already a chance that something will be disclosed. The shot lasts until it is clear that nobody is on the captain's deck or on the bridge (figure 43).

During the whole sequence we can hear continuous music of a dark tone that slightly changes its chords from dark to lighter and back again. The viewer's expecta-

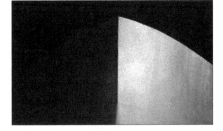

Figures 41 & 42

Figures 43 & 44

tion is satisfied only in the next shot, which starts the elevating movement all over again from a still higher position, which already represents a specific point of view. This time the vertical movement shifts into an in-depth movement, closing in on the two persons on the front deck of the ship (figure 44).

We can only guess what is happening between them, because we join them at the end of their conversation, but the suspenseful visual and acoustic introduction of the scene already tells us that something very bad will happen. The reason why it is absolutely justified to say that the visual and acoustic effects 'tell' us what will happen is that when we finally see the two men on the deck we realise that while the camera was ascending to the level of clear sight of the deck these two had already been there discussing something, which was hidden from us. So, in actual fact the ascending movement of the camera *functions as an action preparing us for an exciting and tragic outcome*. Instead of narrating the preparations for the outcome, Tarr gives us a dark and suspenseful atmosphere with the help of one of his revealing camera movements, amplifying the suspense effect through visual composition and acoustic arrangement. The image and the sound *tell* us what the narration hides.

This example clearly shows that slowing down the narrative has nothing to do with the strict duration of time. It has to do with the relative density of action during a given time span. A five-and-a-half-minute-long almost totally monotonous camera movement hides an action sequence that could easily last even twice as long; still the viewer would not feel it as slow as the camera movement that covers it. Whether or not it is boring is a question of spectator psychology, but there is absolutely no doubt about its being slow *and* suspenseful.

The other way of making these long following movements interesting is to invest them with some particular aesthetic quality through rhythm, composition or peculiar visual elements. One example is the scene in *Satantango* where Irimiás and Petrina are walking toward the police station, the camera following them from behind. Their monotonous walking is accompanied by a strong wind blowing a lot of garbage, especially papers, around them. This visual element is so particular that it keeps the viewer's interest alive for more than two minutes while nothing else happens. Another example is the scene from *Werckmeister Harmonies* when Mr. Eszter and Valuska are walking in the street. In this case it is the particular rhythm of the sound of their steps and the rhythmic wavering movement of their bodies that create an aesthetic quality out of the monotonous movement.

Slowness of narration is clearly accentuated and radicalised in the second-period films, and it comes to represent a cornerstone of the Tarr style. It is one of the main ingredients of the circular structure, a structure producing the feeling that the return is inevitable.

Circular form

Circularity of dramatic form characterises stories in which characters go through a series of events but these events do not get them closer to the solution to their initial problem. Not only does this remain unresolved, but at the end they lose the perspective to resolve it that they may have had at the beginning. At the end of the film they find themselves in a situation that is the same as or worse than before. Circular dramatic form is traditionally based on the exploration of a given environment by the protagonist, looking for a solution. In Tarr's case, this applies more to the films made after *Almanac of Fall*, and to *The Outsider* among the early films. In *Family Nest* and in *The Prefab People* the physical environment plays no particular role, and the human environment is very restricted. There are only a few characters in the stories, and everything remains in a confined physical and human environment. Still, in *Almanac of Fall* the same conception prevails, but the environment is already emphasised to a much greater degree than in any of his earlier films by the theatricalised sets.

As mentioned earlier, it is with *The Prefab People* that circular form becomes explicit or even self-conscious in Tarr's films. By an 'explicit' circular form I mean a narrative which in one way or another emphasises a return to the same place. That is what we find, for example, at the end of *Almanac of Fall*, where in spite of the fights they have had with each other, we can see the four main characters together again celebrating, while the fifth character, Tibor, who arrived later in the story, is taken away by the police. Or in *The Man from London*, where at the end Maloin returns the money he found, thereby falling back into his miserable situation, from which he hoped the money would help him to get out. Self-conscious circularity may appear through some stylistic or narrative element that explicitly calls the viewer's attention to this structure. The best example is the narrative frame of *The Prefab People*, in which we can see the same scene at the beginning and at the end of the film.

However, in *The Prefab People* as well as in *Almanac of Fall* circularity is rather a formal element and does not greatly inform the dramatic structure. And in Tarr's first two films, circularity is not even a formal element; these narratives make a rather static impression. What we see in all of these films are different interactions between the characters, which disclose the nature of their relationships. No incident moves the protagonists toward a solution to their initial situation. What we have is rather an inner development of a psychic situation from which the characters cannot escape, which is why before *Damnation* the stories are mostly confined to a narrow space, in most cases an apartment. In a sense, they end up where they start, but in reality they don't move forward too much; they rather sink deeper into their trap situation. The stories end when all the relevant aspects of some characters or of a given relationship are explored by slightly changing the situations and altering the characters' interactions.

The thematic motif that appears in *Damnation* and that is missing from the early films is the one the circular structure is based upon, the illusion that there is hope for a big change. It is due to this story element that the linear development of the stories provides the illusion that it is developing in some direction. At the end, however, instead of leading to a solution the plot brings the characters downward, which makes the end result all the more disappointing: nothing is resolved and the chance or the only chance for them is gone. That is when they realise that everything was going the wrong way from the beginning. A passage at the beginning of Krasznahorkai's *Satantango* that is repeated at the end of the novel explains clearly this idea:

> … for by then he will have learned already that he got involved in a card game with swindlers where everything was settled in advance, and at the end of which he will be robbed of the only weapon that was left for him, the hope that one day he'll find his way home.[4]

This thematic element is missing from the early Tarr films. Not that some of the characters do not have some hope that they can live a better life. These are not big ideals, however, just very concrete small steps toward some kind of improvement of their lives, and they characterise only two of the four early films. Irén hopes to be able to move out of her father-in-law's apartment, and Judit hopes to get a job in Robi's factory. But we know at the outset that this is not their main problem, and what their main problem is, they cannot see. The protagonists of *The Outsider* and *Almanac of Fall* do not have any big ideals to follow; they just want to continue their lives as they are. That is why these stories are static rather than circular, even though the idea of circularity appears around the end of this period.

From *Damnation* on, by contrast, the characters' situation has real potential for change, sometimes radical change, but at the end, where the characters start out from and where they end up is not very different, or is different only in that it is worse. Most of the time the only thing that really happens during the story is that the only hope for the characters to escape their pathetic situation disappears. But, unlike the early works, these films have a linear plotline, which finally brings the characters back to where they started, but as the plot develops it seems to have the potential to change their situation for the better. And this linear plotline is what turns out to be a circle.

The more hope gets frustrated, the more explicit the circular structure, and this is why single-protagonist dramas are more frequent in the second period. Three of the four early films are ensemble plays centred on a group of characters, and even the one that has a single protagonist, *The Outsider*, locates most of its scenes within multi-character situations, which means that we almost never see the protagonist alone. From *Damnation* on, until *The Man from London*, single protagonists are more emphasised, certainly, due to the literary background of the stories, in which the exploration of the environment is based more on spatial elements, and involves many more characters, even crowds in some instances. *The Turin Horse*, however, returns to the early formula: an extremely confined space with an extremely low number of characters, and a radically repetitive story pattern given variation according to the permutation principle.

In the following section I will discuss the different manifestations of the circular structure in the individual films. As I have already dealt with this more or less in detail regarding the early films, and since circularity is more explicit and spectacular in the second-period films, this time the focus will be on this particular corpus.

Two recurrent thematic motifs which do not appear before *Almanac of Fall* can be identified in the second-period Tarr films: conspiracy and betrayal. The earliest appearance of this thematic motif is in Tarr's work for television, *Macbeth*, made in the same year as *The Prefab People*. Even though this was a Shakespeare adaptation, the choice as to which Shakespeare piece to adapt was his own. This choice clearly shows Tarr's interest in the themes of conspiracy and betrayal in the early period. This is another element that makes *Macbeth* a key film in the early period, foretokening the second-period stylistic system. *Almanac of Fall* makes a step in this direction, but *Damnation* was the film in which this new thematic orientation was the main determinant, and this remained the main determinant for the next three films.

Topic 3: Betrayal and conspiracy

Damnation

This is a story about a man named Karrer, who has nothing else to do in his life but to wait for the woman in his life, a local bar singer who is married. They live in an incredibly run-down small town that was once an industrial centre, but now everyone is poor and appears unemployed. Karrer tries to convince her of his love, but she rejects him violently. Although she supposedly doesn't love her husband either, Karrer does not represent any improvement for her, and she wants to get rid of him for good. Karrer is given an opportunity to make some money by smuggling something from abroad for the owner of the pub where he is a regular. Instead of taking this opportunity, he recommends his lover's husband for the job, knowing that this would remove the husband from the scene for two days. As in this way he actually also helps the husband ease his very delicate financial situation, Karrer hopes that the woman will show him some gratitude. And that is indeed what happens. The husband has no choice other than to take the opportunity, and the woman goes to bed with Karrer as 'compensation'. But when the next day Karrer behaves as if this were the beginning of a relationship, the woman violently rejects him again, calling him a 'dirty little snooper'. A little later, however, they make love again, but when Karrer sees the woman 'compensating' the bartender too for providing this opportunity for her husband, he understands that he will never really have this woman. He decides to go to the police and reports the bartender's illegal trafficking business.

During the film, Karrer is told several times that he will end up in a bad way. Actually, all those who tell him this will end up in a bad way, but the story has no happy ending for Karrer either, of which he is entirely aware. This woman was the last thing of value in his life, however rude she was to him. After Karrer understands that he means nothing to her, he has nothing to lose, and brings down everyone around him, including the people who could possibly give him some hope in life. His trap is closed, and he was the one who closed it.

This story is not similar to any of Tarr's narratives of the early period. It does not consist of scenes whose function is to reveal different aspects of a given situation which fundamentally remains the same from the beginning to the end. *Damnation*'s plotline has a linear development with a real chance for change. Karrer seems to be given an opportunity to escape his miserable existential and psychic condition. He goes after it, but expects everything from someone who despises him and does not want him. Right at the beginning of the story he is told several times to leave the woman alone, because she will only bring him down. Also, at the beginning there is a scene in the bar where the woman sings her extremely bleak song 'Everything is Over'.[5] This is also a sign for the viewer not to expect any positive outcome from the story. At every step Karrer or the viewer or both are alerted in one way or another by different signs that something bad will happen, yet the story progresses slowly in a monotonous way, as if following someone marching toward his inevitable downfall. Thus, the narrative discloses the possible negative outcome right at the outset, but makes the viewer believe that Karrer might escape his destiny, because he ignores those signs and pretends that there is some hope nevertheless. As he explains to his lover and to her husband when he offers them the job: 'At the same time there might just be a way to arrest this inevitable ruin. Mainly with money and not by playing the hero. Needless to say, it doesn't help the inevitability of this breakdown. It can merely cover over a crack for a moment.'

He tells them what he tells himself: the only hope they have is to push back the inevitable bad ending a little. His only hope is to slow down the process leading to his downfall, or, in other words, *slowness is his only hope*. We can see now how the only positive element of the story is intimately linked to slowness. Slowness postpones the tragedy, thereby making the characters and the viewer believe that there remains some hope. On the other hand, slowness together with suspense raises a presentiment of something inevitable to come. This is what I called earlier the most important aspect of Tarr's narrative art: encouraging belief in an illusion without hiding the truth. Narrative circularity finishes the work of slowness: it is with the help of the circular structure that the viewer becomes conscious of this process. At the end, the viewer realises that everything was clear and uncovered right from the beginning, yet he or she fell for the same illusion as the characters and thought that something better could come out of all this.

After Karrer makes his deposition to the police, he finds himself in a situation that is more hopeless than his situation at the beginning. His act of destruction, aimed at harming the people who deceived him, has also become an act of self-destruction. He had one thing to lose at the beginning of the story – the hope that he could conquer this woman – and he lost exactly that. However, the viewer has a special perspective on all this. The first shot in the film shows Karrer sitting in front of the window, staring at the wire carriages that come and go in front of his house. As the carriages go back and forth endlessly on the same track, the image already suggests that there is something immutable and eternal in this world which makes any progression or change illusory. For Karrer this is his natural environment; for the viewer by contrast, this is a statement about this environment. It is with that statement in our minds that we follow Karrer making an attempt to change his life. The fact that he fails is shown only

Figure 45

by another image of circular movement. As he returns from the police station in the rain, a gutter-dog attacks him, and he starts barking at the dog, squatting down and moving around the dog (figure 45).

This scene, with the ruins of a collapsed building behind Karrer and his lowering himself to the level of a dog, represents the situation his story ends up in.

The film's story does not fit into the earlier Tarr films' thematic pattern. No exterior circumstances are indicated as constraining the characters (as in *Family Nest*). No particular personal relationships are exposed in detail which are to be blamed for the character's final situation (as in all the early films). This situation is not socially typical in any way (as in the films up to *The Prefab People*). It is as if the forces that motivate the characters' acts were exterior to them, like the forces of nature, which equally constrain nature, society and individuals. One cannot evoke society, history, morality or psychology to explain why things happen, just the way they happen. Causes and effects go round and round and everything is part of the same web of circumstances that makes it impossible for anyone to step outside of this infernal circularity. This conspiracy-like structure is what evokes the universality of this human condition, which is not specifically moral, social, historical or psychological. It is not geographically located either. It is also natural (no consolation in natural beauty), meteorological (constant rain and mud) and physical (run-down environment): universal, in one word. The character of the checkroom attendant lady is the representative of this apocalyptic vision in the film. She alerts Karrer several times through biblical citations to his inevitable perdition. Karrer listens to her carefully each time, but he cannot help proceeding his own way. Forces of nature that are the same inside and outside tell him to.

The story's recurrent thematic element is betrayal. Everybody betrays everybody else in this story. The singer cheats on her husband, but betrays her lover too by having sex with the bartender. The husband betrays the bartender by stealing from the package he had to smuggle into the country; in turn, the bartender has sex with his wife. And Karrer betrays every one of them by reporting their business to the police. In this respect *Damnation* is a variation of *Almanac of Fall*, but also an important step forward. The main difference is that in the previous film the characters betray one another in order to stabilise their position. In *Damnation* the characters are treasonous because they want to get out of their current position, which is too stable, seemingly eternal and unchangeable. This difference shows better than anything what the element of hope means with respect to how Tarr's films change after *Almanac of Fall*. From now on the characters have an idealistic perspective that, in their imagination, leads them way beyond their current social and existential conditions. As the singer says to Karrer: 'I will be applauded by audiences of big cities…' And it is this ideal that turns out to be the greatest delusion of all. *Satantango* is the most perfect manifestation of this idea.

Satantango

This is the second-period film where the theme of conspiracy is developed and exposed fully. This is also the film in which circularity is the most fundamental structural element at different levels of the narrative. Krasznahorkai's original novel already contains this element in a spectacular way. It is safe to say that one of the most important reasons why Tarr found the manuscript of *Satantango* inspiring was the explicit and all-embracing concept of circularity, which became increasingly important at just the same time in his own films too.

The novel consists of two parts, each part consisting of six chapters. The numbering of the chapters goes from chapter I through chapter VI in part 1, and it goes back from chapter VI through chapter I in part 2. The title of chapter I of part 2 (i.e. the last chapter of the novel) is 'The Circle Closes'. Moreover, the first two and a half pages of the novel are word for word the same as the last two and a half pages. And the novel ends in the middle of a sentence, suggesting that the whole story starts over again in exactly the same way. Circularity for Krasznahorkai, just like for Tarr, does not appear in a static closed form, but rather in the form of an eternal return of the same situation, always flashing the possibility of a change and always falling back to the same misery. In a particular way, the same idea is expressed in *The Prefab People*, where the film emphasises not only the return but also an endless continuum. The closing of the circle does not mean a singular occasion of one particular story, but rather an eternal continuous movement starting all over again. Krasznahorkai's and Tarr's stories are not tales of people or life conditions with problems that can be solved, thereby changing those people and their life conditions; they are about unchangeable situations which do not go away but just return in another form.

Satantango's narrative structure is the most complicated of all Tarr's films. In fact this is the only non-linear narrative, where the events are not represented entirely in chronological order. Especially in the first two-thirds of the film, parallel plotlines are narrated one after the other, so that the narration always goes back to the same point in time, which means *Satantango*'s narration consist of several cycles. In some instances events are recounted twice from different points of view, and in one instance the narration goes back to the same point three times through different plotlines. This is the event when the villagers gather in the pub, dance and get drunk. The narration arrives at this moment from the doctor's plotline and from Estike's trajectory, and it is recounted directly from the villager's point of view too.

Some viewers may feel this narrative structure to be 'chaotic'. Whether *Satantango*'s world is chaotic or not is a matter of subjective feeling. What is certain, however, is that the narrative structure of the film, which is very complex and non-linear in the beginning, gradually straightens out and becomes entirely linear at the end. From the point where the villagers start an argument in the manor, the narration proceeds in a strict chronology, with no more time loops and repetitions. Although the time relationship between two of the last three episodes – the villagers being separated at the train station and the clerks editing Irimiás's report on the villagers – is not specified, there are no events contradicting the suggestion that they are represented in their real chronological order, since the episode featuring the clerks at the police station takes place in the evening, while the episode featuring the villagers and the doctor takes place during the day. The last chapter, 'The Circle Closes', is definitely the last event series in the story's chronology too. So, while the first part of the film abounds in time loops and repetitions, the second part becomes increasingly simple, and in the last 94 minutes of the film what we find is a linear and chronological narration. The image I would use to describe *Satantango*'s narrative structure is that of a whirlpool. It starts as a wide and slow stream that goes round and round, as if there is no progression in it, and we return several times to the same point from different angles; later the streams become narrower, and there are fewer returns: we return only once to Irimiás's farewell speech; and at the end the parallel streams are all moving in the same direction: there is no return, just a strong 'suction', which pulls everything downward.

What is unusual in *Satantango*'s narration is not the existence of parallel plotlines, but the fact that they follow each other in such a way that the viewer is surprised at the discovery of their simultaneity. This effect is created as the result of several factors. One is the extreme length of the individual linear episodes. In *Satantango* the shortest linear episode is thirteen minutes long, and the rest range between twenty-five and sixty minutes in length. Another factor is the extreme slowness created through the radical continuity in the representation of the events. Radical continuity implies absolute linearity, and if such a scene goes on for more than thirty minutes the viewer is likely to forget about anything that is happening in the meantime. A third factor is that the fact that the events in the different episodes overlap is revealed only at the end of each episode. This way the viewer loses the sense of simultaneity of the episodes. Yet another factor is that the exact timeframe of the overlaps is sometimes very difficult to reconstruct, and sometimes it is clearly impossible.

The chronology of the story:
One morning, Irimiás and Petrina go to the police station, where they have a meeting with the captain. At the same time in the village Estike goes out with her brother, Sanyi, to bury some money in the ground to make it grow into a money tree. Both events take place during the daytime when the rain is not falling. Later Irimiás and Petrina drink in the pub in town, where Kelemen sees them. Halics visits Estike's mother. Estike tortures and finally kills her cat in the attic of their house. In the meantime a heavy rain starts. Halics leaves their house, and Estike finds out that the money has disappeared; someone has stolen it. Kelemen returns to the village, enters the pub, and reports to the bartender on his meeting with Irimiás and Petrina in town and on the road to the village. Halics is already in the pub.

It is around that time that Futaki wakes up in Mrs. Schmidt's bed, but they are surprised by Schmidt's unexpected early return. Futaki has a hard time sneaking out of the house, but he returns later as if he has just arrived. At the same time the doctor watches the whole scene (Schmidt returning, Futaki sneaking out and hiding before returning to Schmidt's house). Halics crosses the space, probably going home from the pub to relate the news about Irimiás's return to his wife. Futaki and Schmidt start an argument over the distribution of the money the villagers earned and that Schmidt and Kráner want to steal, but Mrs. Halics arrives with the news that Irimiás and Petrina are approaching on the road, and maybe they have already arrived at the pub. Mrs. Schmidt leaves for the pub to check out what has happened; Schmidt and Futaki follow her later.

The doctor spends almost the whole day in front of the window in his chair, taking notes and drinking. At some point in the day, around noon probably, Mrs. Kráner visits him, announcing that from now on she will no longer bring him lunch. The doctor throws her out. Realising that he has run out of brandy, he puts on his coat and leaves the house to buy alcohol. He walks in the heavy rain, and enters a hangar where he meets two prostitutes. In the meantime the villagers arrive at the pub to be there when Irimiás and Petrina arrive. First, they distribute the money Schmidt and Kráner originally wanted to steal in the morning, then they start to drink heavily. That is when Estike's mother arrives and tells the bartender that she cannot find her daughter. She also drinks, and then leaves the pub. It is already dark outside. The villagers start dancing, and that is when the doctor arrives in front of the pub. There he meets Estike, who peeps inside the pub through the window. She carries a dead cat in her arms, yells at the doctor, and then runs away. In the background we see Irimiás, Petrina and Sanyi arriving. The doctor tries to run after her, but very soon he gets out of breath, and finally he collapses, and is unable to get up again. He remains there lying on the ground until the next morning, when Kelemen finds him, and loads him on his cart.

The time that elapses from this evening until the next morning is missing from the narrative. This is when Irimiás and Petrina meet the villagers in the pub, and we don't know where Estike spent the night. We meet her again, still walking with the dead cat under her arm, and soon after that she poisons herself. There is another jump in time: we don't see when and how Estike's body is found and carried to the pub. The next plot event is when the villagers gather around Estike's dead body, and Irimiás makes a speech. The result of the speech is that everybody hands over his or her share of the money to Irimiás, who promises them he will immediately start the project which will help them get out of the village and start a new life. He tells them to pack up everything and move immediately to a neighbouring manor, which will be their new home where they will start their new business together. Estike's coffin is loaded on the bartender's car, and the villagers go home and pack up. They hit the road while Irimiás and Petrina go back into town. Petrina tries to convince Irimiás to flee with the money rather than continue to play games with the villagers. But Irimiás knows that this story can't finish that way; the villagers should not discover immediately that they have been duped. The villagers arrive at the abandoned manor, which is a huge, entirely empty estate with no doors or windows and no furniture in it. They spend the night there. In the meantime Irimiás and Petrina arrive in the town in Steigerwald's pub. They spend the night there. Irimiás has Payer come to see him, and wants to buy explosives from him. The next morning the villagers have a fight, because Irimiás didn't show up at the time agreed. Some of them are convinced that Irimiás has deceived and abandoned them. Shortly afterwards Irimiás and Petrina arrive, and announce that they have to postpone the realisation of the project, and for the time being the villagers have to be separated and dispersed in the region before they can gather again to start the project.

They are driven to a railway station, and each of them is assigned a place to go to stay. At the police station two clerks edit Irimiás's report on the villagers. The doctor returns from hospital after three weeks, sits at his desk writing his notes, and leaves the house as he can hear bells ringing. He walks to the lonely chapel, where a madman rings the bell. He goes home and boards up the window.

The structure of the narrative:

The film does not replicate the explicit circular structure in the numbering of the novel's chapters, even though the film also consists of twelve chapters and the titles of the episodes are the same, and they are in the same order as in the book. Structurally, one can discern the two-part division in the film too. The narrative structure of the first set of six chapters is considerably different from that of the second set of six chapters. The narrative is woven of different parallel plotlines all through the film, but the individual chapters are completely linear, with some jumps forward in time. In the first part, however, the order of the episodes does not follow the chronology of the story, and they contain considerable jumps back in time, or time loops, as well as repetitions of plot events represented from different perspectives. Moreover, all of the episodes of the first half take place in the same timeframe describing the events of one whole day, from the point where Irimiás and Petrina go to the police station on the one hand to where Estike and Sanyi hide the money on the other, and to the point where Estike commits suicide on the one hand and Kelemen finds the doctor on the other. But only chapter 5 (C5), telling Estike's story, covers the whole timeframe. The rest of the chapters from the first set cover only time fragments of this timeframe and consequently are contained in the timeframe of this one. From this point of view C5 is the 'master story' of the first part of the film, and all the other stories are just fragments converging on the ending of this one: Estike's suicide.

In the second half, by contrast, there is no 'master story' covering the whole timeframe, and the episodes follow one another in a chronological order, except C9, which jumps back in time to the beginning of C8. But this is the only jump back in the second part. Other than that, C8 picks up where C7 finishes, and C10 where C9 ends. The order of C10, C11 is not specified, but as stated earlier, there is nothing that would contradict the suggestion that they are represented in their chronological order, and this is also what logically fits in the structure of the second half of the film, while C12 is also the last chronological event series of the story. After C6 the narrative becomes considerably less complicated than before, and after C9 it becomes absolutely linear. The narrative's process is one of a gradual simplification. It starts as several parallel streams in a rather mosaic-like structure, and these streams are gradually canalised into one single stream, ending up in a simple gesture of closing down everything: the doctor's act of boarding up the window, making everything dark.

The different chapters in part one are organised such that from the end of each one the narration jumps back to an earlier point in time. Futaki's and Schmidt's story of C1 starts sometime before noon, and goes on till late afternoon; C2 jumps back to early morning and runs till late at night; C3 jumps back to sometime before noon, just where C1 started, and runs till early next morning; C4 jumps back again to around the time when C1 and C3 started and runs till early afternoon; C5 jumps back to early morning and runs till early next morning (this is the only one that covers the entire twenty-four hours); C6 jumps back to late afternoon and runs till late at night. The only pattern in this arrangement is the constant jump back in time at the beginning of each chapter. This is how the narration creates an opportunity to see some events more than once. These events include Futaki's sneaking out of the house, which we see twice, and Halics's crossing the doctor's yard, which we also see twice. One of the functions of these repetitions is to help the viewer locate the given episode in time in relation to other episodes. Another function is to gradually reveal the integrity of the repeated events. For example, we see Futaki sneaking out of Schmidt's house, but that is all we see in this chapter. We learn how he did it from another chapter, where we see him from the doctor's point of view. The same goes for the dance episode. We can see in the doctor's episode that Estike is looking inside the pub through the window, but we don't know what she sees. That is the first appearance of the dance scene, but we can hear only the music, and we do not have any information about what is happening. In the return of this scene we have Estike's point of view and see the villagers' drunken and reckless revelry. And the third time, we see her looking inside through the window, which shows that her face was visible from the inside, so someone could have seen that she was there. The repetitions have yet another function, which is most important in the dance scene, because this is the only scene where the narration returns as many as three times. That is where three of the four thus far independent plotlines converge. And the reason is that this is the last point where Estike could have been saved. If anybody from the drunken company saw her peeping inside the pub, or if the doctor didn't push her away, or if afterwards he were able to stop her, things would probably have turned out differently.

Estike's death has a very particular place in the narrative system of the film. It has no direct motivational relationship with any other event. As shocking as it is, this event is not what the story is about. In conventional dramaturgical constructions, deaths, especially children's deaths, are triggers of dramas or ultimate motivations for solutions to dramas. In this case such a horrible event – the suicide of a mentally retarded child who nobody, including her alcoholic mother, took care of – remains marginal relative to the main plotline's constructional logic. The only real tragedy that occurs in the film is not at the dramaturgical centre of the story, and it does not even change the course of the events. In Irimiás's speech, in which he so eloquently characterises the villagers' moral responsibility in the tragedy, Estike's death is only a good opportunity for him to humiliate and disarm the villagers with his rhetoric, appealing to the remnants of their human feelings in order to con them out of their money. The fact that Estike's death does not change anything in the story is a statement in itself, but what is an even more explicit statement is that it is utilised by Irimiás for his most sordid purposes. The only dramaturgical function of Estike's death is to make it easy for Irimiás to deceive the villagers again. However, the narration makes Estike's plotline stand out in an indirect way, and makes it the structural gravitation point of this part of the film. One thing to note here is that this story is made the 'master story', as mentioned before, owing to the fact that this is the one that covers all of the narrative time that elapses in the first part, in relation to which the other plotlines cover only time fragments. The other thing to note is that all other plotlines converge at the last point where Estike could have been taken care of. This is a very particular narrative procedure. A story that covers the entirety of the narrative time and at which other plotlines converge remains nevertheless a marginal event with respect to the causal structure of other narrative events. This way the narration creates a dramaturgical ambiguity: an event which is not taken into account in other narrative events is, nevertheless, given priority by the narrative structure, as if the narration were structurally compensating for the diminished significance of this plotline, missing from the causal logic of the story. Or, to put it in other terms, if Estike's death has little importance for everyone in the story, it is still given the greatest symbolic importance in the narration of the film.

This is also the reason why the narration becomes considerably simplified after this event. Irimiás's return, his 'miraculous resurrection', coincides with Estike's death. While Irimiás is the ultimate evil, the unscrupulous conman, in this story, Estike is the ultimate innocent: humiliated, abused and ignored to a point where death becomes more appealing to her than survival. The resurrection of the figure of evil is accompanied by the disappearance of the innocent. But this is not a direct causal relationship. Estike's death is not caused by Irimiás's return; it is accompanied by it. But this coincidence is not a random event either. It is like a natural *order* of the things in this world, whereby a certain moral balance does not allow both elements to exist at the same time. In a peculiar way, Irimiás refers to this in his speech when he says, 'Don't forget the child who may have to perish to make our star rise.' Other than being an extremely cynical statement, appropriating Estike's death for the sake of an ideological manipulation, this sentence also alludes to the fact that this is a very good opportunity for Irimiás to gather again the villagers, by referring this time to their guilty feelings. Estike's death does not contribute to Irimiás's plan, but it makes it simpler for him to manipulate the villagers emotionally. This is why the narrative structure becomes considerably simpler once she is out of the story. Without Estike, the villagers' downfall is irrevocable.

The narrative circle – the order is restored:
The most conspicuous tool with which the novel achieves the circular form is the repetition of the first two and a half pages at the end in a way that gives the impression that the novel itself is nothing else but a quote from the doctor's diary. This device is preserved in the film, but the effect it has is not quite the same as in the novel. For one thing, the film, unlike the novel, does not start with this text. In the film there is a long prologue before the story starts. For another, it is very unlikely that viewers will remember after more than seven hours just what the exact text was somewhere at the beginning of the film (whereas in the case of the novel it is just a matter of comparing the first and the last pages). For yet another thing, and most importantly, in the novel the repeated text is introduced as the text the doctor is beginning to write just at this moment. This is what gives the impression that the reader is starting to read the novel all over again. In the film, in both cases the text is recited by an off-screen voice while the screen is black (the same question, whether or not the viewer would remember

that the two voices are different, can be raised in this regard too). We do not see the doctor writing the text, which would be impossible anyway, since he made his room completely dark. Therefore the viewer cannot have the impression that the narration starts over again as written by the doctor. Rather than creating the feeling of the narration's return to the beginning of the story, this repetition creates the impression in the film that the doctor has remembered and is reciting the beginning of this story before everything comes to an end.

Clearly, the signs of circularity in the film's narration are much less explicit than in the novel, and technically speaking, the narrative does not return to its starting point. With the villagers leaving the settlement, this story is over at this particular location. This is what is emphasised by the doctor's act of boarding up the windows. This signals the end of the story as well as the end of the film, whereas in the novel only the book ends in the end; the narration seems to continue forever. The film's narration also lacks the self-referentiality of the novel's ending (which returns as a text written by one of the novel's protagonists), which enhances the reality effect a film text usually has as compared to a literary text. Seen from this angle, the weakening of the formal features of the circular structure fits better into the series in the Tarr film, because it reduces the literariness and increases the reality effect of the story. The idea of circularity is transposed onto another level in the film, much like in the earlier Tarr films. The narrative is not circular in the strict sense, only in the sense that the main characters find themselves in the same position they were in at the beginning, or in a worse position; and the apparent progression of the story turns out to be a return to a trap from which there is no more hope of escape.

The main idea behind Tarr's kind of circular form is a process of the disintegration and the restoration of some kind of ordinary life-world. This is the same idea that we find at the beginning of Tarr's career, only there this process is represented as rather static. *Family Nest* and *The Outsider* depict a life situation that does not change, only gets more hopeless. In *The Prefab People* and in *Almanac of Fall* the process becomes circular in the strict sense of the term, which means that the story returns to its starting point. From *Damnation* on the stories become structurally linear, with a clear plot development. The starting and ending situations are not the same, and the trajectory of the protagonists brings them to an end-situation from which there is no way out. These stories are all about the vanishing of the last hope. The difference between the starting and ending situations is that the latter's structure seems to be more merciless than the former's. In the beginning, the protagonist's effort is always directed at dismantling some kind of order that keeps them trapped in a given position. In most stories (*The Turin Horse* is the exception) this process necessarily involves destructive or illegal moves, because the characters are in such a low position that it seems impossible that regular or legal actions could ameliorate their situation. In *Damnation* illegal trafficking and adultery; in *Satantango* embezzlement of the community fund and imposture; in *Werckmeister Harmonies* retuning the piano and destroying the town; in *The Man from London* appropriation of the stolen and smuggled money – these are the moves that hold the promise of changing the ruling order. In all cases the 'order' proves to be stronger, and the protagonists wind up in the same or a similarly bad situation, and without any hope of improvement. Paradoxically, the 'only hope' for them is a specific unlawfulness, the breaking of the laws and rules, which in itself is a guarantee of their failure, because, given their social and economic position, they are so much weaker than the ruling order. They are doomed to fail right from the outset, because they start the change in the wrong way, by trying to dismantle the order which makes them prisoners of their situation, and against which they cannot win. As stated earlier, Tarr's main narrative procedure in the second-period films is to drag the viewer into the same illusion the protagonists fall for. The films make the viewer believe that things can change even though the initial steps (cheating or stealing) are dangerous. The viewer somehow knows that nothing good will come out of this, but she is ready to follow the story because of the empathy the protagonists' situation invites. So, after all, it is the viewer who finds herself in the same situation at the end as the one she was in at the beginning, even though the protagonists' situations may change. The viewer's assessment of the protagonists' situation is emotionally established in the beginning, it is then questioned, and in the end it is restored. But in the meantime the viewer goes through the same hoping for a better life as do the protagonists, although she knows right at the outset that this hope is unfounded.

This form of circular structure is more complex than what we find in the early Tarr films. It is no longer the case that the protagonists follow a simple circular trajectory; rather they gradually come to understand a complex situation from which there is no escape. What is understood is that what seems to be hopeless in the beginning is also hopeless in the end. This understanding is made possible through a systematic and slow disclosure of the web of relations constituting the structure of an unchangeable situation. We come to understand that in fact everything is what it seemed in the beginning. It is not a strong power (natural, social or political) against which the characters are helpless. It is an indefinable 'order' of things and human relations which is impossible to go against. This web-like structure is quite explicit in *Satantango*. The idea is explicitly referred to in two chapter titles – 'The Spider's Work 1' and 'The Spider's Work 2'. Also, at the end of 'The Spider's Work 2' a spider appears in close-up as it makes threads connecting a bottle and a glass on the table. This is how the narrator's text comments upon this:

> And to the tender sound of an accordion the spiders in the pub launched their last attack. They sewed loose webs on top of the glasses, the cups, the ashtrays, around the legs of the tables and the chairs. Then they bound them together with secret threads so that in their hidden corners they notice every little move and every little stir until this almost invisible web is not damaged. They sewed a web on the sleepers' faces, their feet, their hands. Then hurried back to their hiding place, waiting for an ethereal thread to move to start it all again.

The spider's web metaphor brings several things to mind here. Firstly, the unmovable, unchangeable nature of this world, which remains the same in spite of the fact that many things happen. Secondly, the fact that even if the villagers finally leave the settlement, an invisible web will keep them in their places, wherever they might go. Thirdly, the invisible nature of a structure that is under unnoticeable surveillance and that reacts immediately when something in this structure moves and makes sure that what tries to move remains a captive of the web. Fourthly, the fact that the web restores itself immediately after it is disturbed; it is flexible and reactive, so in whatever way the characters' positions may change, the web will be swiftly extended to these new positions.

But this is only the metaphorical level of such an idea in the film; the idea of the hidden web appears also on a very concrete level, in Irimiás's plan to separate the villagers to destroy their own network and create a new one which is invisibly connected to another secret network, that of the police. The villagers ignore the fact that they are treated as parts of a police informer's network, which makes it impossible for them to escape, since they are now on the files of the police. While in the beginning they were only prisoners of their economic and social situation, now they become prisoners of a vast web or network that will never let them go. This is what gives the idea of circularity a more general meaning. Poverty and social depravation or even moral corruption are not sufficient and strong enough to make it impossible for the protagonists to escape. But if all the ways ahead of them are interconnected and none of them leads out of the web, however hard they try, they will remain captives of the system. The villagers may go as far as they can from their original starting point, but they are still part of Irimiás's conspiracy, which means the police's conspiracy.

Werckmeister Harmonies: 'The conspiracy of the details'
This film occupies a very special place in Tarr's career. This is his only film with a story that crosses the borderline between the level of personal relationships and that of social or political relations. To be sure, this level is as unspecific as in other second-period films, having no concrete historical or geographical coordinates. Nonetheless, in no other Tarr film is there any reference to political and military power or to social unrest.

Werckmeister Harmonies is special in yet another respect. No other Tarr film has a protagonist represented in such a way as to engender unequivocal empathy. In *The Outsider*, the only single-protagonist film in the early period, András may have the viewer's sympathy, but it is very difficult to imagine ourselves in his place, simply because his character's main features are a serious undecidedness and a lack of engagement and of precise goals. Other first-period Tarr films are multiple-protagonist structures with characters lacking the potential to engender sympathy or empathy. The same can be said with regard to *Damnation* and *Satantango*. *Werckmeister Harmonies* is the only film which focuses not only on a single protagonist but on a protagonist who does not have any traits that would make him repulsive, ridiculous, frightening or despicable.

The script of *Werckmeister Harmonies* was based on the second part of Krasznahorkai's second novel, *The Melancholy of Resistance* (*Az ellenállás melankóliája*), published in 1989. It is very difficult not to remark upon the novel's date of publication: the year of the overturn of the communist regime in Hungary, and in other Eastern European countries. This series of events is generally referred to in a broad way as 'the fall of the Berlin Wall', the first milestone of which was the creation of the first non-communist-led government in Poland on 24 August 1989. In Hungary the official day of the turn was the proclamation of the Hungarian Republic on 23 October, which declared political discontinuity with the hitherto existing legal entity of the Hungarian People's Republic, established in 1949. The opening of the Berlin Wall by the East German authorities was announced two weeks later, on 9 November. In Czechoslovakia, mass demonstrations demanding the resignation of the communist regime started on 17 November. In Romania a series of demonstrations started on 16 December, followed by violent fights and bloodshed resulting in the execution of the Romanian communist leader and his wife. Although large-scale economic reforms and radical changes in foreign policy began in the Soviet Union in 1985, which led to the rise of grassroots political movements in Hungary and Poland around 1987, nobody foresaw even in the spring of 1989 that this process would lead so quickly to the collapse of the communist regimes in Eastern Europe. In this period, the prevalent general feeling in these countries was a sense of the slow disintegration of a world which had been non-viable for too long, yet had seemed never-ending. So, the process of erosion also seemed endless, and no one had any idea about the aftermath. In Hungary, at least, a potential spontaneous popular unrest was considered by all parties as dangerous rather than as desirable, mainly due to the tragic experiences of past revolts against communist regimes in 1956 in Hungary, in 1961 in East Germany, in 1968 in Czechoslovakia, and in 1981 in Poland. Thirty-three years of experience confirmed that on each of these occasions the communist regimes' reactions were violent, and the result was destruction and the establishment of an even more cruel order of repression. Accordingly, the wish to overturn the communist regime by force was viewed as purely destructive rather than heroic and revolutionary, and so the slow erosion of an authoritarian, corrupt, cynical and unproductive social and political system seemed to be the future for generations to come.

This is the political sentiment expressed in Krasznahorkai's novel, without specification of any historical or political details. It depicts the irrational and destructive rage of a mob fuelled by a shady and irrational ideology, with no identifiable social or political goals. This is why Krasznahorkai's novel is not political in the sense that it could be linked directly to the concrete historical events of the period in which it was written. It contains only a remote reflection of this period, representing a situation in which the frustration of the people is not articulated in political terms, only by excessive emotional response. It is not directed against some form of order, but against order as such. As is clearly stated in the 'Prince's' discourse:

> Whatever they build and will build ... whatever they do and will do, is disappointment and a lie. Whatever they think and will think makes one laugh. They think because they are afraid. And he who is afraid, knows nothing. He wants, says he, everything to become a ruin. Ruins contain every construction, thus disappointment and lies are like air in the ice, that is what it is like. Everything is contained only in half in construction; in ruins, everything becomes a whole.[6]

The 'Prince's' ideology is focused on the common recurring and most frightful element of every social unrest or revolution, the desire for destruction as a self-contained goal.

Political ideologies appropriate this desire and utilise it to their own ends, whether or not the destruction is justified. This is what is symbolised by the whale, the biggest attraction of the circus. To show something really 'big' can be enough to gather people around it; and if their dissatisfaction is great enough they will follow whatever ideology is presented to them. And herein lies a paradox contained in the novel: the emotional response is justified, as the political order is represented as repressive and corrupt, as shown in the third part of the novel. A justified emotional frustration ignites a justified movement, which is in turn unjustified by its sole rationale, which is mere destruction. Therefore restoration of the order is desirable, but what will be restored is the same repressive order, which must be overturned again, and the circle is closed. The order is unnatural and repressive, but overturning it causes death and destruction and will bring back the same unnatural and repressive order.

More explicitly than *Satantango*, this novel ends with the restoration of 'the order' as an even more oppressive system of powers from which there is no escape. The whole circular logic appears as unavoidable and as a process of nature. The forces of order appear as the forces of nature. Already in *Satantango* there are many allusions to large-scale natural processes like the geographical history of the Great Plain region in the notes of the doctor's diary. In *The Melancholy of Resistance* the parallel between the forces of nature and the forces of society is even more explicit, inasmuch as the last chapter of the book ends with a detailed description of the chemical process that takes place during the disintegration of a dead body. Krasznahorkai describes these processes as a battle the aim of which is to destroy the biological structure of a living being, and he makes it seem like the continuation of the preceding violent events on the social scale. The description makes disintegration appear as the inevitable final goal of everything in the world of the living, which includes human relations as well as society. Disintegration is hidden in the smallest particles of the organism on the small scale and of the social organisation on the large scale. The relationships of the details have their own natural order that cannot be overruled and that makes things proceed in their own way rather than in the way we want them to. This is what Krasznahorkai calls in the book 'the conspiracy of the details': an artificial structure, like a social order, cannot help but succumb to this conspiracy. Artificial and social orders are unnatural and oppressive; natural order, on the other hand, is impersonal and destructive. The same conception can be found in this novel as in *Satantango*: social order is a conspiracy, abusing human desire, feeding it with deceptive ideologies the only goal of which is to maintain the existing oppressive hierarchy. The only power that is greater than this is the unstoppable natural process of disintegration, the result of which is decay as well, and thus the circle closes.

The same paradox is represented on the most sophisticated and abstract level in Mr. Eszter's attempt to return to the musical order of nature by retuning his piano to a world of harmonies that is different from the artificial one European music has been using over the past three hundred years or more. He claims that our whole musical universe is built upon forgery, because it gave up the pure and heavenly harmony of the Pythagorean musical system. However, with this tuning according to clear intervals, the musical art of the past is destroyed, and becomes unbearable to listen to. So, finally,

Mr. Eszter can't help but restore the 'unnatural', artificial order of musical harmonies introduced by Andreas Werckmeister in the seventeenth century. He appears in the novel as someone who destroyed the clear intervals of the tones for the sake of an all-embracing equalised system: 'Werckmeister divided … the universe of the twelve half-tones to twelve equal parts, so that – to the understandable satisfaction of the composers, and after the quickly evaporating resistance of the uncertain desire for the absolutely clear intervals – the situation has become sealed.'[7] Thus, the paradox of the repressive order versus the destructive resistance doomed to failure is represented both on the most brutal and physical level and on the ethereal spiritual level. The novel's title, *The Melancholy of Resistance*, refers to the state of mind generated by this paradox.

Tarr used the second part of the novel, entitled 'Werckmeister Harmonies', where the two processes – the social destruction and the restoration of the order on the one hand and the intellectual process (tuning to another system and retuning) on the other – are placed in parallel. The plot has very little linear development. The protagonist is a slightly mentally retarded young postman, Valuska, who, thanks to his job, meets different people at different locations in the small town. He comes and goes, visits places, and brings news from here to there. He takes care of the elderly composer and musicologist, Mr. Eszter, whose ex-wife, Tünde, left him and now lives with the alcoholic police chief of the town. One night a circus arrives in town. Its biggest attraction is a whale. Another attraction is 'The Prince', a dwarf speaking some foreign language – Slovakian, in fact – and protected by the circus's caretaker, who has the appearance of a bodyguard. More and more people follow the circus from town to town, and rumours spread regarding the destruction caused by this ever-growing dangerous crowd. The dwarf acts as a 'spiritual leader' of the mob and fuels their angry ferocity with his sinister ideology of universal destruction. The circus director is unable to stop him, even though originally it was his business idea to call the dwarf 'The Prince'. Valuska visits the circus in the main square of the town and he is also scared by this mob, still quiet for the moment. A group of citizens, including the police chief and Tünde, ask Mr. Eszter to be the leader of their movement aimed at restoring calm in the town. His ex-wife sends him a message saying that if he refuses to take responsibility in this, she will move back into his house, and sends her suitcase back as a warning via Valuska. The second time Valuska visits the main square, the director announces that the next show is cancelled and asks the crowd to go home. The third time he goes to the main square, it is already dark. He sneaks into the huge carriage containing the whale, and overhears the director and the dwarf's argument, during which the dwarf declares his disobedience to the director, and his intention to continue to excite the mob to destroy. That night, the crowd devastate the town, set fire to buildings, lynch people on the street and patients in a hospital, and break into and loot shops. The next morning the military, led by the alcoholic police chief and his mistress, Tünde, occupies the town. When Valuska goes home, his landlady warns him that he is on the list of those wanted by the forces of order, and suggests that he flee before he gets caught and then hanged. Valuska escapes, but a mysterious helicopter arrives, circles above his head, slowly comes lower, and hovers over the ground in front of him. Next we see Valuska in a psychiatric ward as Mr. Eszter pays him a visit, and tells him that he will be cured and that he can come to live with him, even though his ex-wife and the police chief occupied his whole house too. He also tells him that he retuned his piano to the conventional tempering system, and now it is like an ordinary piano again.

Metaphorical narration:
The plot has a linear development, yet most of the plot elements are causally unrelated, or their relationship is puzzling. There is no relationship whatsoever between the riots and Mr. Eszter's act of tuning his piano to the pre-Werckmeister system, yet he restores his piano when after the military coup the social order is restored. These are two parallel events that are similar on a very abstract level, and their relationship is only based in this similarity, not in their causal relationship. It is unclear why Valuska is wanted by the military, since he has a good relationship with Tünde and Mr. Eszter, the leader of the civil group; moreover, he did not do anything wrong, and everybody knows that he is harmless. Tünde's blackmailing of Mr. Eszter is also very strange, even absurd. It is unclear how Mr. Eszter's decision about whether to become the president of the civil group is related to Tünde's moving back into his house. This is a manifestation of an absurd logic that is also manifested in the crowd's riot, the social motivation of which is unclear, and can hardly be explained solely by a circus dwarf's speeches. The fact that the military commander reports to Tünde and asks her opinion about military tactics is also one of the story's absurdities. All these events and relations are impossible to explain on a concrete and practical causal level; they make sense only on metaphorical terms. Since the most important events fall into this category, we can say that this film – unprecedented in Tarr's oeuvre – has something that can be called a *metaphorical narration*. It is only from this perspective that the film's many other elements, which are puzzling on a concrete level, obtain meaning.

By 'metaphorical narration' I mean a kind of narrative where metaphorical interpretation is not only an option but the only possible way to get the narrative to make sense. In this case, the metaphorical level of the narrative is not a 'surplus' or an extra level, but the only meaningful level. Metaphorical narration is based on impossible or highly unusual connections between events that are not motivated by genre conventions such as those of science fiction or comedy. Metaphorical narration particularly characterises styles such as surrealism, dada and absurd drama. In Tarr's case absurd drama is the closest reference in his films of metaphorical narration.[8] But only two of Tarr's films are of this kind: *The Turin Horse*, where the whole narrative is permeated by this kind of narrative mode; and *Werckmeister Harmonies*, where this mode appears for the first time. The rest have very concrete narrative meanings that can be interpreted on the basis of everyday logic, and the viewer does not have to resort to metaphorical interpretation to accept them, even if in some rare cases individual events seem excessive in their improbability, like the rape scene in *Family Nest*. But in *Werckmeister Harmonies* the above-mentioned events are not only improbable but clearly nonsensical or absurd from an everyday perspective. Metaphorical narration is another way for Tarr of reaching universality on the interpretative level.

This is clearly shown by the first scene of the film. Valuska is in a pub with a bunch of weary drunkards. 'Show us', they demand, aware that the pub will soon close. 'Showing

Figure 46

them' involves Valuska arranging a little scene with the participation of the pub's clients which represents the Earth and the Moon as they revolve around the Sun. A total eclipse is created as the Moon gets between the Sun and the Earth, and then the Moon slowly moves away, so that light and warmth come back again (figure 46).

At the end of the show all the people in the pub join the 'Earth' and the 'Moon' who revolve around the 'Sun', enjoying the returning 'warmth' and 'light'. Apparently this is a regular ritual in this place, since the drunkard who asks Valuska refers to it without explaining what he is talking about. The repeated and ritual nature of the show is even more explicit in the novel: 'when they told him and encouraged him to show "how this thing is with the earth and the moon" was absolutely not unexpected for Valuska, since that is what they also did yesterday, and the day before too, and who knows how many times over past years…' This introductory scene has two interpretative levels. One is the eternity of natural laws and processes, engendering the alternation of coldness and warmth, darkness and light, which allows the return of hope, and assures us that nothing is closed down forever. (In the novel the text explains that this ritual is performed every day before closing time to divert the bartender's attention from closing. Moreover, the people in the pub do not allow Valuska to change anything in the ritual; they want to watch it unaltered over and over again.) This ritual, then, metaphorically represents the stability of nature for those it is performed for. A second metaphorical aspect of this ritual is the one that connects the individual human being with the cosmos. The show brings the cosmic nature of human beings down to the deepest and most hopeless levels of human existence. Since this is the most important aspect of all of Tarr's films, this ritual is the most telling metaphorical representation of this aspect of his oeuvre.

This introductory scene is different from other introductory scenes of second-period Tarr films. In other films the introduction's main function is to attune the viewer to the rhythm and emotional atmosphere of the subsequent story. Except for in *Satantango* and *Werckmeister Harmonies*, the first scenes represent some static situation from which the plot develops: Karrer sits by the window and stares outside; Maloin watches the ship that has just arrived in the port; the father arrives home with his horse. *Satantango*'s introduction has the same 'attuning' function, except that the scene – cows come out of the cowshed and slowly wander around – makes neither concrete nor metaphorical reference to the subsequent story. *Werckmeister Harmonies*' introduction has no place in the subsequent narrative flow either. The story never returns to this pub again, none of the characters return later in the story, except Valuska of course, and there is no mention of the show again in the story, except someone asking Valuska a little later in the post office, 'How are things in the cosmos?'

The scene that could be seen as an introduction similar to the other films' introductions is the second scene: Valuska leaving the pub and walking along the street to go to Mr. Eszter's house. It is a single 80-second tracking shot similar to the introductory shots in the rest of the second-period Tarr films, attuning the viewer to the rhythm and atmosphere of the whole film. Hence, we can say that this film has two introductions. The first is an unusual metaphorical one; the second is the regular 'attuning' type of introduction. The only explanation for the existence of the metaphorical introduction is that many parts of the subsequent story can be interpreted only metaphorically, so this kind of introduction is necessary, alongside the regular attuning type of introduction.

Other than the metaphorical introduction there are four important events in the film that seem excessively strange or make no sense on the level of everyday logic. They are all part of the film's metaphorical narrative structure. The first is Tünde's gesture of sending her suitcase back to Mr. Eszter's house as a threat that she will move back if Mr. Eszter is not willing to become the leader of the civil group. This gesture is nonsensical, all the more for the fact that after Mr. Eszter accepts Tünde's conditions she moves back anyway, and with her lover the police chief. Tünde and the police chief's moving into Mr. Eszter's house makes sense on a metaphorical level, where it symbolises the loss of any intellectual and personal independence, which is confirmed by another metaphorical gesture: resetting the piano to the conventional temperament.

The second instance of a metaphorical structure in the film is the end of the ravaging scene in the hospital. When the mob breaks into the hospital, destroying everything and beating up the patients, they find a naked old man in the shower. The sight of this naked old body seems to cool down their anger and destructive impulse. They stop smashing the hospital and behaving aggressively towards the patients, turn back and slowly leave the place. On the level of psychological realism, this change in behaviour makes no sense. A mob carried away by rage in the middle of lynching and breaking is not likely to be impressed and stopped in its tracks by the sight of the naked body of an old man. On the contrary, the perception of helplessness and weakness usually fuels violent impulses. Among all the metaphorical scenes this is the least realistic; therefore this is most vulnerable to spectatorial rejection. In fact many spectators feel that this scene is rather unrealistic and, with the melancholic music added, is even embarrassingly implausible and sentimental.[9] Others are clearly moved by this scene and, turning to the metaphorical interpretation, consider it the expression of the ultimate absurdity of violence. The next important metaphorical scene is the helicopter hovering in front of Valuska when he flees the town. It is unclear whether this helicopter is real or only Valuska's hallucination, since in fact it does nothing except hover in front of Valuska, and nobody descends from it to capture him, which would be the obvious realistic motivation for its appearance. Because of this ambiguity, its presence can be most plausible interpreted on the metaphorical level, at which it represents Valuska's going crazy. Finally, the last clearly metaphorical gesture in the film is Mr. Eszter's resetting the piano, which has no realistic motivation; this gesture only represents a complete surrender before the return of the oppressive power.

The theme of conspiracy, which is just as central to this film as it is to *Satantango*, also becomes rather metaphorical, unlike in *Satantango*, where it is very practical and concrete. In *Werckmeister Harmonies* there are three instances of group organisation.

The first is related to the mob, whose movement is organised, or at least initiated, by the dwarf. This movement does not seem to have any specific goal other than that referred to by the dwarf: destruction of everything. However, in the eyes of the town citizens this movement looks like a conspiracy against their order. The second is the organisation of the civil movement against the mob, but this cannot be called a 'conspiracy', since it is public and aimed at upholding law and order. The third is the most interesting. It concerns Tünde's different manoeuvres to grasp power, these manoeuvres being closely connected with the official power through the police chief. The fact that she gives orders to the military shows that in fact she is behind the forces of law, which makes her acts the most 'conspiracy-like'. Tünde uses the military and politics for her own personal ends. She benefits from the chaos caused by the mob, and manipulates not only the civil movement, but the law enforcement powers too. Not surprisingly, the idea here is the same as in *Satantango*: conspiracy is not a complot against law and order; rather law and order are the means of conspiracy for those who control the means of oppression and who aim to keep down those who do not.

Circular trajectory:

In *Werckmeister Harmonies* circularity prevails not only at the macro level of the narration, but also on a micro level, as seen in Valuska's trajectory in the film. The narrative follows Valuska's route from one place to another, which is dictated partly by his duties, partly by his interests. There are ten different locations in the story, six of which are recurrent. There are two locations that we return to the most. One is the square where the circus is and where the mob is gathering, appearing four times. The other is Mr. Eszter's apartment, appearing three times. Valuska's home, the hotel and the hospital appear twice, while the other locations, the pub, Tünde's home, the police chief's home, the hardware shop and the railroad tracks, appear only once each. In most cases the film shows Valuska walking from one location to another, which makes the streets of the small town an important location and the most frequently pictured one in the film; however, we don't see the same street segment twice, even though Valuska obviously returns to the same places. There are as many as eleven scenes in which Valuska is walking on the street, sometimes at length, sometimes just for a couple of seconds. There are nineteen location changes in the film, and only five of them are 'sharp', where we do not see Valuska walking on the street between the two locations. It is through Valuska's constant movement between places, giving the viewer a sense of motion, that the circular structure becomes perceptible. The narrative is organised in three major sequences of locations, which can be described as three big circles. These circles are framed by two special scenes, the first and the last. The first is special because none of its elements return in the film, and it does not participate in the narrative causal order. The last is special in that it is the only one in which Valuska is missing. This way there is a remarkable rhythmic symmetry in the narrative structure at the level of sequence length (the numbers show how many locations the given sequence contains): 1-4-8-5-1. The following are the location sequences of the narrative (the abbreviations stand for pub (p), Mr. Eszter's house (Eh), post office (po), hotel (h), square (sq), Valuska's home (Vh), Tünde's home (Th), the police chief's home (pch), hospital (h), shop (sh) and railroad tracks (rt). Two dashes mean a street sequence; one dash means a 'sharp' location change):

```
p --
Eh -- po -- h -- Eh -
sq -- Vh - Eh -- h -- sq -- Th - pch -- sq --
H - sh -- Vh - rt - H -
sq
```

All three sequences are framed by the return of the same location. The first sequence takes place between Valuska's two visits to Mr. Eszter's house, the second of which closes the first part of the narrative. The second part and the second circular sequence starts with Valuska's first visit to the square, and ends with his third and last visit there. The third part and the third circular sequence starts with the scene of the ravaging of the hospital, and ends with Valuska's and Mr Eszter's scene in the hospital. This way the narration creates structural circularity (in the narrative) through physical circularity (in Valuska's movements, his returning to the same locations), which can be interpreted metaphorically (the return of the oppressive order). This is the most consistent and complete circular system of all of Tarr's films.

The Man from London

In an interview Tarr called *Werckmeister Harmonies* a 'too pleasant fairy tale', after which he felt he had to make something 'more dry and cruel'.[10] In the mid-1990s Tarr was approached by an American producer wanting to do a film with him. Tarr didn't like the script proposed; instead, he suggested making a film of a George Simenon short story he had read many years before, *The Man from London*. Together with Krasznahorkai they wrote the script, and the producer purchased the rights of the short story. However, the film was ultimately produced by his own production company, which he had established in the meantime, *T. T. Filmműhely*. To set up the co-production consortium was not particularly difficult, at least not more so than for any other previous film. What was unprecedentedly complicated was finding the appropriate location for the shooting. The original literary work mentions a small French port of call, Dieppe in Normandy. What Tarr needed was an enclosed hilly harbour area where the port is closely connected with the railway. Today's Dieppe had nothing of that sort. Tarr took several months to travel around Europe to find the right location for his film. Finally, he found Bastia, Corsica's northern port. The problem with that choice was that shooting in Corsica meant a considerable rise in expenses, not least because of the very expensive set element, the watchtower, which had to be constructed in Hungary, transported to and assembled in Bastia. Producers tried to talk Tarr out of this location, but Tarr was intransigent. He needed a real location where he could show the port, Maloin's house on the hill and the watchtower at the port in one shot, and he also needed to 'see' the tower from Maloin's house. Paradoxically, these particular images were left out of the film. Finally he managed to convince everyone of the merit of his idea, and the production started under the supervision of Humbert Balsan as executive producer. What could not have been anticipated was Balsan's unstable psychological state, and the financial situation of his production company, which was on the verge of bankruptcy. A couple of days before shooting would start Balsan committed suicide. Right after learning about Balsan's death, Tarr still hoped that he did not have to stop, so he started shooting. As if this situation alone was not difficult enough, the work itself did not start well either. Two days after starting, the director of photography, István Szaladják, unexpectedly announced that he would discontinue his work on the film. He claimed that the psychological atmosphere generated by Tarr's working methods as well as the impossible working conditions the Corsican crew had created made it impossible for him to stay. Being a practising Zen Buddhist, he found too much tension in the production, which he couldn't accept.

In spite of having lost both his executive producer and his director of photography in a matter of days, Tarr did not give up. He summoned Fred Kelemen, a former student of his from Berlin, to immediately replace Szaladják. But things went wrong in other ways too. The Corsican and Hungarian crews were in constant disagreement, their arguments becoming violent at times. Negotiations did not go well with the bank, and it was not long before shooting had to be suspended, and the crew repatriated to Budapest. The tower had to be dismantled and stored somewhere in Corsica in the hope of an eventual continuation. Over a year later shooting could resume, after lengthy negotiations with new banks and even with the Hungarian and French governments. None of Tarr's films were easy to produce and most of them, especially in the second period, were financial gambles. But the difficulties that afflicted the production of *The Man from London* were unprecedented. And that is what exposed Tarr's extreme intransigence and extraordinary battle skills. After the collapse of the financing for the film, he was able to rebuild it within a year without having to compromise whatsoever.

All of this raised the expectations for the film in terms of critical success. Everybody wanted to see that all this trouble had been worthwhile. But the film fell short of this expectation. At its Cannes screening the audience's response was rather hostile, and it received many poor reviews. Even though in his review in *Cahiers du cinema* Cyril Neyrat considers the 'quasi unanimous whistling of the French and international press' as an event that 'counts among the dark pages of film criticism', and talks about a 'general blindness',[11] the good reviews, such as his, could not change the general atmosphere of disappointment. Yet I think that it would be to hasty to say that the lack of a breakthrough success influenced Tarr's decision to give up filmmaking after his next film. Obviously, no one knows, including Tarr himself, what would have happened had this film been a big success. Judging from previous cases of lack of success, and considering Tarr's stubborn character, what others say does not count for much regarding decisions about whether or not to make a film, or about what films to make. Neither is there some 'objective' quality of his film that can be identified as leading to his decision. He does not consider this film as 'worse' than any other of his films. It is the future rather than the present or the past that counts in this decision. As mentioned already in the introduction, what Tarr says about this is unequivocal: he has nothing more to say. In other words, he feels that the Tarr style is no longer productive, and he could certainly see this before anyone else.

Circles of randomness:

If it were not clear so far that Tarr and Krasznahorkai consciously look to construct circular processes everywhere in the stories, *The Man from London* presents a striking example. The way they modified the original plot in the script is very telling in this respect. Simenon's novel tells the story of Maloin, a railroad switchman working at the port of Dieppe, controlling the railroad traffic from a watch tower. One night he becomes aware of two men fighting over a suitcase near the edge of the jetty, not far from his tower. One of them pushes the other into the water together with the suitcase. The man sinks, and the one who pushed him tries in vain to recover the suitcase, before leaving. Maloin descends from his tower and manages to pull the suitcase out of the water. To his great surprise the suitcase is full of banknotes. The next morning he meets the man, named Brown, he saw on the jetty, who is obviously looking for the suitcase. Maloin has a feeling that the man suspects that he has the suitcase, but he decides to keep the money, and tells nobody about what happened. Yet he starts spending the money. He buys an expensive fur for his daughter and forces her to quit her humiliating job at a shop. His wife becomes furious, as she does not understand Maloin's seemingly irrational and irresponsible acts. As the days pass, Maloin regularly sees Brown on the street; he has nowhere to go, nothing to eat, and somehow knows for sure that Maloin has the money, but never approaches him directly. Maloin gradually develops some sympathy for him, because he reckons that he is also responsible for Brown's desperate situation. When a private detective arrives from London to look for him, Brown becomes a fugitive, and looks for a hiding place, choosing a shed on the waterfront, which happens to be owned by Maloin. Maloin wants to help Brown by bringing some food to the shed, but Brown thinks he has come to deliver him to the police, and attacks Maloin as he steps into the shed. Maloin has to defend himself, and before he can explain the situation, he inadvertently kills Brown. In the meantime Brown's wife also arrives from London, and it turns out that she knew nothing about his husband having robbed his patron. Maloin reports what happened in the shed, and gives the money to the detective. And this is where Simenon's story and Tarr's story differ considerably. In the novel the detective proposes to save Maloin from the French police by testifying that Maloin found Brown dead in the shed and did not kill him. But Maloin refuses this solution and gives himself up to the police, accepting the murder charge. In the film, instead, not only does he accept this solution, but he accepts a little bit of money too from the detective.

Although it seems like a minor change at the end of the story, it changes everything regarding the structure of the plot. Simenon's story has a linear development leading from a miserable existential situation and an alienated psychological state toward moral gratification, which changes considerably Maloin's life in all respects: he goes to prison but he gains moral integrity by discovering in himself the feeling of solidarity with the outcast, and his capability of acting accordingly. By contrast, in the film, Maloin's trajectory is circular. With the choice he makes at the end, he falls back into the same hopeless existential situation he started out from, without any moral gratification. Simenon's Maloin was nobody and became somebody, even if he was a criminal in the eyes of the police. Tarr's Maloin hoped only to become somebody, but did not go all the way, and remained a poor nobody, losing even his self-esteem.

Uniquely among Tarr's films, this story is constructed upon coincidences. In no previous Tarr film do coincidences play a role. This is how the conspiracy theme could easily develop together with the circular structure. In this story the two most important events are coincidences: Maloin sees the two men fighting on the jetty, and Brown hides in Maloin's shed. There is no intentional conspiracy behind the events here, like in *Satantango* or, in a less direct way, *Werckmeister Harmonies*. Yet Maloin cannot avoid his destiny any more than the protagonists of the previous films. The 'order' of things keeps him, too, captive in his situation, from which there is no escape. The only difference is that this time no one and nothing can be held responsible for this except 'the conspiracy of the details', which this time is in the form of the power of randomness.

Speechless drama:
The incorporation of coincidences into the narration is not the only way in which Tarr moved away from his earlier films. Another very important change in the narration is the dramatic tension caused by silence in the film. Dialogues are always a central element throughout Tarr's career, especially in the early period. Two of his films have nothing but dialogue scenes in them (*Family Nest* and *Almanac of Fall*), but the rest of his films in the second period are full of lengthy dialogue scenes as well. One of the most important changes in his career is also related to the status of dialogues: prewritten and poetic dialogues in the second period took the place of the improvised everyday-style dialogues of the first period. But that was not the only change regarding the dialogue. Between *Almanac of Fall* and *Damnation* the quantity of the dialogue decreased dramatically. While in the first film the rate of dialogue scenes is 90% relative to the film's running time (107':119'), in the latter this rate is only 41% percent (47':115'). In other words, in more than fifty percent of the film the characters do not talk. This rate remains relatively stable during the whole second period until *The Turin Horse*, in which there are virtually no dialogues.

The Man from London is special in this respect. Although the dialogue scenes take up approximately as much space overall in the film as in the previous second-period films (a little less than fifty percent), the impression created in the viewer is of a conspicuous lack of dialogue. This is due to two things. Firstly, in these dialogue scenes there is much less information than in the previous films. The characters remain speechless during big portions of the dialogue scenes, as for example in the scene with Maloin and Henriette in the bar. This is a four-minute scene in a single seven-minute long shot. The dialogue portion of the sequence is divided into three almost equal parts: between Maloin and Henriette's two dialogues, another dialogue is inserted between the bartender and a woman, which is basically the bartender's monologue. Maloin and Henriette speak in very short, mostly one- or two-word sentences. During the whole time they say altogether fifteen such brief sentences. When the camera travels sideways to show the bartender and the woman's dialogue, keeping Maloin and Henriette in the background of the picture, they don't speak at all. The bartender's monologue is in sharp contrast to Maloin and Henriette's dialogues, which last twice as long and contain half as many words.

In other scenes only one person speaks, and the other just listens, as in the scene with Morrison and Brown, or the one with Morrison and Mrs. Brown. On the other hand, in the longest dialogue scenes, which are with Morrison, the saying of a simple sentence takes twice as long as it normally would because he speaks extremely slowly. If Morrison spoke at a normal pace, his scenes would be much shorter, and the dialogue-scene rate would certainly show a considerable decrease compared to the previous films. What is remarkable therefore in this respect is that Tarr did not change dramatically his *mise-en-scène* as far as the dialogue scenes are concerned; he only extracted most of the dialogue out of the dialogue scenes. Thereby he reached an effect that is new in his career.

Together with this effect, another thing creates the impression that there is very little dialogue in the film. This is the highly dramatic *mise-en-scène* style. This consists in staging scenes where there is a high tension between the characters, yet they speak very little or not at all. The tension is increased by the total lack of or excessive reduction of dialogue. This is a technique that Tarr had never used before. This technique stems from the narrative inasmuch as Brown and Maloin's exchanges are wordless, as Brown never approaches Maloin directly, yet Maloin feels that Brown knows that he has the money. In all the scenes where Brown and Maloin meet there is this tension between the metacommunication and the lack of dialogue.

Lack of communication characterises most scenes in the film. This is most conspicuous with regard to the relationship between Maloin and his wife. There are three scenes with the two of them. The first is when Maloin goes home after the night he found the suitcase. This is a five-minute scene, and each of them has two short sentences to say to the other about their daughter. Neither talks about the other or him- or herself; there is no sign of tenderness or of any human contact. The second is a three-minute scene at the dinner table, where the two of them start an aggressive verbal fight. Maloin, obviously irritated by having seen Brown, who is clearly after him, starts nagging his daughter without any obvious reason. His wife does not understand his behaviour and defends the girl. Instead of explaining his state of mind or simply backing off, Maloin turns his anger against his wife and yells at her with excessive violence. Technically, this is of course a kind of dialogue, but it serves only to vent tension and rage. The third scene with Maloin and his wife is the one when she discovers that her husband took their spare money to buy an expensive fur for their daughter, and furiously demands an explanation. Maloin is not any more communicative than before, so this scene too is just a scene of their yelling at each other instead of engaging in reasonable discussion. It is obvious that their problems could be solved by simple words which explain their feelings or at least calm down the other person, enabling the development of a human dialogue, but this is exactly what is missing in this film. Nobody speaks really to anybody else.

The dramatic speechlessness has a visual consequence too in the film with respect to Tarr's use of close-ups. Close-ups have always played an important role in Tarr's films, precisely because of the overwhelming role of dialogue in the films. Now that dialogues are reduced, and dialogue is missing from the dialogue scenes, the close-ups show not people who speak but people who are silent. Tarr did not change the rate of close-ups in this film, so these images convey a very different atmosphere: that of an inner tension that cannot find a proper way to dissolve.

Communication is just the exercise of power or manipulation of the other person. It is a little bit like most of the dialogue in *Family Nest*, where most of the time the characters, instead of exchanging ideas or attempting to come to a mutual understanding, used conversation to fight the other person. But this kind of use of conversation is more striking in this film, because there is so little. The character who is referred to in the title, Brown, the man from London, speaks only a few sentences in the film, during his conversation with the detective. He otherwise remains speechless. Likewise, his wife, who arrives in Dieppe from London to look for her husband, says only one sentence: 'Where is my husband?' Other than yelling at her husband, Maloin's wife has only three short sentences, two said to her husband, one to her daughter. The person who talks at the greatest length is Morrison, the private detective from London. His dialogue scenes are in fact lengthy, but not because he says a lot of things, rather because he speaks extremely slowly. The effect this has is, again, to create the impression that it is not the information that counts but the tone. It conveys a feeling of an unavoidable fate. This is the same effect slowness has in general in the Tarr films.[12]

The scene in which the silence is the most striking, even embarrassing, is when Maloin enters the shed. He remains in there for one and a half minutes, with the camera staying close in front of the door, and we can hear only the sound of the waves. When Maloin comes out of the shed heaving, the viewer is not in a position to know what happened inside, since there are no sounds coming out of the shed. The viewer is perplexed and has to wait until the next scene to find out what happened. And yet, even then the viewer does not know in what circumstances Brown died. When Morrison tells Maloin in the last scene that this was a case of self-defence, we can only imagine what happened, but we cannot be sure (unlike in the novel, where the scene inside the shed is described in detail). This is another scene where one type of sound (that of the waves) takes the place of speech or of some other sound that would develop the situation. There is a striking lack of acoustic information: in other words, silence.

Lengthy monologues are missing too in this film. Even though dialogue scenes become reduced in the second period, the main characters of the films deliver monologues of various lengths. In this film nobody speaks more than is absolutely necessary to convey the required information, and sometimes they speak less than that. When this is not the case, as in Maloin's two arguments with his wife, speaking is just a way of venting emotion. There is another case of this kind of use of speech. It is in the scene when Maloin buys the fur for his daughter. The two salesmen grotesquely talk for thirty seconds, very fast and in parallel, to Henriette, trying to sell her the fur. Again, what they say is not very important. It is only the tone of their speech which plays a role in their attempts to impress Henriette. When they see that they have succeeded, they immediately stop talking.

For the second time in his career Tarr effected a radical shift in the function of dialogue. In the first period dialogues were an essential or sometimes the most essential part of the narrative process. In the second period situations are not constructed solely or mainly around dialogues, but they remain an important element, and many times monologues take the place of dialogues (this is most spectacular in *Satantango*, but it is clearly perceptible in *Damnation* and *Werckmeister Harmonies* too). In *The Man from London* the important change is that long monologues are entirely missing, and dialogues are not constitutive elements of the narrative any more. They hardly convey any important information, since most of them have as their only function the expression of emotions. Thus, the way Tarr uses dialogue changes and becomes part of the process of increasing the expressivity of the film.

Topic 4: Being lost in one's life (2)

The Turin Horse

> I wish to make one more film about the end of the world and then I am done with making films.[13]

In many ways Tarr's last film is the most radical of all of his works. And this is not a coincidence. This film is meant to be the closure of a whole career. Should this career in fact continue in the future, Tarr made sure that it could not be a continuation of the Tarr style, which is brought to its extreme point here. The radicalism of this film resides entirely in its narrative and not in its visual qualities, which are similar to those of the earlier Tarr films. For one thing, the permutation principle that characterises Tarr's choices of stylistic tools is made explicit through its expression, for the first time, in the narrative structure. For another, partly as a consequence of the former, Tarr's narrative minimalism reaches a point which is very difficult to develop any further. To be sure, this minimalism is not the most radical in the history of cinema. In the 1970s the European art cinema created many more radical forms (Straub and Huillet, Philippe Garrel, and Chantal Akerman are just the best-known examples). Also, in contemporary art cinema, forms approaching art-gallery video works, such as Benedek Fliegauf's *Milky Way* (2008), are obviously more radical in their minimalism. However, within the realm of the Tarr style, and with regard to Tarr's moral attitude, this film is the one that is reduced to its minimal essential ingredients. Shots are the lengthiest of all Tarr films. *Satantango* was the longest Tarr film, but its shots were not much longer on average than those of *Damnation*, the first extreme long-shot Tarr film. But the shots in *The Turin Horse* are twice as long as in *Damnation*, and eight times as long as in Tarr's first film, *Family Nest*. The story has no linear development; it consists of repeated events, and during most of the time we see only two protagonists who barely talk to each other.

The story, written by Tarr and Krasznahorkai, is based on a short essay by Krasznahorkai published in 1990, *Legkésőbb Torinóban* (*At the Latest in Turin*). The story takes as its starting point a biographical fact about German philosopher Friedrich Nietzsche. In 1889, Nietzsche was found weeping, embracing the neck of a horse on a street in Turin, Italy. This was his final mental breakdown, from which he never recovered. He was mentally ill until his death in 1900. The first paragraph of Krasznahorkai's essay tells this story in a reconstruction according to which the horse was being brutally beaten by the coachman when Nietzsche embraced it, as if protecting it. The last sentence of the paragraph is this: 'What happened with the horse, we don't know.' The film script, taking this paragraph as its starting point, tells the story of what happened with the horse. Krasznahorkai's story obviously cannot be a historical reconstruction, since historically nothing is known of the identity of the coachman or of the destiny of the horse. It is rather an apocalyptical vision of a meteorological, human and social catastrophe, a total collapse of the world following this incident.

Other than this first paragraph, which is inserted as a voice-over at the beginning of the film, there is no mention of the German philosopher or of the incident in the film. One could ask what is added by involving the great German philosopher in this story. The first thing that comes to mind is one of Krasznahorkai's fundamental story patterns, which is the immediate relationship between the most abstract, subtle and highest level of the poetic and philosophical sphere and the lowest and most desperate human existence. This relationship can be found in all of the second-period Tarr films. In this story, Nietzsche is the representative of the most poetic visionary philosophy of a new human existence, and the beaten horse represents the most humiliated, helpless and miserable subhuman existence. Not only do the two meet, but their encounter is the only human connection occurring in the story, or, more precisely, in the film (since it occurs before the story begins). And since the last human connection is the manifestation of the final mental collapse, the apocalypse occurring in the story can be interpreted in a way as a result of or as a metaphor for Nietzsche's mental breakdown, as if Nietzsche's collapse were a premonition, the first sign of this apocalypse. Or else, as if the latter were a consequence or the physical continuation of the former. So, the fact that the story is about the specific horse provoking Nietzsche's reaction, and not just about any horse beaten by its master, makes Nietzsche's story and the horse's story reflect each other. That this story is about the horse gives Nietzsche's story a moral aspect, and Nietzsche's story gives the horse's story a philosophical dimension.

The narrative is broken into six parts, which cover six entire days. The events taking place during this time are the simple everyday activities of two people, the coachman and his daughter, in a small and poor farm. The events do not add up to form a goal-oriented sequence; they are highly repetitive and have the simple aim of satisfying the needs of everyday survival. There are altogether twenty different events, of which ten reoccur at least once. The action recurring the most often (six times) is one of them sitting in front of the window and staring outside. The second most frequent event, recurring five times, is the two of them eating potatoes and the father changing his clothes with the help of his daughter. During the whole time a constant and extremely strong wind blows outside, which means everything they do outdoors requires extra effort. The events of the day are very small, mostly everyday activities that do not make the narrative go forward, like washing, sewing, doing leatherwork, and so on. There are two instances of extraordinary events. On the second day a neighbour comes over to buy brandy, and gives a long speech about the collapse of everything. The other extraordinary event is the arrival of a company of gypsies, who stop for water and give the daughter a religious book before the father sends them away. Later on the daughter starts reading from the book out loud. Both extraordinary events are related to the two lengthiest monologues of the film, which emphasises the extraordinary nature of speech in this story. The only thing that represents a developing process is the dying of the horse and the natural conditions, which become more and more severe and strange. First, the bark beetles stop eating the wood. Second, the horse will not pull the carriage any more. Third, the horse won't eat. Fourth, water disappears from the well. Fifth, when the farmer decides to leave the property, they pack everything up and leave the house; then they suddenly turn back without any obvious reason. The next step is that the horse won't even drink. And finally, in the middle of the day, everything becomes dark and even the fire goes out.

The most spectacular thing about the narrative is that there is no progressing element in it related to the characters. The characters have no intentions, goals, plans, or desires that could become the motivational basis of the narration. This total lack of human motivation is unique even in Tarr's career. Two films are the closest in this respect to *The Turin Horse*. One is *The Outsider*, in which the lack of specific goals is the driving force of the narrative, and the other is *Werckmeister Harmonies*, where the main character, Valuska, becomes the victim of the events around him without ever playing an active part in anything. In both films, however, human actions make the story develop. By contrast, in *The Turin Horse* not only do human actions not play a part in what is going on in the world, but also no attempts are made by the characters to influence the events. They are absolutely helpless as they face the dying of the horse, let alone the wind and the disappearance of the water and the light. There is nothing they can do about these things, and they have no plans for survival.

The only thing they try is to go away, but this seems hopeless too and they turn back. Neither the scenario nor the film makes it clear why there is nowhere else to go. The scenario reads: 'They stand there motionless for some time, and as time goes by it becomes increasingly obvious that no matter which direction they may take it will be just totally hopeless.' In the film, even those uncertain clues disappear. As they get to a certain distance from the house, we see them in long shot as they disappear over the horizon. For almost forty seconds we see only a lonely tree on the horizon and the leaves blowing in the strong wind. Suddenly they reappear on the horizon, and slowly return to the house. Tarr does not try to explain what it means that 'it becomes increasingly obvious' that all directions are equally hopeless. He does not even show the moment of the decision, as if this were not even a decision they made, rather the effect of some exterior power which brings them back from where they wanted to leave. This must become obvious from the simple fact that they return. They don't speak, they don't express any emotions, they just adapt to the circumstances. And as they unpack everything again, and the daughter sits down in front of the window, and we see her face from outside, framed by the window through the haze of the storm, the spectator surely understands the overall hopelessness of their situation, which no human act can change (figure 47).

This film is different in many ways from the previous Tarr-style films. First of all, there is no circularity in the narrative. Even though this is the most repetitive of

Figure 47

all Tarr films, neither explicit nor implicit circularity characterises the story. He thus returns to the static character of his early films. The characters go through a simple linear trajectory, which is neither long nor complicated. It extends from the point where the father arrives home, through the moment they realise that there is nowhere to go, to the point when everything becomes dark. If someone felt the need to find the idea of circularity within this film, the only way to do it that I can think of would be through an interpretation of this story as something like a 'counter creation'. The fact that this story lasts six days obviously refers to God's creation of the world in six days, starting with the sentence, 'Let there be light'. This story tells of the last six days of the created world, when gradually everything disappears and finally even the light goes out. This is the end, when everything falls back into the darkness from where everything was created. This film closes the circle of creation, as it were. Clearly, the idea of circularity appears here on a very high interpretative level, but nowhere can it be detected in lower level structures.

Secondly, none of Tarr's usual topics are present in the story. This is an apocalypse, not an everyday hell. There is neither conspiracy nor betrayal in the film, since everything that happens is a process of nature rather than the result of human action. Also, this is Tarr's only film where no human relationships develop. The two main characters, father and daughter, basically have no human contact with each other. They speak very little, and when they speak they relate only the necessary minimum of information about the immediate physical environment, or give orders to one another. The few other characters who appear in the film for a very short time have no relationship whatsoever with the main characters. The neighbour who comes for brandy delivers a long monologue, but there is no reaction to it. The gypsies who arrive, even though they want to take the daughter along at first, are very quickly sent away.

Thirdly, as a consequence, the narrative element that is so crucial in the early period, and that remains important until *The Man from London*, the dialogue, disappears almost entirely in this film. We saw in relation to *The Man from London* in what ways and to what extent the dialogue disappeared from the dialogue situations or lost the function of conveying information and served only to vent emotions. In *The Turin Horse* there is only one real dialogue situation, the one with the neighbour, but in this scene there is only a monologue. The rest of the scenes are not dialogue situations, and the few and very short dialogues that occur in them refer to external events rather than human relations.

This is what makes the neighbour's speech so spectacular. In a story where the characters almost never speak, a long monologue becomes exceptional, especially if it is as abstract and philosophical as the neighbour's monologue. This pattern is well known from earlier Tarr films, especially from *Damnation* and *Satantango*. Characters make speeches in situations where the tone and the content of the monologue seem displaced. The viewer wouldn't expect weary characters in conditions of extreme poverty and in the midst of rude human relations to deliver highly abstract or poetic monologues. In this film this paradox appears in its most extreme form, since the neighbour's philosophical monologue appears in a situation in which it is not only unexpected, but also totally unrelated to everything the viewer knows about this world. This is exactly the main role of this monologue. It is the only source that gives the viewer any information about the world outside. Without this monologue the whole story would be out of context, given that Nietzsche's story is just an occasion and not a real context.

However, this monologue is also too obscure to provide exact information about what is happening outside, especially because the neighbour speaks about some large-scale political happenings from a moral point of view, and it is hard to see how these are related to the dying of the horse, the well's drying up, or the disappearance of the light. This context is rather metaphorical. Since the neighbour speaks about the final victory of evil powers over moral order, which causes everything to go wrong, we must suppose that the natural events taking place in the story are, somehow, also part of this general break-down. The collapse of the moral universe means in fact the end of the world in the concrete sense. So, once again, just like in *Werckmeister Harmonies*, most of the key events of the story are related metaphorically rather than causally, which makes this film another Tarr film with metaphorical narration.[14] No wonder that the father has only one thing to say in response to the neighbour's speech, which puts an end to it immediately: 'This is nonsense.'

Related to the reduction of dialogue, the role of music and noises increases considerably in this film. Since *Almanac of Fall* composer Mihály Víg has had a distinguished role in all Tarr films. This role is fundamental in this one. There is an almost constant musical accompaniment in this film, and the character of the music is indicative of the film's structure and atmosphere. There are no individual numbers in the music. We hear a repetitive minimalist music constituted of variations on a single three-note musical motif using different instruments, orchestration and harmonies.

Whatever remains of Tarr's narrative motifs becomes radical owing to its being reduced to its very essence. Narrative slowness is more radical here than it is in any other Tarr film because no clues are provided for the viewer as to where the narration is going. All the means by which narration can be slowed down are used in this film: extensive repetition; real time and detailed description of everyday acts; representation of monotonous movements; and extensive representation of *temps mort*.

There is no other Tarr film in which narrative repetition is as prevalent as in this film. In this respect *Almanac of Fall* is the most similar to it. In *Almanac of Fall*, the narrative structure is constructed upon the permutation of dialogue situations. However, the variations of the dialogue add up to create a developing process of human relations, whereas in *The Turin Horse* repetition of scenes means repetition of the same scene in the same way, where the difference between the scenes appears only on a very small-scale visual level, and the repeated events do not generate a progressing series. Real-time representation of everyday events is not as radical as in *Satantango* for the simple reason that this film is not of as excessive a length as *Satantango*, so the time which description of everyday acts can last is much more limited. The everyday-ness of the characters' acts is emphasised more, however, than in any other Tarr film by contrasting them with the extraordinary circumstances. Tarr's usual procedure of making the banal extraordinary is achieved here through this contrast. In the midst of the apocalyptic circumstances the two characters carry on their ordinary everyday activities. Representation of monotonous movements at length is also less radical here then it is in *Satantango*, again because of the film's normal length, and also because of the fact that the characters do not go outside the house much, and if they do, they only go as far as the well or the stable. But still, there is as much monotony in the suspenseless repetition of the same movements of changing clothes or eating potatoes. Finally, extensive representation of *temps mort* is more excessive in this film than in any other Tarr film. In fact, what is represented all through the story is empty time, since nothing is envisaged in the plot, nothing adds up, and the characters' acts lead nowhere. The story represents the time elapsed between two extraordinary events: Nietzsche's final mental break-down, related to the beating of the horse, and the final apocalyptic blackout. But this is not the empty time within a process between two significant events representing important turns in an event series. The empty time in this story will not end. This is the process of time emptying out for good, which is represented on the concrete level by the events contributing to the disappearance or the fading out of the world. The last event, the fade out, therefore, is not an event. It is the end of all events, the end of time. The time of the plot takes place in a kind of 'day after', where the apocalyptic event is Nietzsche's mental break-down followed by an undetermined natural catastrophe where the chances of survival are zero.

This process is somewhat similar to what we see in Antonioni's *L'eclisse* (*Eclipse*, 1962), which also starts with an 'end': the breaking up of a couple. The rest of the film represents the 'days after' the separation, which after all lead nowhere, and the main characters disappear from the story, leaving the camera alone, as it were, on the empty streets. The idea of the disappearance of the light is also present in Antonioni's film in the title, even though the notion of the eclipse suggests only a temporary fading out, whereas in *The Turin Horse* the blackout is not associated with a known temporary natural phenomenon. The story suggests that this is final. Not only does natural light go out, but artificial light is impossible to turn on. The important difference between Antonioni's eclipse and Tarr's apocalypse is that Antonioni's film is about the disap-pearance of human relations, while Tarr's film is about the disappearance of nature, as human relations are already missing at the outset.

This is an absolutely dehumanised world, and all of the differences between this film and the earlier Tarr films are due to this radical dehumanisation. No human act is capable of affecting any of the processes of nature, and attempts are not even made to this end. Living beings are only helpless observers and victims of what is happening. This is also what makes any communication between the characters superfluous. The destiny of the humans becomes similar to the helpless dying of the horse, a pure natural process that cannot be remedied. Although according to the title the horse is the protagonist of the story, the horse remains in the background of the plot events. This story is about the Turin horse inasmuch as the humans around him become reduced to the same helplessness, to the point where there is no difference between them. They become as helpless as the horse, and when they understand that, they start acting like the horse. The final event of the film is that the daughter stops eating.

The power of compassion:

This story is a metaphor for ultimate human helplessness, which is the main idea of the story of Nietzsche in Turin, according to Krasznahorkai. In his original essay, Nietzsche's story in Turin is about the power of compassion. The man, whose philosophy despises 'humanist' feelings like compassion and pity, suddenly, and certainly unwillingly, manifests the deepest compassion for a helpless living being, a beaten horse. This event, says Krasznahorkai, is 'the flashing recognition of a tragic error: after such a long and painful combat, this time it was Nietzsche's persona who said no to Nietzsche's thoughts that are particularly infernal in their consequences.'[15] This is the example which leads to a conclusion about the universality of this feeling: 'if not today, then tomorrow… or ten, or thirty years from now. At the latest, in Turin.'[16]

Herewith, we arrive at the most important thematic element of Tarr's stories, which is not even a topic or a theme, but rather an attitude or an approach to human conditions, which Tarr fundamentally shares with Krasznahorkai. This attitude concerns all of his films, and not only those he made with Krasznahorkai, and this is certainly what makes their collaboration an exceptional success. Both authors have a fundamentally compassionate attitude toward human helplessness and suffering in whatever situation it may manifest itself, and of whatever antecedent it may be the result. This is what connects all of Tarr's films, of both periods, together. This attitude also becomes radical in *The Turin Horse*. In no other Tarr film is the helplessness of the characters laid bare so powerfully as in this film. Although the neighbour attributes the apocalyptic conditions primarily to human intervention, the story contains no events contributing to the apocalypse that could be seen to be caused by any of the characters. Everyone in this film faces ultimate helplessness, and for the first time in Tarr's oeuvre, the characters do not make their own life or others' lives harder. They are entirely at the mercy of exterior circumstances, and these circumstances have no mercy for them. No real human qualities are manifested by the characters of this film; be it good or bad, there is only bare human existence reduced to its simplest physical and biological substance. That is why the last sentence uttered in the film is what the father says to his daughter: 'One must eat.'

If there is no reason why the characters would cause their own miserable situation, there is no reason either why the viewer should particularly like them. Tarr in all of his films generates compassion for his characters not by making them seem to deserve it owing to their behaviour, but simply by making them human. Tarr never judges his characters, and this would be simply impossible in this film. While the characters of the other films have different attributes, good and bad, the father and the daughter in this film are beyond moral characterisation. They struggle for their mere survival, and their cooperation is reduced to the basic utilitarian level, like when the daughter helps his father in changing his clothes.

If the universality of the ultimate power of compassion in Nietzsche's story stems from the philosopher's pity felt for a horse, in the film the viewer is driven to feel the same. If we feel compassion for the characters it is not because of their noble human qualities, but because lives – that of a horse, of a man, and of a woman – are about to flicker out.

This brings us to the problem of Tarr's characters, which I find the most fundamental of all the subjects I have dealt with so far. Tarr's whole attitude regarding his stories and filmmaking in general can be explained through his attitude regarding his characters. This is the topic of the next chapter.

Notes

1   German feminists protested against the film at the time of its release at the Mannheim film festival, where the film won the Grand Prize, claiming that this scene is disgracing for women. Here is Tarr's response: 'And then came eight representatives of the Frankfurt feminist party, saying that this is not true. A humiliated woman doesn't go drinking with her rapists. Sure she does! She is humiliated every day, and still she drinks with the man afterwards. What is worse, she even lives her entire life with him.' Unpublished interview.

2   The viewer obviously doesn't have the information that this story is made up of Irén's real story, and the things she says at the end she knows from real-life experience.

3   See, for example, Gábor Kövesdy (1997) 'A léket kapott élet', *Metropolis*, http://www.c3.hu/scripta/metropolis/9702/kovesdy.htm

4   László Krasznahorkai (1985) *Sátántangó*. Budapest: Magvető, 329.

5   This song was originally written by Mihály Víg in the beginning of the 1980s, and was meant to be a parody of popular kitsch love songs of the time. The lyrics repeat different verbal clichés about expressing negative emotions. Víg was surprised when Tarr chose this song for the film, fearing that the parody effect would prevail over the sadness of the song. But the film has made this song a hit in the Hungarian alternative music world.

6   All translations of excerpts from the novel are mine.

7   Maybe it is worth noting that Krasznahorkai, and following him Tarr, repeats a common misunderstanding according to which the Werckmeister temperament is based on equal intervals. This is wrong. The Werckmeister tuning is called 'good temperament'. Equal temperament became the basis of tuning only half a century after Werckmeister (1645–1706). See Alfred Dürr (1998) *Johann Sebastian Bach – Das Wohltemperierte Klavier*. Kassel: Bärenreiter.

8   More than one review of *The Turin Horse* at the Berlin Film Festival in 2011 mentions Beckett. See for example Jonathan Romney (2011) *The Turin Horse*, *ScreenDaily*, 15 February.

9   Lajos Jánossy in his review describes this scene as 'metaphysical kitsch'; in *Magyar Narancs*, 8, 4, April 2001.

10 Vincent Malausa (2008) 'Interview with Béla Tarr', *Transfuge*, September, pp. 20–6.

11 Cyril Neyrat (2008) 'Le gardien du vide', *Cahiers du cinema*, September, 28.

12 It is noteworthy that the character of Morrison in the film is borrowed by Tarr from another Hungarian filmmaker's works, György Fehér's two films, *Szürkület* (*Dawn*, 1990) and *Szenvedély* (*Passion*, 1998), where the same actor, István Lénárt, played a neurologist and an attorney, respectively. Originally, it was Fehér's idea to instruct Lénárt in both films to use extreme slowness in his diction. Tarr used the same character pattern in *The Man from London*. Fehér and Tarr worked in close collaboration starting from *Damnation* up until Fehér's death in 2002. Tarr is credited in Fehér's films and Fehér is credited in Tarr's films until *Werckmeister Harmonies*, so Morrison's character in *The Man from London* can be regarded also as an homage to Tarr's close friend and collaborator.

13 Vincent Malusia (2008) 'J'ai perdu toutes mes illusions', *Transfuge*, September, pp. 20–6.

14 It is probably worth mentioning that *Werckmeister Harmonies* and *At the Latest in Turin* were written in the same period, and published within only a couple of months of each other (May 1989 and January 1990, respectively).

15 László Krasznahorkai (1990/91) 'Legkésőbb Torinóban', *Alföld*, 29.

16 Ibid. 30.

CHAPTER SIX

The Characters

In the previous chapter I came to the conclusion that the radicalism in *The Turin Horse* is mainly due to the way Tarr handles his characters, which is different in many respects from his other films. This chapter deals with the last important aspect of the films of Béla Tarr, his characters. The reason why it is possible to discuss this aspect separately is that Tarr's characters belong to the general conception of his films rather than to the individual stories. Obviously, each story has its particular characters, yet they represent identifiable types and in many ways they are very similar to each other.

Tarr's most fundamental artistic attitude can be summarised by the idea of *compassion without moral judgement*. This idea explains also the dialectics of distance and participation mentioned already and to which I will return in this chapter.

Tarr belongs to the tradition of modernist filmmakers who tell stories about the suffering of sinners. Some of these filmmakers are religious, like Bresson and Tarkovsky, and some of them are not, like Fassbinder and Tarr.[1] The most religious of them all, Bresson, is also the coldest and most distanced. His films reach a feeling of compassion from afar, and require a big effort by the viewer. His sinners are real ones: thieves and murderers. Tarkovsky is a semi-religious filmmaker; his sinner characters are sinners only from the point of view of their own conscience. His films are much warmer, and require much less effort from the viewer to arrive at the feeling of compassion. The beauty of his images and the elements of nature help the viewer 'perceive' the spirituality of the world that embraces his outcast characters. Fassbinder is not religious at all, and his films are the most sentimental. In his films the characters express their suffering, and the expressivity of their acting is either counterbalanced by means of cinematic alienating effects or emphasised by visual expressivity. Tarr is not a religious filmmaker either, and his films, especially in the second period, are also rather sentimental. He, like Fassbinder, alternates expressive and sometimes radically sentimental visual and acoustic effects with alienating ones, while at the same time making it very hard for the viewer to acquire the feeling of compassion, because of the extreme slowness of the narration and the alienating effects.

At the level of character representation, typically these filmmakers choose characters who are either not likable or are not represented in such a way that the viewer identifies emotionally with them. The reason for this is that emotional identification results in easy moral absolution. We tend to understand and forgive those who we come to like, and it is much more difficult to forgive and understand those who we do not like. And it is not forgiveness of the characters that these filmmakers expect from the viewer, and they do not want the viewer to like them either. It is understanding and suspension of moral judgement they want to elicit.

Social status

The most general trait of the Tarr characters in all of his films is that they are vulnerable both socially and psychologically on the one hand, and that they are not very likable or simply evil on the other. That the Tarr characters are not very likable sounds like a subjective statement. Yet it is not, and I will try to show that the 'unlikability' of the characters is part of a well-defined conception and can be illustrated by a very specific characterisation.

The characters' vulnerability is first of all social. Socially, all of Tarr's characters belong to different groups within the working or lower middle class, and there is not much difference between the social status of the characters within a single film. There are only two instances when supporting characters in the story come from a supposedly different social class. One is the last sequence of *The Outsider*, when we see a celebration of local political leaders, some of them from abroad, and the other is in *The Man from London*, where Morrison comes from a different world. One could also think of *Almanac of Fall*, where Hédi, who is at the top of the hierarchy among the characters, is certainly the richest of all, but this difference is not manifested here as social difference. She belongs to the same world as the other characters. We can find a similar spectrum of a particular lower class in *Satantango* too. While most of the characters belong to the same low social status, a somewhat higher level also appears through the different agents of the police, but they do not represent a very big social difference either.

The characters of *Family Nest* all belong to the working class, just like the characters of *The Outsider*, although in the latter film, even this low social status is very unstable. The protagonist of *The Prefab People* also works in a factory, yet at a somewhat higher level (he is a technician), and his wife stays at home with the children. Financially, they are better off than the protagonists of the two previous films, but their social perspectives are very limited. Not much is known about the social status of the characters in *Almanac of Fall*, because their professions are not specified, except for Anna, who is a nurse, and Tibor, who is a teacher. But the mere fact that they are obliged to share Hédi's apartment informs the viewer about their low social status. The same is true for *Damnation*, where a very narrow range of lower-middle-class characters is displayed, some of them with unspecified occupations. In the films up until *The Man from London* we find the same social structure: a narrow range of lower-middle-class and working-class characters living at a small distance from extreme poverty.

In sum, Tarr's characters represent the socially lowest or close to the lowest stratum of everyday people. They are not the 'real' poor people or the socially outcast. They are the people whose energies are invested in keeping themselves from falling lower, in keeping this status with no opportunity to ever get any higher. The chance of getting into a better situation financially appears in only two films: *Satantango* and *The Man from London*. In both films, as mentioned earlier, this turns out to be just an illusion. Tarr's choice of representing this particular social group is so consistent that it needs an explanation.

This consistence is certainly not due to any specific cinematic convention, since in Hungarian cinema one cannot find any consistent interest in this social group, especially not over the past thirty years. To be sure, at the time of Tarr's debut, in the mid-1970s, there was a fashion for lower-middle-class or working-class protagonist characters in the documentary-fiction wave Tarr belonged to. However, so many circumstances have changed since then, the society, the political system, and most importantly, Tarr's cinematic style, that it would be hard to attribute his consistent focusing on this social group to this tradition.

Another possible explanation could be based on some political agenda concerning this particular social group. Tarr does not have a specific political agenda in his films that can be discerned in any period regarding any concrete political issue. Some of his films are political in the very broad sense that his stories represent the hopelessness of sometimes excessively deprived people, but, especially in the second period, nothing in his films refers to any identifiable social or political circumstance. The only exception is *Family Nest*, but as I have attempted to show, this film already concentrates on the human relations rather than on the social conditions.

The explanation for this consistency that I find convincing is to be found in the positioning of this social group at the narrow borderline between relative poverty and sheer misery. Tarr places his characters in situations in which their social status is precarious but not so difficult that their own moral behaviour does not make any difference. This would be the case if they were much higher or much lower socially. Moral behaviour makes no poor man rich, and the immorality of the rich almost never makes them poor. The social status of Tarr's characters is associated to some extent with the moral and existential autonomy necessary for human dignity, and a social vulnerability, which automatically provokes compassion. This is an area where the situation of the characters still has an identifiable social aspect – low social status, poverty, deprivation – yet their destiny is not entirely dependent on this. They are socially vulnerable not because they are at the bottom already, but rather because they are constantly in danger of falling to the bottom. This is where their own behaviour makes a difference. Obviously, for the overwhelming majority of the viewers of Tarr films, the extreme poverty of socially outcast people represents a different world, for which they eventually feel some (predominantly social) responsibility. The acts of the people existing at this social level are viewed as driven by their social position in the first place, rather than their autonomous personal attributes. If they happen to be 'good' people, the romanticised view of the 'goodness of poor people' cannot be avoided. If they happen to be bad, we tend to interpret their acts as the necessary result of their social situation. If the characters are of a middle class or a higher position, their acts are considered 'free' of social constraint, and they are provided with a maximum of moral independence and lack social compassion. Tarr places his characters at the border where the characters' moral behaviour may have an important impact on their social status. They are not free of social constraints, yet their choices make a moral difference.

In most cases that is what happens in the stories, especially in the early period. The protagonists' moral choices have a decisive impact on their social position. In *Family Nest* the behaviour of Laci and probably Irén largely contributes to the situation of their family becoming more unstable, inasmuch as Irén and their daughter are obliged to become illegal squatters. It seems that it is Laci's and his father's behaviour that make the difference for Irén between the precarious situation of being obliged to share a little apartment with four other people and being out on the street with her little daughter. In *The Outsider* András's social marginalisation is a direct consequence of his careless and irresponsible attitude. He loses his jobs, and also the women who could keep him in relative security. In *The Prefab People* Judit and Robi's poisonous relationship leads to Robi leaving the family. Although it is not specified what this means socially for them, it is not hard to imagine. The only opportunity Robi was given that could have led to an improvement in their situation involved his leaving his family and going abroad, so this was not an option. In *Almanac of Fall* Tibor's theft lands him in jail, which is the final step of his social downfall. This last step is what separated him from ruining himself entirely. In *Damnation* everybody betrays everybody, which will certainly result in the general financial and social collapse of the whole company, including Karrer himself. In *Satantango* the greed and the stupidity of the settlers make them lose whatever little remains for them at the end of the story. This is what makes the difference between having a miserable home and becoming homeless, between having a little money and having nothing, between being attached to a community and being separated from people who may have been unlikable but who were at least familiar.

The consistency with which Tarr depicts only this particular social environment leads us to conclude that the most important aspect of it is the precariousness resulting in excessive helplessness, and the fact that a bad choice can turn a bad situation into a catastrophe. Up until *Satantango* Tarr represented the interaction between morality and social position. From *Werckmeister Harmonies* on he becomes more fatalist: a bad choice is not even necessary for things to go wrong. In the films before *Werckmeister Harmonies*, Tarr plays these two factors against each other, trying to keep a balance. Whenever viewers could become too carried away by social compassion, the characters do something which is morally unacceptable. And similarly, whenever viewers would be inclined to judge a character too harshly for his or her morally questionable choice, they are reminded of the character's social vulnerability. The viewer is never allowed to sympathise with these people just because they are socially vulnerable, but Tarr never allows the viewer to make a simple moral judgement on them either.

The episode when the settlers arrive at the manor to meet Irimiás is a case in point. After they leave their homes with the few belongings they have, they walk for hours in the heavy rain to meet Irimiás in the old manor to start a new life. When they arrive it is already dark, and they look around their 'new home'. This is a ten-minute long sequence where they discover this space in silence, and we see their disappointed and dispirited faces. What they see is a devastated, entirely empty huge old building, the home of a one-time lord of the region now half in ruins. The walls are bare, with no windows or doors and no furniture, of course. This is when the viewer starts to realise that something is very wrong here. But they have no choice; they have to wait, and they accommodate themselves for the night.

None of them were likable characters from the outset, and when they left the settlement, they broke their own furniture rather than leave it 'for the gypsies' (not to mention that three of them, Schmidt, Kráner and Futaki, wanted to steal the money from the community), yet when we see them like this in this environment, knowing that they have left everything behind, we are likely to feel some kind of empathy for them. And, to make this feeling dominate, Tarr makes his own attitude very clear. They all lie down in the same room, close to each other. Then the camera starts panning slowly from a high angle along the bodies of the sleeping characters on the floor, showing them one after the other in a six-minute-long shot. This point of view suggests very strongly an exterior position, from which they look more vulnerable and defenceless than ever before. In the meantime a voice-over narrates the dreams of each of them, and soft, melancholic music is heard. This is a very strong compassionate gesture provoked by their current situation, regardless of what they have done before and regardless of the fact that they are also responsible for their own misery. This segment of the narrative is interrupted by the next chapter, which is a long flashback (the last one in the film), but the subsequent chapter continues where the narrative left off one chapter earlier. The company wakes up in the morning and waits for Irimiás to come. But he is late. And this is where our compassion for them, provoked by such powerful visual and acoustic means, is dissipated immediately, in a scene where Kráner and Schmidt start beating up Futaki, charging him with having set them up, while the others just watch. Now they have both our compassion for their desperate situation and our contempt for their repulsive, irresponsible and violent behaviour. But then comes another turn. When Irimiás finally arrives and tells them that their project cannot be started right away and they have to be separated, first Kráner asks for his money back. Irimiás is diabolical here. He immediately complies with the request, but with a tone which finally drives Schmidt to order Kráner to give the money back to Irimiás, and when Irimiás refuses to accept the money, Kráner himself starts to beg him to take it (figure 48). Finally, all of them are ashamed of 'not having perseverance' and of being 'unfaithful' to 'the cause'. Once again, we look at them as desperate and helpless people who are being abused by an unscrupulous conman. In this example the narration changes perspective three times concerning the viewers' emotions toward the characters.

This limbo has a direct impact on the effect the long takes have on the viewer, as referred to already in chapter three. Whether the viewer feels involved in the space along with the characters or, on the contrary, feels detached from the situation depends very much on what phase the 'empathy swing' is at in the narration. Sometimes, this is clearly manifested

Figure 48

in the camera movements themselves. The above example is a case in point. When the company arrives at the manor it is already dark, and they discover the place with the help of lamps. The viewer can see only as much as they can see; we move forward with them, and their faces are frequently shown in close-ups. There is even a 360 degree turn around the head of Mrs. Schmidt, which really makes the viewer feel he or she is in the space. We have the same effect in the scene when the camera moves around showing the sleepers. However, the next morning, when the conflict starts, the camera is distanced to the point that it leaves the space where the action is taking place, showing the outside of the building and entering the place on the other side of the room.

In the films where the characters' attitude and their social status are counter-weighted, Tarr's method is to alternately represent the characters as suffering and as causing suffering to others. Sometimes they are clearly despicable, yet, without any exception, each of them has at least one scene where we can see their vulnerability. This is particularly striking in *Family Nest*, where the immorality of some of the characters is beyond forgiveness. Laci, with the rape, and his father, with turning Laci against Irén and evicting Irén from the apartment, clearly cross important moral limits. Still, both have a scene at the end where we see them vulnerable and suffering. All of this does not make their acts acceptable, but it does provoke the viewer's compassion for those people who are not only in a miserable social situation, but also have horrible personalities, which makes their own lives harder too.

This balance is not missing entirely from the last three films either. Just as in the previous films, the characters' attitudes in *The Man from London* as well as *The Turin Horse* do not easily generate sympathy. All of the main characters in both films are uncommunicative, closed and rude to others. They do not do much they can be disliked for, but they also do very little they can be liked for. But since their acts do not make much difference to their situation, there is not much opportunity for the narration to play with the viewer's contradictory emotions. Much of the compassion the viewer may have for them stems from their hopeless situation. Maloin's act of taking the money cannot be considered as stealing, especially given the fact that he knows that the person who claims this money committed a serious crime to get hold of it, so supposedly, he is not the owner of the money either. If the viewer does not like him it is not because he took the money; it is rather because of the way he treats his wife, and the fact that the viewer can see Brown's helplessness. On the other hand, in several scenes we can see Maloin's inner struggle with his own conscience (for example when he nervously pulls and pushes the switch levers, or when he wakes up in the evening fearing he will see Brown), for which the viewer sympathises with him, because he did not commit a crime, and the poverty of his family is manifest. The same swing between sympathy and antipathy characterises *The Turin Horse*: we do not like these characters but deeply sympathise with them on account of their miserable situation.

Werckmeister Harmonies is the only exception in this respect. As I mentioned already in the previous chapter, this is Tarr's only film where it becomes possible for the viewer to identify with the main character without serious reservations. Valuska is Tarr's only good and entirely harmless character who becomes a victim without having done wrong, and without having been rude to anybody.

Personal traits

One of the constants of the Tarr characters is that their personal traits carry no reference to their past. In a few films there is some information about some past events of the lives of some of the characters, but this information never carries any weight regarding our understanding of the given character. There is mention of András's childhood in *The Outsider*; there is a story about the suicide of Karrer's wife in *Damnation*; and finally, there is mention of Irimiás's and Petrina's lives as vagabonds in *Satantango*. In all of Tarr's films the characters live in the present with no past and no future. This way of handling the characters' personalities is typical of the direct-cinema-style films and their concern with social issues. Even though only two early Tarr films could be characterised as belonging to this category, Tarr's character formation remained the same all through his career.

One obvious explanation can be found in the circular thinking. If Tarr wants to show that his characters are stuck in a situation from which there is no escape, there is definitely no need to evoke the past, since the past does not contribute to the understanding of the present. What we see is the same as was always there, and what will be forever.

Another explanation, not unrelated to the previous one, focuses on the fact that Tarr's characters are not depicted with psychological depth in spite of the fact that, especially in the early period, the films are based on personal relationships manifested in dialogue rather than in acts. The reason for this apparent paradox is that the communication of Tarr's characters consists in manipulation and power games rather than in changes of ideas or expression of feelings. As a result, no matter how long we listen to a character's monologue or dialogue, the real personality of the character remains hidden. When characters talk about themselves the goal is most of the time to manipulate someone else; otherwise they either fight or talk nonsense.

This is most palpable in *Almanac of Fall*. The characters have very intimate conversations with each other, which could be an occasion for them to open up, to be sincere, and to inform each other and the viewer about their innermost feelings and thoughts. Instead, they use intimacy to reach the position in the hierarchy they want to reach. They use different means to achieve their goals, but fundamentally they are very similar to each other. All of them are basically determined, reckless, unscrupulous and sly. And regardless of their age and sex, each of them is ready to use physical violence if they think it is necessary. Probably the two most honest and straightforward characters of all Tarr films are András from *The Outsider* and Valuska from *Werckmeister Harmonies*. However, we do not know much about them either, because András's main traits are indecision and inconsistency, and Valuska does not speak of himself at all. In sum, if Tarr decides that his characters' human contacts consist primarily of manipulation, power games and fighting, there is no need for him to go too much into the details of the characters' psychological lives and pasts.

Another general trait of the Tarr characters is their fundamental sensibility. No matter how manipulative, mean or violent they are, most of them have a dream or desire, which finally causes them to fall. This aspect of the Tarr characters is mainly characteristic of the second-period films. One can think of Karrer's desperate love in *Damnation*; the settler's naïve, almost religious faith in Irimiás; Valuska's innocence and Mr. Eszter's fantasy about the absolute pure tones; and finally Maloin's honesty. However, we can find some elements of this in some of the early films too. András's artistic talent, which makes him different and sensitive, but cannot develop, in *The Outsider*; Laci's weak personality and his dependence on his despotic father in *Family Nest*; Judit's desire to do something with her life in *The Prefab People*. The two films where this aspect of the characters is missing are *Almanac of Fall* and *The Turin Horse*. In the first film the characters' expression of their desires cannot be taken seriously, firstly because their only purpose with their conversation is to manipulate their companions, and secondly because none of them ends up in a worse position at the end of the story, except Tibor, the outsider. It is noteworthy that it is him who speaks the most and most eloquently about his desire to become a good person. In *The Turin Horse* the characters basically do not speak, and so the viewer does not have any information about their inner lives. Although there is not such a direct relationship between personal vulnerability and the final downfall in the early Tarr films as in the Krasznahorkai stories, the same character structure exists in these films too. This shows again the close relationship between Tarr's and Krasznahorkai's visions, which has made their cooperation so easy.

In many of the second-period films Tarr's characters seem to be displaced. I talked about this effect at some length with regard to *Satantango*, where this is the most apparent. Three films are concerned with this: *Damnation*, *Satantango* and *Werckmeister Harmonies*. In these films one or more characters talk or look like someone coming from another world. The man reciting a poem in the run-down and dirty community place during the small-town evening party to a woman apparently not of his kind is the clearest example of this effect. But the checkroom attendant is also a mysterious person definitely not of her environment. In *Satantango*, as pointed out earlier, the faces of the characters betray their appertaining to someplace else, not the social and cultural environment where they are, and this is particularly true regarding Irimiás. In *Werckmeister Harmonies* Mr. Eszter definitely does not belong to this world, and Valuska's fine, naïve and poetic attitude indicates he also belongs to another world, which is also manifest in the fact that he cannot cope with what happens around him and collapses mentally.

Most of Tarr's characters are in a marginalised position. Not only are they marginalised socially, but they also choose to be outsiders even in their own marginalised social group. Most often these characters assume a passive observer position. András in *The Outsider*, Karrer in *Damnation*, the doctor in *Satantango*, Valuska in *Werckmeister Harmonies* and Maloin in *The Man from London* are cases in point. In the case of the doctor and of Maloin the observer position is manifested in a literal sense too. The doctor does nothing but scrutinise the others and make note of what he sees, and Maloin has a tower from which he can see everything that happens around him. I have discussed András's outsider situation in detail already, and Karrer is also an outsider who has no connection to the world other than his hopeless love for the singer. This is how he puts it:

> Something tells me that the next moment I'll go mad, but I don't go mad the next moment, and I have no fear of going mad because fear of madness would require me to cling to something. Yet I don't cling to anything, I cling to nothing but everything seems to cling to me, wanting me to take notice, to see the hopelessness of things.

Attachment problems of this kind are very typical traits of more than half of the Tarr protagonists. This problem is in one way or another central in all of the early Tarr films. András in *The Outsider* is the epitome of this. Laci's weak personality also suffers from this problem. It is part of Robi's problem in *The Prefab People* too, and obviously all of the characters suffer from alienation and self-centredness in *Almanac of Fall*, even though they keep making speeches to the contrary. In *Satantango,* in *Werckmeister Harmonies* and in *The Turin Horse* this problem is not relevant, since no intimate human relationship appears in the stories, and any desire for it is missing too. In *The Man from London,* however, it reappears in the rude and aggressive communication lacking any tenderness between Maloin and his wife. It can be asserted that whenever Tarr represents couples, their relationship is cold, alienated, rude and aggressive.

In the first-period films the human relations between the characters are much more detailed. In fact those films are built upon the dynamics of personal relations. The dynamics of relations are not missing from the second-period films either, except probably *The Turin Horse*, but the relationships are simpler, much less detailed and do not change. There is some development in the relationships between the characters, which contributes to the circular structure. Irén and Laci, although they were not separated in the beginning, have not lived together for two years, and they end up separated. András finishes his relationship with his wife, having left his relationship with his girlfriend at the beginning of the film. Robi and Judit find themselves in the same situation in the end, and even the breaking up scene is almost the same. The company in *Almanac of Fall* go through violent fights, but finally they end up creating new alliances with each other. All of these characters go through a series of conflicts with each other which provides the dynamic for the narrative, and in the end they find themselves in a similar situation to that they were in at the start. This is true in a certain way for *Damnation* too. This story is also driven by the dynamics of the relationship between Karrer and the singer, although their relationship is stagnant, and it does not vary during the film. (The fact that she sometimes goes to bed with Karrer and sometimes does not is not a sign of change in their relationship; this is how they live.) From *Satantango* on, the stories are no longer constructed upon the dynamics of personal relationships. The characters have a specified way of communicating with one another, which does not change during the story, and has little influence on what is happening. The characters are mostly rude to each other, and their relationships are merely instrumental. Love, tenderness, compassion, curiosity and confidence are missing from them. The relationship in which there is the most tenderness is the relationship between Mr. Eszter and Valuska.

From all of this we can conclude that Tarr is certainly less interested in personal relationships in the second part of his career than in the early period, which does not mean that he is less interested in his characters. Despite the less detailed characterisation, his compassionate attitude toward the suffering of his characters is not any weaker than it was in the beginning of his career. *The Turin Horse* clearly demonstrates this.

Character dynamics

It follows from the circular construction that Tarr's characters do not develop during the story. This is, however, not a trait unique to Tarr. Lack of character development is an important element of specific currents of the modernist art-film tradition. It is particularly typical of modern French cinema – especially the films of Bresson, Resnais and Godard – and of much of the New German Cinema, in many respects a national variant on the French New Wave. It is less typical in Italian cinema. Neither the films of Antonioni nor those of Pasolini lack some character development, and lack of character development characterises the films of Fellini starting only from the end of the 1960s. Tarr's own references to Godard and Fassbinder are telling of his methods in this respect too.

There are some slight differences between the individual films, however. The films in which there is no character development whatsoever are *The Outsider*, *The Prefab People*, *Almanac of Fall*, *Satantango* and *The Turin Horse*. In all of these films the characters manifest their most important traits early in the story, and not only do they not change, but no important traits come out later on either. Take the example of Irimiás from *Satantango*.

Irimiás is one of the most complex characters in all the Tarr films. He is a conman but he has several positive or remarkable traits that allow him to deceive people. He is very intelligent, he is calm, he has a real talent for making speeches and convincing people, and he has an unquestionable sense for poetry and for philosophy. He can see through people easily, which allows him to manipulate them. On the other hand he is arrogant and unpredictable, he has contempt for everyone around him, he is an unscrupulous liar, he is a potential terrorist, and he has no compassion for others. The second chapter of the film starts by introducing Irimiás and Petrina. The first thing we hear from Irimiás is a surprising observation about the different clocks on the wall and a poetic commentary about time:

> The two clocks show different times. Both wrong of course. This one here is too slow. The other, as if it showed the perpetuity of defencelessness. We relate to it as twigs to the rain: we cannot defend ourselves.

The film introduces Irimiás as a very interesting and remarkable character. After chapter one, when the other characters talk about him as their saviour, the viewer's first impression is also something rather positive. But very soon all of this turns into the opposite feeling, and one comes to understand that in reality this calm and philosophical subtlety is the source of Irimiás's deceptive power. Right after this scene we learn that Irimiás and Petrina are criminals and that they have also become undercover agents. In the subsequent pub scene they turn out to be dangerous and violent. All of Irimiás's complex and paradoxical character is revealed in this chapter. After chapter two he does not surprise the viewer any more; we just continue to enjoy his poetic speech and admire his manipulative skills, while at the same time being appalled by his cruel unscrupulousness.

The films in which there is some degree of character development are *Family Nest*, *Damnation*, *Werckmeister Harmonies* and *The Man from London*. Among these films *Werckmeister Harmonies* is the only one in which the main character goes through a considerable change during the film, even if this change is nothing other than his becoming mentally ill. In the rest of these films the main characters undergo some kind of shift at the end of the story which does not represent a real personality change; still they behave like never before. Laci bursts into tears, which we did not expect based on his earlier behaviour. Karrer reports his friends to the police, so destroying everything around him, including his own dreams. And after having ignored and avoided Brown, Maloin suddenly becomes compassionate and brings food to him in the shed, which causes the tragedy.

None of these changes come as a result of a progressive development of the characters, stemming from their reactions to the change in the environment. The only film where there is some progression indicating some change is again *Werckmeister Harmonies*, where two scenes preceding the second hospital scene can be interpreted as indicating such change. One is the scene in the ravaged hardware store, where Valuska, sitting on the floor, is reading something like a diary of the cruel vandalism perpetrated in the town; the other is the scene on the railway track with the mysterious helicopter hovering in front of him. In neither scene does Valuska explicitly manifest any quality radically different from before, but the inadequacy of his perception of the world is of the kind that can only be attributed to psychosis. Realistically one cannot imagine that someone in the brutal and barbarian mob lynching and killing people, destroying everything around them and setting fire to a whole town, is writing a diary in a very literary style, all while a helicopter, clearly a paranoiac hallucination, is hovering above him. In the rest of the films nothing predicts any change in the characters' behaviour, and when such change does suddenly occur, it indicates not the possibility of positive change but rather a break-down whereby the circle closes.

In conclusion we can say that Tarr's characters are rather unchanging from beginning to end. They are characterised by only a few traits, which are developed entirely in the beginning, and in the rest of the story they just try to survive, without trying to reflect on or adapt to the circumstances. All of them are in a precarious social situation, and they are not in possession of the moral or mental tools with which to improve their situation. The only plans they can think of to get into a better position are carried out at the expense of others, which makes their communication a process of constant fighting and manipulation: a power game. They are extremely vulnerable psychologically and socially, which makes their incapability at the level of cooperative human communication another obstacle in handling their own difficulties. This latter detail is what makes the viewer watch them from a distance, judging their acts when they do wrong, but never judging their entire personality, which is the source of the quality they all share and what is most important for Tarr to express: their human dignity.

In the depths of the Tarr films

One may like many things in the Tarr films. In my opinion all of his films explore the same basic problem: the problem of human dignity in extreme moral and existential circumstances, which makes a moralising attitude impossible. These films represent an existential situation from which there is no escape, which is in itself demoralising, and which is rendered even more serious by moral failures. Tarr represents those characters in situations who are at the terminal phase of their struggle for saving their human dignity. They are about to lose this struggle, and their survival has long ago been taken out of their hands, but as long as they live, they try to save their dignity.

In the Tarr films human dignity is not based on morality. It is based on the fact that in spite of their absolutely hopeless and desperate situations the characters remain what they are, however low what they are brings them. Eventually, this can go as far as self-destruction, like in *Damnation* and *Satantango*. But Maloin's dignity is also hidden in his 'weakness', inasmuch as he feels pity towards Brown, and after the tragedy he cannot help giving back the money. Tarr is able to eliminate Simenon's moralising sentimentality at the end, because the story would be about Maloin's human dignity even with this ending, only this ending emphasises more the origin of the dignity in Maloin's weakness.

Most viewers of the Tarr films find these films 'depressing' and 'negative'. In 2011 on the occasion of a screening of *The Turin Horse* for the participants of a conference, someone from the audience asked the usual question:

'Why are your films so pessimistic?' Tarr's answer was a question:
'Tell me if after the film you felt stronger or weaker?'
'I felt stronger' was the answer.
'Thank you. You answered your own question.'

If we consider only the topics and the circumstances of the narratives of the Tarr films, there is nothing to see but negativity and excessive hopelessness. If we consider Tarr's characters, something else appears, which might be the source of the catharsis of these films. Human dignity means the same thing at the deepest bottom of hopelessness as it does in more lucky circumstances. One can always have a chance to continue to live a life full of hope and dreams, as if these circumstances did not exist, while all the time bearing in mind the last sentence of *The Turin Horse*: 'One must eat.'

Hotel Magnezit
The reason why this short film from the early period is discussed in the last section of this book is because this is the film where Tarr's attitude toward his characters appears in the most concise and powerful way. This fact proves also that this attitude was the basis of his filmmaking credo right from the beginning and in whatever circumstances

and genres he worked. *Hotel Magnezit* is an approximately twelve-minute short film which was a second-year film school assignment which required him to make a television play. This was the only time Tarr worked in a studio, but Tarr used his then-usual improvisation style with everyday people, and one of the actors was a former colleague of his from the shipyard.

The film consists of a single scene in a dormitory of a workers' hostel. One of the inhabitants is being officially banned from the hostel because of some theft he admittedly committed, allegedly together with his comrades. The story runs from the point where the decision is communicated to him up to the point where he leaves the dorm. The man is startled by the fact that he is banned and tries to defend himself, calling on his roommates to rescue him. Instead of defending him, they start to put the blame on him. They immediately claim he owes them money, and one of them wants to occupy his bed too. Very soon, he finds himself all alone among the mates who he works with, who he goes to the pub with, and who were his accomplices in the theft. As the argument develops he finds himself more and more isolated and humiliated, and the question now is not whether or not he can keep his place in the dorm, but whether or not he is able to leave the dorm with dignity. We learn that he is a one-time air force officer, and now he has not only lost everything he had in his life, but is considered as the lowest of those of the lowest possible social status, humiliated by those he still has around him. In the end he bursts into tears, pulling a piece of paper out of his wallet to prove that in fact he was an air force officer. This film is about a man's desperate struggle to save the remnants of his dignity in spite of the circumstances and the people around him. This man has fallen out of the society of 'honourable' people, and the last token of his lost status is this piece of paper proving that once he was a respectable person. As he cannot save his place, all he wants is to leave the room with honour. Since this scene has no narrative context, the film illustrates more than any other what is the most important issue in all Tarr films: the struggle to save human dignity.

The author's point of view

All of this, as I pointed out in the introduction, is the point of view of a viewer, and no doubt a privileged viewer for that matter. If this were a critical essay, a reference to this personal aspect would suffice to make this point valid, even if it did not meet another viewer's point of view. This book, however, describes, comments on and interprets Tarr's films in relation to his whole oeuvre, and in this respect the author's point of view does not seem negligible, as much as it is available. It is particularly important in the case where a given viewer's point of view clashes with the intent of the author. In this particular case I cannot deny that the way I formulate my feelings and judgements of the characters is not identical to the way the authors of these films would do. It seems to me necessary to briefly comment on this discrepancy, since we are talking about the most fundamental issue of the Tarr films, and because it is possible that another viewer's approach may be closer to the author's approach than mine.

I have expressed my opinion several times in this book that Tarr's characters – with the exception of Valuska and András – are not likable, and the main point of this chapter was that despite this, these films still manage to create empathy towards them, which is the foundation of the viewer's feeling of respect for their human dignity. I think that the great artistic power of the Tarr films is partly a result of this tension. It became clear from my conversations with Tarr and Hranitzky that they think the concepts of 'respect' and 'dignity' are too weak, and do not capture what they think the viewer should feel. Their intention regarding their characters is more than that: it is the expression of love. They do not talk only about their subjective feelings for their characters and the people who inspired them. It is important for them that their emotional attachment be felt in the films too. They refuse the idea of any distance from their characters (the existence of this distance is an important claim of this book).

When I talked with Tarr about this discrepancy, he came to the conclusion that it may be the result of differences in personal attitude. Those who feel any distance do not perceive the films *per se*; they interpret it rather with the bias of their bourgeois or petty bourgeois mentality. So, the distance is not in the films; it is a given viewer's attitude towards people in such existential situations. Bourgeois values are for him the expression of the distance from lower social classes, and of the idea that mere possession of material goods makes someone more valuable. Tarr's opinion is that the world is unjust, because the world of the lower classes is as rich as that of those at the top of the hierarchy. They emphasise that they like to be among these people, and they want to express this emotional relationship in the films.

Now the question is whether we are merely talking about a difference in spectatorial attitude or about a discrepancy between authorial intention and the impact of the work of art. Or, even more interestingly, whether we are talking about very special attitude by the authors which they call 'love', but which does not cover the everyday usage of this word. I think that the third option is the most likely one.

It would be hard to think about this in terms of a difference between spectatorial attitudes, since on one side we have the author's opinion and on the other side we have a spectator's opinion. The author's feelings in this case are based on his own intentions rather than on the impact of the work. This means the difference between intention and the realisation of the intention. This is the second option. But this option does not have a lot of explanatory power, because unrealized authorial intentions usually result in falling short of a powerful artistic impact. It is very unlikely that as self-conscious and extremely careful an author as Tarr would achieve such a powerful effect unknowingly, just by chance. The third option is very simply that what Tarr means by 'love' is something different from that suggested by the everyday meaning of this word. What Tarr is talking about here is a political conviction, a subjective and emotional translation of a social responsibility for the outcast, the helpless and the poor which is so strong that it becomes a personal engagement. The feeling of 'love' is the subjective expression of this engagement. It is not the 'love' we talk about in ordinary life when we refer to an intimate bond between people. It is a political role Tarr has considered as his own ever since his adolescence. It is more than a political conviction. It is a real human relationship, even if it does not involve specific people. Tarr actually likes to be among these people, he talks their language, and he can inspire confidence. Ágnes Hranitzky put it this way: 'When Béla enters into a village pub five minutes later a drunken giant will hug him and cries on his shoulders.'[2] Being poor and being an outcast and marginalised is a personal matter for Tarr; it is not only a social situation but rather a psychological state that can be the result of any kind of a situation.

One might wonder what this attitude is based on, since neither Tarr nor Hranitzky comes from this social environment, they do not live this kind of lifestyle, and their value system is different. Except for the two years when Tarr worked in the shipyard, he has never lived in a proletarian environment, and these people never see his films. Tarr's answer to this is that he understands life and himself better when he is among these people. In this, he has not changed a bit since his youth, when he visited workers' hostels to show his films to the workers. This is what he wants to say in his films, and he does this with full devotion and emotional identification. This answer confirms again that here we are concerned rather with a political approach at the foundation of which there is a psychological identification. This identification is not political, but deeply personal, the source of which is beyond the scope of this book.

This attitude is similar to the attitude of one of his favourite directors, Fassbinder. The main theme of Fassbinder's early films is the feeling of being emotionally rejected, whatever the source of this may be: social situation, sexual orientation or cultural identity. Fassbinder's early cinema is fundamentally informed by the suffering caused by emotional coldness, and this remains an important topic even later on. In his *Merchant of Four Seasons* (1971) what particularly hurts the protagonist, Hans Epp, who is despised by his family, is his mother's emotional rejection. It is no wonder that Fassbinder very quickly arrived at the genre of classical melodrama. One can feel a similar empathy for the pain caused by emotional coldness in Tarr's films too. However, with the possible exception of *Werckmeister*, the emotional identification with the heroes is not as direct as in Fassbinder's films. Tarr's are not melodramatic heroes; their suffering and their emotions are more hidden and covered by a struggle for dominance. We never see the Tarr heroes as helpless and emotionally desperate as the heroes of Fassbinder. Tarr's heroes never collapse as deeply as some of the Fassbinder protagonists, because they always try to defend themselves as if they have some hidden agenda, even if they do not. They always pretend that they have some control even when in fact they do not, and, with the exception of Karrer, they never beg for love. They never uncover themselves entirely; they always keep something hidden that seems to keep them on the surface. It is very telling that when some of them in fact collapse (as in *Family Nest* and *The Prefab People*), the film immediately simulates an interview situation; that is, the author immediately steps outside the emotional situation, giving it a form in which he only records the outflow of the emotions, and stops identifying with it. This is what I mean by the difference between identification through 'love' and the distance comprised in the representation of 'human dignity'.

What Tarr and Hranitzky call 'love' for their heroes is in my opinion a result of an attitude that is politically left wing and aesthetically avant-garde, which finds its source in early 1970s leftist cultural critique. Tarr has identified with this attitude from the beginning of his career. This 'love' is an identification with the social position of the outcast and the socially helpless, a moral interiorisation of this position, which was for a very long time the position Tarr chose most often in his profession, as mentioned in chapter one.[3] It is this position that Tarr likes, and he feels the people close to him –

not necessarily in person – bear this position with dignity. Refusing melodrama is the source of the dignifying quality of this situation. The aesthetic price Tarr has to pay is that his films lack emotional warmth; the benefit is that the social aspect remains very strong. Tarr's films are never melodramatic. What creates a distance from the characters is the documentary style in the first period and the circular structure in the second. One way to say it is that Tarr is probably more shy than Fassbinder in terms of overt emotions; another way is that we come into contact with the characters through their complex cultural and social positions, which makes the direct emotional contact weaker. First we see them in their social positions and then we realise their human relations. Not to mention the irony that is felt in more than one second-period film.

That this dilemma is not only my invention is shown in an interview conducted with Tarr in 2011:

Q: For me the most exciting thing in your films is that I can never decide which is their deepest level: the love or the dark hopelessness. Can you comment on this?

T: I cannot tell either. I would say that both have to be present, because if only the first one is present, it will generate kitsch, if only the second is there, it is just pure frightening. One is worthless without the other. And people have both. Everybody has some likable qualities and at the same time the darkest immorality can also be found in them. It is a question of circumstances. We become dirty by the power of constraints, and if there are no constraints, freedom brings out some good from everyone. (…)

Q: I feel that love mentioned earlier is less and less found in your films. Do you agree?

T: No. Also, because when we make a film, we like the people we work with. Shooting has generally a good atmosphere, this film was also very good to make. And this atmosphere can be seen on the screen too. If there is an actor who I like, such as János Derzsi, Erika Bók or Mihály Kormos, I cannot film them so that the love is imperceptible. You don't have to say this, but this is what gives the film a secret tension. In *Almanac of Fall* the characters were ready to kill each other, to destroy each other entirely. And even in this film there is the other side too in that they are thrown together and love each other.[4]

Several things can be remarked on in these excerpts. First, Tarr himself has some amount of uncertainty with regard to the weight the idea of 'love' has against 'desperation'. Although in this particular phrasing he does not talk about identification versus distance, he accepts that expression of love is not that dominant and unambiguous. Second, in the second part, he does not speak about the characters of his films but rather about the actors who play them as the objects of his emotions. This misses the point, since nobody questions Tarr's and Hranitzky's feelings for their actors. The question is about their characters. Third, the last sentence interprets the word 'love' in a very strange way. Tarr talks about 'being thrown together' and love in the same way, which is odd, because in everyday parlance love is something other than being constrained together and dependent on each other through this constraint. Being thrown together in spite of their mutual wish to destroy each other is a real trap situation, however, and the most current in the Tarr films. But it is very odd to say that someone is ready to destroy another person entirely, yet still loves him or her.

To conclude, it is my opinion that Tarr exposes a dual moral situation in his films. This is based on the understanding of the bad deeds of people constrained in bad situations, inasmuch as he considers these acts as the consequence of the circumstances. It is in spite of this that he presents his characters as having a dignity equal to that of 'good people' living in more fortunate circumstances. The authors' positive emotion is a result of a personal empathy for and understanding of this moral situation.

Notes

1   Fellini had this theme in his pre-modernist period in the 1950s and utilised the classical melodrama form for it. *La strada* (1955) is the most typical example.
2   Personal conversation.
3   Ironically, he keeps this marginalised position even as the president of the Hungarian Filmmakers Association. He was elected president just when this organisation had come into conflict with the Hungarian government on the subject of a new film financing system. Until 2010 this association was politically very powerful, and Tarr was not involved with it in many ways. When the association became politically marginalised, Tarr became its president; in other words his politically marginalised position has not changed very much.
4   Bújdosó Bori: *Tarr Béla: filmmel semmit nem lehet elérni.* http://www.origo.hu/filmklub/blog/interju/ekskuziv/20110215-tarr-bela-filmmel-semmit-nem-lehet-elerni-interju-a.html.

Conclusion

In about 1986 Béla Tarr jokingly remarked on his festival participation: 'Since I have become Béla Tarr, I am treated decently on international festivals.' In Hungarian the first name and the family name are in reverse order as compared to other European languages; that is, the family name comes first and the given name comes second. So, when Hungarians address a foreigner they usually reverse the order of their names, so that the foreigner knows which is which. When we see or hear a Hungarian name written or uttered in reverse order, we know that the person evoked either is an expatriate or is mentioned in a foreign context. 'Becoming Béla Tarr' stood for 'now having an international reputation'. Somehow, this *bon mot* was retained in my mind, probably because it signalled an important split in the role Béla Tarr has played on the Hungarian and on the international stage. At the time Tarr was gaining an international reputation and growing in status, his acceptance at home was far from being comparable to the respect he enjoyed abroad. For about sixteen years Béla Tarr was not the same as Tarr Béla.

For the international art-film audience the names of three Hungarian filmmakers may sound familiar: Miklós Jancsó, István Szabó and Béla Tarr. For those in the audience that have appreciated the contemporary cinema of the last twenty years, there is only one name: Béla Tarr.

In 2002 a panel of seven British film critics named the forty best art-film directors in the world.[1] Béla Tarr, the only Hungarian on the list, is at 13th place, before masters like Lars von Trier, Kitano Takeshi, Alexander Sokurov, Michael Haneke, Aki Kaurismaki, Quentin Tarantino, Pedro Almodovar and Wong Kar-Wai. Ranking is not that significant. Being listed with these names is indeed.

One can always claim that such lists are ephemeral, subjective and one-sided, but if we have a closer look at the list, three things become striking: first, the top five places are occupied by American filmmakers; second, names such as Godard, Resnais, Antonioni and Bergman are missing from it. To be sure, Antonioni had been inactive for a long time by that time; Bergman not so much, but he also had withdrawn from the international film market since 1982. But Godard and Resnais were active contemporary filmmakers, and they still are. The third thing one can say is that there are two British directors on the list in the top eleven. All of this leads to the conclusion that one cannot claim that this list reflects an elitist, old-fashioned modernist art-film taste, and that it even may show a specific national sensitivity too. If this list is biased, it is certainly not in a way which would easily favour the kind of films Tarr makes.

In 2007 fifty-one American film critics and academics were asked to compose a list of the top twenty-five non-English-language films of all time.[2] From the fifty-one lists a list of a hundred films was composed according to the frequency of the films on the individual lists. *Satantango*, the only Hungarian film, is the 97th on the list.

In 2000, a list of the 'best 12 Hungarian films', composed by Hungarian film critics, did not contain any films by Béla Tarr.

Such lists, just like festival awards, obviously cannot be taken seriously as guarantees of aesthetic quality. They represent a momentary general aesthetic taste, which may change considerably from time to time and from country to country. But the discrepancy between the appreciation of Tarr's films on the international and on the national level is striking. And I am not talking about the discrepancy between an elite's taste and the popular taste. This would be obvious and needs no explanation. What I am talking about here is a discrepancy within a Hungarian art-film audience, which right from the appearance of the Tarr style in 1988 became divided about its value. I mentioned already in chapter one that during the 1988 Hungarian Film Week *Damnation* received incredibly negative comments from the jury while, at the same, receiving the international critics award. And this was not the only case. In 2001 a controversy appeared in the Hungarian press in which some young critics, on the occasion of the release of *Werckmeister Harmonies*, attacked not only Tarr, but also the critics who had been sympathetic to Tarr's works over the past years.[3] Until about the middle of the 2000s Tarr not only was ignored in the wider context of Hungarian film culture but on occasions was subject to harsh and passionate attacks too. Even in 2008 on the occasion of the 39th Hungarian Film Week, *The Man from London*, the only imaginable candidate, was not accepted to be the opening film of the festival by the board of directors.[4] What is responsible in the Tarr films for such a curious discrepancy, which means that the only Hungarian filmmaker receiving high-prestige awards and recognition in a given period is ignored and damned in his own country?

On both occasions those criticising Tarr mentioned the unconditional and absolutely negative attitude with which Tarr creates his stories and represents the world. Obviously, nobody could claim that the negative attitude these critics see in Tarr's films is just an illusion. This book has listed a number of arguments underpinning the opinion that the general atmosphere of Tarr's films has indeed a considerable negative ingredient in it. The narration is slow; the environment represented is poor, shabby, dirty and run-down; and the stories' atmosphere is bleak. The characters are sad and frightened; they often suffer and often cause others to suffer; nobody in any of the films smiles or laughs; and nobody is cheerful. The visual atmosphere is dark, with no colours. The stories do not develop, just turn in cirlces, and there is no hope in them for anybody.

The difference is definitely not to be found in the fact that those who like the Tarr films cannot see their depressing side. It may appear as though the difference in the appreciation of these films is to be found in the personal attitude of the appreciator, whether or not he or she likes this particular atmosphere. This could be the case indeed, but to argue for this seriously, we would have to make a psychological survey of the different viewers of the Tarr films. Not to mention that the discrepancy between national and international appreciation definitely cannot be explained by this psychological factor, unless we claim that international critics like more depressive films than most of their Hungarian colleagues.

We could also say that probably the image Tarr makes of the world, which is composed of sceneries that vividly remind us of the Hungarian landscape, is offensive to someone living in Hungary and having very different everyday experiences. The only real experience a foreigner may have of Hungary, on the other hand, may be what he or she can see in these films, so he or she may not find the films in any way offensive, not living in Hungary, and may consider only the aesthetic quality of the films. This claim is also not entirely ungrounded, although no official explicit statements that I know of can corroborate it. In private, many people have this view, and some of Tarr's own statements may support this stance. When in an interview he was told that his films are often about ugly landscapes and ugly people, he said: 'That is my nation.'[5] It is well known that Tarr was nominated in 2002 for the highest national decoration which is awarded by the government, which, conservative and nationalist at the time, rejected Tarr's nomination. He obtained the decoration a year later, when another government was in power. This shows that even though the Tarr films can in no way be regarded as political, there exists a view that identifies their radically negative attitude with an opinion expressed about the nation. And on this view the national sentiment overrules aesthetic quality.

Someone could also argue that, after all, foreign critics are not unanimous either in highly appreciating Tarr; there are just many more foreign critics than Hungarians, and those who like the Tarr films mainly work at high-prestige, high-visibility newspapers or film journals, just like their Hungarian colleagues, among whom those who like Tarr also usually work at the elite film magazines. According to this argument the reason why Tarr's international reputation developed earlier than his national recognition is that this elite taste is stronger outside of Hungary than it is inside Hungary. This is also partly true. In Hungary Tarr has a very restricted audience, even among high-brow intellectuals, which in a small country such as Hungary means really just a handful of people.

Taking all of the above into account, we still need an explanation for Tarr's outstanding international reputation.

One part of the answer could be that Tarr did not just make 'interesting' or 'good' films. He created an original version of stylistic features that are part of recognisable and important international art-film currents. Inexpressive acting and quasi-religious dialogues: Bresson; slowness and partly static compositions: Ozu, Bresson and Tarkovsky; long takes: Antonioni, Jancsó and Angelopoulos; complicated continuous camera movements: Resnais, Jancsó and Angelopoulos; self-reflective citations: Godard; representation of cruel human relations without psychology: Fassbinder. The first thing a critic with a taste for international art-film culture would see in *Damnation* at the end of the 1980s was that this film reached back to the great period of modernist art cinema, but was not a follower of any single current. It created a style that was familiar yet never seen before.

The other element is the 'added value' to this stylistic mixture, which was threefold. First, an incredibly grim, depressed atmosphere; second, a landscape entirely unknown to the international audience yet very typical of a geographical and historical region: Eastern Europe; and third, a historical situation: all of this appeared when international art-film culture had just started to rediscover the value of these elements in the films made in regions far from Western Europe: Iran, Taiwan, Hong Kong and Japan. Although Hungary was not part of these regions, it became exotic itself owing to the historical event of the collapse of the communist regimes in Eastern Europe. Thus Tarr was seen not as part of the good old European art cinema tradition, but as one of the first representatives of a globalised art cinema the centre of which was not France, Italy or Sweden any more, as had been the case from the beginning of film history, but countries outside of Europe or small European countries like Denmark and Hungary.

The third element is a consequence of all this. With Tarr's films a very strange form of realism emerged in art cinema. This form is unprecedented in European modernist art cinema. It consists of an accumulation of the effects of the real to the point where the real becomes exaggerated and starts creating strong negative emotions. Even in Hungary there is only one film that could be remotely compared to it. This is a 1979 film by András Jeles, *A kis Valentino*, which has run a totally opposite path to *Damnation*. It has received no international recognition whatsoever, but it has become a widely appreciated Hungarian cult art movie. With very different stylistic tools, Jeles also created an exaggeratedly sinister picture of society which simultaneously had a strong realist effect, but with the help of its stylistic tools it rendered the realist image visionary, creating strong subjective emotional effects without ever resorting to highly fictional or conventionally melodramatic narrative motifs. When asked in an interview why his films are full of mud and dirt, full of people getting drunk and falling over, Tarr's answer was: 'I would create the same impression if I made a movie about some other people. This is our nation. This is our role. That is what I see.'[6] This is a real world filtered through an admittedly subjective approach, which turns a specific social experience into a universal image about the world. Some films of Russian and Romanian cinema of the 2000s rely very much on the same structure, without Tarr's radical stylistic solutions. This kind of realism is not a correct and balanced representation of a social environment. It is an excessively biased, emotionally intensified vision of it, which at the same time remains remarkably close to the ground and never turns into surrealism. Tarr's utilising natural elements such as rain, wind and mud are good examples of this. Tarkovsky has often been mentioned in this book, and with reason. He also used these natural elements in his films, especially in his Russian films. However these elements have a very different role in the Tarkovsky films. They represent nature's blessing, the manifestation of a transcendental world. In the Tarr films rain is what it is for those who have no shelter: it makes life even harder. Wind is what it is for the poor: it dries up wells; it makes moving forward even more difficult. Mud is what it is: the lack of a civilized road, something that doesn't let people leave.

I claimed in the introduction that there is nothing Hungarian in Tarr's films of the second period. But what these films accomplished in the 1990s was not unprecedented in Hungary. The cinema of Miklós Jancsó in the late 1960s and early 1970s became widely known and acclaimed for a very similar set of reasons. For about ten years – from the mid-1960s to the mid-1970s – Jancsó's cinema represented Hungarian cinema's innovative spirit. Without entering into the details we can summarise the importance of Jancsó's films of this period as offering a style that radicalised a well-known international art-film tendency, the long-take continuity style initiated by Antonioni in the 1950s, and at the same time integrated it into typical and recognisable national traditions. This latter process involved using topics from national history and representing a characteristically Hungarian landscape. For the international audience Jancsó's films had an idiosyncratic regional atmosphere, expressed through the stylistic texture, which was one of the most prominent currents of international art cinema. On the other hand, the themes of these films – the turmoil of national history – were represented in a recognisable but unspecific way, so that they became atemporal and ahistorical, and could be transposed into very different national and historical contexts.

Tarr's method is very similar, with some important differences. He took the same track Jancsó took twenty-five years before him. He radicalised the long-take style again, but in a period when it was not a current practice. He also depicted a landscape which was very typical of a region, yet remained unspecific as regards concrete space and historical time. Tarr managed to reach the same level of universality, not on the level of national history as did Jancsó, but on the level of sociological representation, without ever eliminating the specific regional atmosphere. This is the reason why one can share Tarr's vision of Eastern Europe without having any knowledge about Eastern Europe, because Tarr's vision brings something universal of this region into relief: the image of the underdog, the image of a helpless life.

Notes

1   http://film.guardian.co.uk/features/page/0,11456,1082823,00.html
2   http://eddieonfilm.blogspot.com/2005/12/foreign-art.html
3   See *Magyar Narancs*, 13:14 (2001).
4   The official explanation was that due to 'logistical difficulties' it was decided not to have a screening at all at the opening ceremony, which was unprecedented in the past thirty-eight years. When, following this decision, Tarr announced that *The Man from London* would be premiered the day before the opening ceremony of the festival, the 'logistical difficulties' disappeared immediately. Now it was Tarr who refused to change his mind, and the film was screened independently of the Hungarian Film Week.

5   Jonathan Romney, 'Places off the Map', interview with Béla Tarr on the stage of the NFT in London. In: *Béla Tarr*. Published on the occasion of the retrospective of Béla Tarr's films at the MOMA in New York, 15 October 2001, p. 44.

6   Ibid. 45.

FILMOGRAPHY

Vendégmunkások (*Guest Workers*), 1971
(lost)
Amateur film

Az Utca Embere (*The Man of the Street*),
1975 (lost)
Amateur film

Családi Tűzfészek (*Family Nest*), 1977
B&W, 100 minutes, Balázs Béla Stúdió
Script: Béla Tarr. Cinematography: Ferenc
Pap, Barna Mihók. Editor: Anna Kornis.
Music: János Bródy, Mihály Móricz,
Szabolcs Szörényi, Béla Tolcsvay, László
Tolcsvay. Cast: László Horváth (Irén),
László Horváth (Laci), Gábor Kun
(Laci's father), Mrs. Gábor Kun (Laci's
mother), Gábor Kun Jr. (Laci's brother),
Irén Rácz (Irén's girlfriend), Mrs. János
Oláh (Valika), Mrs. János Szekeres
(Irén's sister-in-law), Krisztina Horváth
(Krisztike), József Korn (clerk), Dr.
Adrienn Kádár (paediatrician).

Hotel Magnezit, 1978
B&W, video, 12 minutes
Examination film

Cine Marxisme, 1979 (lost)
Examination film

Szabadgyalog (*The Outsider*), 1980
Colour, 122 minutes, MAFILM
Objektív Stúdió, Magyar Televízió
Co-author: Ágnes Hranitzky. Script: Béla
Tarr. Cinematography: Ferenc Pap,
Barna Mihók. Editor: Ágnes Hranitzky.
Music: András Szabó, Hobo Blues Band,
Minerva, Neoton Familia, Orchestra of
Tündér presszo and restaurants Ipoly
and Balassa, Balassagyarmat, Ludwig van
Beethoven. Cast: András Szabó (András),
Jolán Fodor (Kata), Imre Donkó
(Csotesz), Ferenc Jánossy (Kázmér, the
painter), István Balla (Balázs), Imre
Vass (worker), László Náton (a patient),
László Kistamás (a friend of András).

Macbeth, 1981 (lost)
Examination film

Diplomafilm, 1982
Colour, examination film, 41 minutes
Script: Béla Tarr. Cinematography: Barna
Mihók. Editor: Ágnes Hranitzky.
Consultant teachers: Miklós Szinetár,
János Dömölky. Cast: Judit Pogány
(Judit), Róbert Koltai (Robi), Gábor P.
Koltai (the child).

Panelkapcsolat (*The Prefab People*), 1982
B&W, 82 minutes, MAFILM Társulás
Stúdió
Co-author: Ágnes Hranitzky. Script: Béla
Tarr. Cinematography: Ferenc Pap, Barna
Mihók. Editor: Ágnes Hranitzky. Cast:
Judit Pogány (Judit), Róbert Koltai (Robi),
Gábor P. Koltai (the child), Kyri Ambrus
(singer), Barna Mihók (bartender).

Macbeth, 1982
Colour, TV play, 62 minutes, Magyar
Televízió
Script: Ágnes Hranitzky and Béla Tarr
after William Shakespeare's *Macbeth*.
Cinematography: Ferenc Pap, Buda
Gulyás. Music: András Szabó, Gépfolklor
Band. Set design: Lyvia Mátay.
Costumes: Emőke Csengeri. Director's
consultant: Ágnes Hranitzky. Cast:
György Cserhalmi (Macbeth), Erzsébet
Kútvölgyi (Lady Macbeth), János Ács,
Gyula Maár and József Ruszt (Witches),
Lajos Őze (Banquo), János Derzsi
(Macduff), Djoko Rosic (Duncan),
Miklós Székely B. (the killer), Ferenc
Bencze (the porter).

Őszi Almanach (*Almanac of Fall*), 1984
Colour, 115 minutes, MAFILM Társulás
Stúdió
Co-author: Ágnes Hranitzky. Script: Béla
Tarr. Cinematography: Sándor Kardos,
Ferenc Pap, Buda Gulyás. Editor: Ágnes
Hranitzky. Music: Mihály Víg. Set design
and costumes: Gyula Pauer. Cast: Hédi
Temessy (Hédi), Erika Bodnár (Anna),
Miklós Székely B. (Miklós), Pál Hetényi
(Tibor), János Derzsi (János).

Kárhozat (*Damnation*), 1987
B&W, 122 minutes, Magyar Hirdető,
Magyar Filmintézet, Magyar Televízió,
MOKÉP
Co-director: Ágnes Hranitzky. Script:
László Krasznahorkai, Béla Tarr.

Cinematography: Gábor Medvigy.
Editor: Ágnes Hranitzky. Music: Mihály
Víg. Set design and costumes: Gyula
Pauer. Cast: Miklós Székely B. (Karrer),
Vali Kerekes (singer), Hédi Temessy
(checkroom attendant), Gyula Pauer
(bartender), György Cserhalmi (the
singer's husband), Péter Breznyik Berg
(the man reciting a poem).

The Last Boat, 1989
Colour, 32 minutes, episode of *City Life*,
Rotterdam Films
Co-director: Ágnes Hranitzky. Script: László
Krasznahorkai, Béla Tarr (based on László
Krasznahorkai's short stories 'The Last
Boat' and 'In the Hands of the Barber').
Cinematography: Gábor Medvigy.
Editor: Ágnes Hranitzky. Music: Mihály
Víg, Wolfgang Amadeus Mozart. Cast:
Miklós Székely B., Michael Mehlmann,
László Kistamás, Gyula Pauer.

Sátántangó (*Satantango*), 1994
B&W, 430 minutes, Mozgókép
Innovációs Társulás, Joachim von
Vietinghoff Filmproduction, Vega Film
Co-director: Ágnes Hranitzky. Script:
László Krasznahorkai, Béla Tarr (after
László Krasznahorkai's novel *Sátántangó*).
Cinematography: Gábor Medvigy.
Editor: Ágnes Hranitzky. Music: Mihály
Víg. Design consultant: Gyula Pauer.
Set design: Sándor Kállay. Costumes:
Gyula Pauer, János Breckl. Cast: Mihály
Víg (Irimiás), Dr. Putyi Horváth
(Petrina), Miklós Székely B. (Futaki),
László feLugossy (Schmidt), Éva Almásy
Albert (Mrs. Schmidt), János Derzsi
(Kráner), Irén Szajki (Mrs. Kráner),
Alfréd Járai (Halics), Erzsébet Gaál (Mrs.
Halics), Erika Bók (Estike), György
Barkó (headmaster), Peter Berling (the
doctor), András Bodnár (Sanyi Horgos),
Ica Bojár (Mrs. Horgos), Péter Dobai
(the captain), Barna Mihók (Kelemen),

Zoltán Kamondi (bartender), István Juhász (Kerekes), Gyula Pauer (Payer), Mihály Ráday (narrator voice).
Producers: György Fehér, Joachim von Vietinghoff, Ruth Waldburger

Utazás Az Alföldön (*Journey on the Plain*), 1995
Colour, 35 minutes, Magyar Televízió
Co-director: Ágnes Hranitzky.
Cinematography: Fred Kelemen. Music: Mihály Víg. Reciting Sándor Petőfi's poems: Mihály Víg.

Werckmeister Harmóniák (*Werckmeister Harmonies*), 2000
B&W, 145 minutes, Goess Film, Von Vietinghoff Filmproduction, 13 Production
Co-director: Ágnes Hranitzky. Script: László Krasznahorkai, Béla Tarr (based on László Krasznahorkai's novel *Az ellenállás melankóliája*). Cinematography: Gábor Medvigy, Jörg Widmer, Patrick de Rander, Rob Tregenza, Emil Novák, Erwin Lanzensberger, Miklós Gurbán. Editor: Ágnes Hranitzky. Music: Mihály Víg. Costumes: János Breckl. Design consultant: Gyula Pauer. Cast: Lars Rudolph (Valuska), Peter Fritz (Mr. Eszter), Hanna Schygulla (Tünde), Péter Dobai (police captain), Alfréd Járai (Harrer), Irén Szajki (Mrs. Harrer), Ferenc Kállai (circus director), Gyula Pauer (Hagelmayer), Dr. Putyi Horváth (porter).
Producers: Franz Goess, Miklós Szita, Joachim von Vietinghoff, Paul Saadoun

Prologue
B&W, 5 minutes, episode of *Visions of Europe*, T.T. Filmműhely
Co-director: Ágnes Hranitzky.
Cinematography: Robby Müller. Music: Mihály Víg.
Producers: Béla Tarr, Gábor Téni

A Londoni Férfi (*The Man from London*), 2007
B&W, 132 minutes, T.T. Filmműhely, 13 Production, Cinema Soleil, Von Vietinghoff Filmproduction, Black Forest Film
Co-director: Ágnes Hranitzky. Script: László Krasznahorkai, Béla Tarr (based on Georges Simenon's novel *L'homme de Londres*). Cinematography: Fred Kelemen. Editor: Ágnes Hranitzky. Music: Mihály Víg. Set designer: László Rajk, Ágnes Hranitzky, Jean Pascal Chalard. Cast: Miroslav Krobot (Maloin), Tilda Swinton (Maloin's wife), János Derzsi (Brown), Ági Szirtes (Brown's wife), Erika Bók (Henriette), István Lénárt (Morrison), Gyula Pauer (bartender), Kati Lázár (shopkeeper).
Producers: Gábor Téni, Paul Saadoun, Joachim von Vietinghoff, Miriam Zachar, Cristoph Hahnheiser

A Torinói Ló (*The Turin Horse*), 2011
B&W, 146 minutes, T.T. Filmműhely, Vega Film, Zero Fiction Film, Movie Partners in Motion Film
Co-director: Ágnes Hranitzky. Script: László Krasznahorkai, Béla Tarr (based on László Krasznahorkai's texts *Legkésőbb Torinóban*, *Megjött Ézsaiás*, *Járás egy áldás nélküli térben* and *Megy a világ*). Cinematography: Fred Kelemen. Music: Mihály Víg. Editor: Ágnes Hranitzky. Cast: János Derzsi (the coachman), Erika Bók (his daughter), Mihály Kormos (the neighbour), Ricsi (the horse), Mihály Ráday (narrator voice).
Producers: Gábor Téni, Elisabeth Redleaf, Christine Walker, Ruth Waldburger, Marie-Pierre Macia, Juliette Leputre, Martin Hagemann

SELECT BIBLIOGRAPHY

The following is a bibliography of selected items I find crucial in the Tarr literature. A thorough international bibliography on Tarr can be found at: http://unspokencinema.blogspot.hu/2007/10/bla-tarr-links.html

Bálint Kenyeres: 'Interview with Béla Tarr'. *Metropolis*, summer, 1997.

Balsom, Erika: 'Saving the Image: Scale and Duration in Contemporary Art Cinema'. *CineAction*, 72, 2007.

Boháčková, Kamila (ed): *Béla Tarr* Praha: Edici Inicialy, 2010.

Bouquet, Stéphane: 'La splendeur de Béla Tarr'. *Cahiers du cinéma*, February, 1997.

Breton, Emile: Béla Tarr, 'le regard du maître'. *Cinéma*, 3, Spring, 2002.

Breton, Émile: 'Quelques jalons dans une oeuvre vouée au noir'. *Vertigo*, 41, 2011: p. 100.

Bújdosó Bori: 'Tarr Béla: filmmel semmit nem lehet elérni'. http://www.origo.hu/filmklub/blog/interju/exkluziv/20110215-tarr-bela-filmmel-semmit-nem-lehet-elerni-interju-a.html.

Buslowska, Elzbieta: 'Cinema as Art and Philosophy in Béla Tarr's Creative Exploration of Reality' Acta Univ. Sapientiae, *Film and Media Studies*, 1, 2009: p.107–16.

Chapron, Joël: 'Le cinéma hongrois rouvre un oeil'. *Cahiers du cinéma*, March, 2004.

Facets DVD: 'Talking about Tarr: A symposium at Facets'. Booklet for the Facets edition of *Satantango*, 2008.

Jánossy, Lajos: 'Egyszer jóllakni?'. *Magyar Narancs*, XIII: 4–5, April, 2001.

Jensen, Jytte *et al.*: *Béla Tarr*. Published on the occasion of the retrospective of Béla Tarr's films at the MOMA in New York, October 5–15, Filmunio, 2001. Authors: Jytte Jensen, Gus van Sant, Jim Jarmusch, Ulrich Gregor, Derek Elley, Jonathan Rosenbaum, Bérénice Reynaud, Jonathan Romney, Stéphane Bouquet, András Bálint Kovács.

Kovács, András Bálint: 'Egy műfajváltásról'. *Filmkultúra*, 1985/1: pp. 25–9.

Kovács, András Bálint (ed.): 'Monológok a Kárhozatról'. *Filmvilág*, 1988/2: p. 19.

Kovács, András Bálint: 'Sátántangó' in: Peter Hames (ed), *The Cinema of Central Europe*. London: Wallflower Press, 2004. pp. 237–45.

Kovács, András Bálint: 'The World According to Tarr' in: the catalogue *Béla Tarr* (Budapest: Filmunio, 2001) see also: http://www.kinokultura.com/specials/7/kovacs.shtml.

Kovács, András Bálint: 'Körbezárva' *Filmvilág*, 2008/1: pp.4–9.

Kővári, Orsolya: *Árnyékvilág*. Budapest: Sprint kiadó, 2012.

Kövesdy, Gábor: 'A léket kapott élet'. *Metropolis*, summer, 1997.

Méranger, Thierry: 'Cadences hongroises'. *Cahiers du cinéma*, November, 2006

Neyrat, Cyril: 'Le gardien du vide'. *Cahiers du cinéma*. September, 2008: p. 28.

Rancière, Jacques: *Béla Tarr, le temps d'après*. Paris: Capricci, 2011.

Richou, Pascal: 'Béla Tarr, le cosmos sinon rien'. *Cahiers du cinéma*, June, 2000.

Rollet, Sylvie: 'Béla Tarr ou le temps inhabitable'. *Positif*, 542, April, 2006: pp. 101–3.

Rollet, Sylvie: 'Théo Angelopoulos, Alexandre Sokourov, Béla Tarr ou la mélancolie de l'Histoire'. Positif, 556, June, 2007: pp. 96–9.

Romney, Jonathan: 'The Turin Horse'. *ScreenDaily*, 15 February, 2011.

Schlosser, Eric: 'Interview with Béla Tarr'. http://www.brightlightsfilm.com/30/belatarr1.html

Signorelli, Angelo, Vecchi, Paolo (eds): *Béla Tarr*. Bergamo Film Meeting, 2002.

Rollet, Sylvie: 'L'archipel de la résistance: Bartas, Loznitsa, Sokourov, Tarr'. *Positif*, 597, November, 2010: pp. 105–8.

Valkola, Jarmo: *Ege Celeste Reinuma: The Image of Women in the films of Béla Tarr*. University of Jyväskylä, Department of Art and Culture; 2012.

Valkola, Jarmo: *Visual Thinking and Various European Cinematic Landscapes. Examples from Peter Greenaway, Theo Angelopoulos, Béla Tarr and Andrei Tarkovsky*. Hungarologische Beitrage: Universitat de Jyvaskyla, 1997.

Valoka, Jarmo: 'L'esthétique visuelle de Béla Tarr'. *Théorème*, 7 (le cinéma hongrois, le temps et l'histoire), 2003.

Vincent Malusia: 'J'ai perdu toutes mes illusions'. *Transfuge*, September, 2008.

INDEX OF NAMES